EXPERIENTIAL LEARNING AND COMMUNITY

Examining the University's Teaching Mission

Institutional autonomy, private interests, and relevance are central themes in the evolving discourse on the nature and role of higher education. Whether pushing institutions to become more responsive to industry and labour market demands or to resist these very pressures, leaders and policymakers insist that universities must adapt. *Experiential Learning and Community* explores the changing role of the university, with a particular focus on how the rise of experiential learning (EL) is reshaping teaching and learning.

Through the lens of EL, universities are balancing two core principles: fostering an engaged citizenry and democracy and equipping learners with the skills needed for a prosperous economy. As EL rapidly expands in various forms – such as work-integrated learning like co-ops and internships, as well as community-engaged student placements such as service learning – universities are extending their reach far beyond the campus.

The book asks: Should universities fully embrace EL? If so, how can institutions and faculty adapt to this fundamental shift in their core mission? Are community partners now equal collaborators with a voice in pedagogy and curriculum? And perhaps most importantly, are students better served by this emergent EL approach to teaching and learning? *Experiential Learning and Community* addresses these questions at a time when universities, communities, and learners urgently need answers.

MICHAEL BUZZELLI is Director of the Centre for Urban Policy and Local Governance and an Associate Professor in the Department of Geography and Environment at the University of Western Ontario.

Experiential Learning and Community

Examining the University's Teaching Mission

EDITED BY MICHAEL BUZZELLI

UNIVERSITY OF TORONTO PRESS
Toronto Buffalo London

Toronto Buffalo London
utppublishing.com
Printed in Canada

ISBN 978-1-4875-6586-2 (cloth)
ISBN 978-1-4875-6587-9 (paper)
ISBN 978-1-4875-6588-6 (UPDF)
ISBN 978-1-4875-6589-3 (EPUB)

Library and Archives Canada Cataloguing in Publication

Title: Experiential learning and community : examining the university's teaching mission / edited by Michael Buzzelli.
Names: Buzzelli, Michael, 1971– editor.
Description: Includes bibliographical references and index.
Identifiers: Canadiana (print) 20250181452 | Canadiana (ebook) 20250181541 | ISBN 9781487565862 (cloth) | ISBN 9781487565879 (paper) | ISBN 9781487565886 (PDF) | ISBN 9781487565893 (EPUB)
Subjects: LCSH: Experiential learning. | LCSH: College teaching—Methodology. | LCSH: Education, Higher—Aims and objectives.
Classification: LCC LB1027.23 .E97 2025 | DDC 378.007—dc23

Cover design: Susan Zucker
Cover image: Cover artwork created by Siena Buzzelli, 2024

We wish to acknowledge the land on which the University of Toronto Press operates. This land is the traditional territory of the Wendat, the Anishnaabeg, the Haudenosaunee, the Métis, and the Mississaugas of the Credit First Nation.

University of Toronto Press acknowledges the financial support of the Government of Canada, the Canada Council for the Arts, and the Ontario Arts Council, an agency of the Government of Ontario, for its publishing activities.

Canada Council for the Arts
Conseil des Arts du Canada

Funded by the Government of Canada
Financé par le gouvernement du Canada
Canada

Contents

List of Illustrations

Tables

Figures

Acknowledgements

I would like to express my profound appreciation and thanks to all of the authors of the chapters in this volume. Nearly all became new collaborators to me by accepting my "cold-call" invitation to share their scholarship in this edited book project. In fact, this book became a new constellation of collaborators who came together for a mutually constructive and enriching journey. We bootstrapped internal reviews of our respective abstracts and early drafts to offer each other advice and support and to understand and develop the project as a complementary whole. Any edited book project can be easily slowed or stalled in alleyways, re-routes and full traffic stops however we kept our focus right the way through. I could not have asked for a more committed, spirited and scholarly group for this experience as editor. To all co-authors: thank you. Merci. Grazie e complimenti. Bedankt en gefeliciteerd. Tack och grattis.

Together with all authors, we are thankful for the support and encouragement we've received from our home institutions in Canada, Italy, the Netherlands, Sweden, and the United States. At the University of Western Ontario – my home institution, I've benefitted immensely from stimulating conversations and debates with colleagues and friends at the Centre for Teaching and Learning who appointed me as University Teaching Fellow, 2018–22. The COVID-19 pandemic was no match for our drive for a critical examination of experiential learning in the community. Moreover, a portion of my Teaching Fellowship award went to the Faculty of Social Science whose administration graciously (and wisely, if I may) agreed to channel some funds to support the publication of this book. And I must acknowledge that the Centre for Urban Policy and Local Governance and the Network for Economic and Social Trends always wrap my work – this book included – in a blanket of encouragement. For that I will be eternally grateful. I should also like to thank Dr. Merlin Chatwin for his careful reading of earlier versions of the text and for diligent construction of the index.

Finally, I know all parties could not be more pleased to see this work published with the University of Toronto Press (UTP). In early 2022, my initial proposal to UTP went to Meg Patterson whose vote of confidence was affirmation of the book idea and the "go-ahead" to approach prospective authors. In early 2023, the project was handed to Jodi Litvin who guided us through key moments in the process including the external peer review and re-review stages. We offer Jodi and the whole UTP team our deepest thanks and gratitude for helping us cross the finish line.

Michael Buzzelli
Director, Centre for Urban Policy and Local Governance
University of Western Ontario, Ontario, Canada
2025, Apirl 21

EXPERIENTIAL LEARNING AND COMMUNITY

1 Introduction: Experiential Learning and Community

MICHAEL BUZZELLI

University of Western Ontario, Canada

Introduction

The university's place in our social architecture is both lauded and contested. Institutional autonomy, private interests, and relevance are "buzzwords" in the highly charged discourse concerning the design and purpose of higher education. Whether marshalling institutions to be more responsive to industry and labour market needs or, indeed, resisting these very pressures, policy-makers and the public insist that universities respond. This volume is situated within this broad framing of the university's social contract and focuses specifically on its teaching and learning mission as it is now being reworked through the expansion of experiential learning (EL).

Through the lens of teaching and learning, the university seeks to activate two foundational principles: on the one hand, to develop an engaged citizenry and democracy while, on the other, to serve the learner's need to build a livelihood for a prosperous economy (Axelrod, 2002). The reader of this volume – sector policy practitioners, institutional leaders, and scholars – might imagine broad agreement on these principles, however, we quickly tip into debate over policy choices and organizational change, including – perhaps especially – when activating EL. For instance, how do programs and professors adapt what is taught and how it is taught? Should student co-op placements or internships be optional or mandatory, and how, if at all, do we recognize these in credentialling? More fundamentally, some ask whether universities should embrace EL at all. From the point of view of teaching and learning, we must also ask about the mechanics of EL "in town." With the rapid growth of EL, teaching and learning may quite literally happen elsewhere. Of course, EL can occur on campus and in the classroom. Internships and community-engaged placements, among other forms of

EL discussed below, increasingly resituate teaching off-campus and in the community. The terms of reference for pedagogy and curriculum are being rewritten. Community partners are presumptive co-authors as to say they are co-educators and co-creators of pedagogy and curriculum. Following the questions above, we may also ask: Is the community merely a canvas onto which the university scribes its own priorities? How are partners "out there" identified and engaged? Do principles of equity and diversity drive partner identification, participation, and feedback?

These questions make it clear that intra-institutional adaptations confront only one half of the challenge of EL. Scrutineering awaits also at the interface of the university and its community (Buzzelli & Asafo-Adjei, 2023). A touchstone in this context is the *US Morrill Act* of 1862: legislation that led to the creation of the American state-system of universities notable for its goal of institutional service to local economies (Kerr, 1966). A rich literature continues to examine the university-community relationship through a variety of themes such as municipal power relations, housing market impacts, skilled labour attraction and retention, and local spending multipliers (Baldwin, 2021; Gavazzi, 2015). But because EL is public by its very nature, the university-community relationship is also of interest to the wider public. The recent experience of UC Berkeley is instructive (Asmelash, 2022): in brief, a legal proceeding initiated by *Save Berkeley's Neighbourhoods*, a local neighbourhood group, successfully argued in Alameda Superior Court in 2021 that the University's decision to grow admissions was displacing residents via rising rents in the local housing market. The case made international media because it seemed the University would have to rescind offers of admission, a degree of local accountability worthy of case study in its own right. The University was exercising its social license as we usually accept and take for granted: independently choosing to raise enrolments and relying upon the local housing market to absorb the impacts of its decisions. The case continues to the present after it reached California's Supreme Court where the group's win was overturned on the University's successful appeal.

Whatever the outcome of this particular legal battle, it signals that the university's accountability in its own community – its presence, influence and operation – is garnering ever more attention and interrogation (Meusberger et al., 2018). The lesson for the rising tide of EL is that we ought to "sit up and listen": an unfamiliar posture for universities in the Global North accustomed to a high degree of operational and strategic autonomy (Buzzelli & Allison, 2017; Axelrod et al., 2013; Hearn, 1996). In some respects, local accountability suggests the university as an institutional type could learn from local technical and community colleges (North America), universities of applied sciences, and vocational education and training (both of the latter in Europe) whose mandate is nearly exclusively teaching-focused. These alternative institutional types and sectors bears their own examination, to be sure, however their curriculum mix (e.g., mechanical and construction trades) also suggests limits to transferable lessons (Weingarten, 2021). Moreover, the size and prestige of the university and its sector throws its EL landscape into high relief: in the face of much more national and global reach, often tied to research and scholarship, the university's educative mission is more proximate and local-facing for EL. The university's buildings and campus must be open to local two-way traffic. Weaving EL into curriculum and even requiring it for credential completion necessarily binds the university to the community, to the relationships it must have in place for EL to operate, fundamentally. Indeed, one might regard the university "going local" with EL as a mission paradox: necessarily creating relationships in order to fulfill its mandate despite not being accountable *prima facie* to the local and regional context from a strictly governance and mandate perspective.

In this context, the expansion of EL in town is reigniting questions about what universities are for, how they should function, and how institutions and systems might be alternatively designed (Newfield, 2016; Collini, 2012; Fallis, 2007). As with Berkeley's enrolment and housing challenges, new accountabilities also lurk with EL such as labour market displacement via paid and unpaid work-integrated learning (Marrone, 2018). In principle, the growth and diversification of EL is not an entirely new challenge. Interdisciplinarity and the scholarship of teaching and learning (SoTL) have each spurred policy research and organizational decision-making. SoTL asks us to interweave the often separate activities of teaching and research. It promotes research on teaching and learning and the dissemination of that scholarship as a legitimate form of inquiry. Among other things, the reward structures within the university would have to reflect SoTL if it is to be facilitated and promoted: the chemistry professor, for example, would be equally supported for publishing her research on teaching and learning as for her chemical research. Similarly, interdisciplinarity raises serious questions about what constitutes core academic inquiry if not from within traditional academic units and, thereby, how units might be themselves organized (Hemstrom et al., 2021). Interestingly, the history of this particular movement – accompanied by healthy debate over differences with trans- and multidisciplinarity – is quite like the current swell of EL: emergent terms that reach beyond semantics to signal meaningful differences in the kinds of relationships and arrangements faced by learners, professors, and administrators in the university and the community alike. At stake is the very foundation of the university's *raison d'etre*: how it fulfills its social contract to develop an engaged citizenry and prepare its learners for their futures, all as it negotiates its curriculum and pedagogy with unseen depth within its community.

Terms of Reference: EL and Community

By now the reader will have gathered that the geographical lens of this volume is the university's local community. Our local focus for *EL and Community* is both shared and varied. Across the chapters of this book, the local community of the university – the city or region within which the university is located – may be a smaller municipality of roughly 160,000 population (e.g., University of Twente in Enschede, part of a region of 620,000; see Chapter 10) or the multi-institutional context of the Toronto metropolitan region (City of Toronto, about 3 million and region of nearly 8 million). What remains shared is our concern with the nature and scope of relationships amongst local partners to facilitate and serve EL. EL does, of course, span all geographical scales (c.f. Curran et al., 2018; Tiessen & Huish, 2014). Our focus on the local is purposeful: the university's proximate community is where relationship density is greatest and learners can most readily access opportunities free from the prohibitive costs of distant and indeed international arrangements (Lazzeroni & Piccaluga, 2015). Equally, our local focus is motivated by the policy discourse of the place of the university in its local community: layering accountability to higher orders of government (i.e., national and provincial or state-based systems) with a rising expectation of local responsiveness. The OECD's recent establishment of the *Geography of Higher Education* program is telling (OECD, n.d.): one might be unsurprised to learn that the spark of the program is to generate policy alignments between higher education and regional economic development. It notes that the OECD project is helpful to us also because it confronts the abundant and evolving terminology in this domain: among others, town-gown marriage or relations; community or societal engagement (reaching beyond the core missions of teaching and research); the third mission (explicit recognition of serving the public good and having social impact beyond teaching and research, and perhaps with a global reach). The concepts are helpful even if their origins differ and their meanings are Venn-like. Academic literature on the university's societal contribution usually concerns research-related impacts and benefits such as technology transfer, entrepreneurial spin-offs, and patenting (Perkmann et al., 2013; Nelles et al., 2005). Our focus, instead, is on the teaching and learning mission.

Turning to that mission, then, what is EL and what does it hope to accomplish? While sharp definitions are usually preferred, the rapid expansion and flux of the field necessitates our use of "EL" to encompass the many and varied arrangements out there. We do so precisely because of our dual interrogation of what the university is doing to develop and deploy EL as well as how this fosters new and different relationships in the community. EL is an "umbrella term" used in this volume to capture co-op placements, paid or unpaid internships, community-engaged learning (CEL), and other pedagogies that will often resituate learning outside of the classroom and into the community (HEQCO, 2016). Specialists may find fault in this wide casting. In fact, that contestation is one of our motivations for this book, a volume, we feel, that will help the reader navigate the growing body of EL arrangements and issues at play. For instance, co-ops and internships can be differentiated or may be seen as only slightly different shades of work-integrated learning (WIL). Yet treating them as one suits others, understandably, who distinguish WIL from CEL, promoting the virtues of civic mindedness in learning for and with the community. However, CEL itself may or may not include community service learning (CSL) in which students undertake work directly for community partners in support of that organization's mission, typically not-for-profits and NGOs (Brabazon et al., 2019). The latter may be the clearest instance of the pedagogy and curriculum acting on one another. And yet at the other end of the continuum, for example, is the policy decision in Ontario to permit institutions to count in-class student laboratory work as experiential, thus, enabling the university to achieve benchmarks for EL delivery without having to adapt much at all. Some might interpret the last instance as a performative outcome of the EL in universities and systems in the context of the new public policy and management. Note that students need not even leave campus for EL. This gets to the core of our approach: in the swirl of ongoing EL development, an inclusive definition is preferred over precise specification, moreover, it may be necessary as precision is elusive in the current flux. We hope the reader will absorb the fundamental point that, from a policy and process perspective, EL arrangements share in common that learning is usually not in the classroom but off campus and in the community. For most observers, EL is the site where university and community are integrated with structured support and learner engagement via work experience, broadly defined (Billett, 2009).

At its core, the current push for EL across institutions and systems in North America, Europe, and elsewhere draws on educational philosophy and theory, particularly John Dewey's foundational work. David Kolb (1984) is usually seen as the spark of the current EL movement: he put forth the now-familiar argument that the student's development and professionalism are elevated when theory and practice are brought together. Co-ops, internships, and CEL enmesh theory and practice through the learner's experience, reflection, and knowledge application in a workplace or community-based research project. Consider the University of Western Ontario's (2019) definition of EL: "an approach that educators use to intentionally connect learners with practical experiences that include guided reflection. EL allows learners to increase and apply disciplinary knowledge, develop transferable skills, clarify interests and values, strengthen career engagement and employability, and collaborate meaningfully with communities." The reader will see in several chapters that authors draw on this foundational history of EL in their respective treatments. At minimum, EL is a practical "trial run" of the learner's aptitudes and interests, if not an opportunity to create professional networks and a direct connection to the labour force upon graduation. Above all others, students find great appeal in the "bonus" of EL's practical benefits: learning by doing, professional networking, and possibly more certainty over future employment, all layered atop foundational university studies. The benefits are not lost on policy and institutional leaders who have embraced the EL movement so fulsomely for the sector. It helps to demonstrate institutional responsiveness to policy mandates and assure learners that their institution is tuned to their needs.

To be sure, EL is not new. In Canada, McCallum and Wilson (1988) document nearly seven decades of cooperative education in universities and colleges. They demonstrate that fully 60 institutions had some presence in this space already by 1987. Often promoted as a Canadian innovation in teaching and learning (Weingarten, 2021), attention usually goes to the particular history of the University of Waterloo as "the co-op university" (initiated co-op education in 1957; 9,111 reported placements by 1987 equalling nearly half of all placements across Canada). The Cooperative Education and Work Integrated Learning Canada was established in 1973 (notably, the Association includes CEL/CSL within WIL). Fast forward to 2015, about 50% of all baccalaureate students in Canada had some exposure to EL in their studies (Galarneau et al., 2020). Of course, Canada was not alone in such developments. The International Journal of Work-Integrated Learning was established in 2000 and its early issues included coverage of various WIL arrangements already at play in New Zealand, South Africa, Australia, and Germany, among others. Notably here, too, the Journal adopts a similarly broad definition of WIL that overlaps with many forms of EL. Perlin (2012) traces the same timeline in a critical examination of the growth of EL in the developed West including the British, French and particularly the US experiences. Both cause and effect of these trends is the increasing institutionalization of EL, such as the growth of professional staff and infrastructure by stakeholders with accountability metrics and even funding tied to EL. For example, in Italy systems have been developed to help frame and track EL placements in part in response to EU and national labour market legislation. Since 2015, Italy's Alma Laurea program has set out contractual obligations and tracking of all EL placements in the country's nationalized Higher Education [HE] system. The current reinvigoration of EL development impels the movement further.

Guide to the Chapters

The chapters that follow are situated in the broad framing of the university's social contract outlined above. As a set, the chapters are situated in alternative contexts, deliver a variety of approaches, and employ different methods. The chapters are nonetheless curated to examine the question of EL in town. All chapters start with the premise that EL and societal engagement are inextricably bound together. In their own ways, authors have sought to understand how this distinguishing pedagogical feature of EL is reshaping both the core mission of the university and its place in the community in new, potentially positive but also unexpected and unwanted ways. The reader will find three sections of chapters addressing a sequence of overarching questions: in the first section, *Learners and the Intra-Institutional Lens*, how the university (re)organizes around the learner and learning to facilitate and develop EL; in *Partners and Networks in the Community*, what are the nature and terms of relationships between the university and local community organisations; in *EL and Local Governance*, the geographical lens is nuanced around the shared theme of environment and sustainability.

In the first section of the volume, *Learners and the Intra-institutional Lens*, Björck, in Chapter 2, critically examines the concept of graduate employability to problematize the very core and motivation for EL. The foundation of connecting theory with practice for the learner's post-graduation labour force entry, we read, relies on facile understandings and assumptions about transferable skills and professionalism. If universities fall short of their own goals and objectives, LaCroix argues in Chapter 3, it can be because management and academics may not have the same understandings of EL and, thereby, how it should be developed and supported. Without the necessary institutional "logic work" of fully articulating goals and objectives, EL programing risks missing its mark or worse. In Chapter 4, Buzzelli demonstrates how the development of EL in Canadian universities appears to have bypassed that internal logic work at the senate level. As institutions have exercised their social license to develop and deploy EL over recent years, Canadian university senates have scarcely had any deliberation about the creation and expansion of EL.

Turning to *Partners and Networks in the Community*, Milley's Chapter 5 bridges the learner and intra-institutional focus with the other side of EL: it's connective tissue of relationships and networks with partner organisations. Milley presents a critical empirical analysis of the influence of the social innovation and social enterprise movements. As with commercial interests in the geography of higher education, social innovation/enterprise can condition the university's internal organization around EL, the relationships created, and outcomes generated. In Chapter 6, Giroux, Eady, and Moreau ask the reader to consider those very external connections more directly by distinguishing "relationship" and "partnership". They write on the need to actively involve community stakeholders if EL is to be impactful and if community partners experience ethical parity. They also introduce a critical step often missed in public policy and programming: the need for evaluation. Bjartveit, Gordon, and Bear Chief (Chapter 7) and Collins-Nelsen, Egert, Maclachlan, and Raha (Chapter 8) further layer the discussion of EL's ethical challenges in the community: the former, in the context of university-First Nations learning and cooperation, a theme of national importance in Canada's process of Truth and Reconciliation; the latter, in the urban context aimed at ensuring the university mindfully reaches under-served (e.g., low SES) communities with EL programming so as to not reproduce inequities. Together, the latter two chapters also elevate a theme touched on at points throughout the volume: equity, diversity, inclusion, and decolonization (EDID). As universities confront their EDID histories and practices (Advisory Committee, 2021; Gaudry and Lorenz, 2018; Songsore and Buzzelli, 2018), the development and expansion of EL should heed the call for accountabilities for learners, learning, and partnerships.

In *EL and Local Governance*, the final tranche of chapters nuance the geographical lens with a shared theme of environment and sustainability education. In Chapter 9, Magnani, Proto, and Manocchi situate graduate-level (Master's) EL in the Emili-Romagna region of Italy. They trace the current growth of EL out of, on the one hand, tensions between local priorities and interests and internationalization (the Bologna process and European higher educational harmonization) and, on the other, the history of specific types of EL in the Italian system ("tirocinio" or "stage"). In the Dutch context, Dix, Baibarac-Duignan, and Jongbloed introduce the reader in Chapter 10 to the emergent model of challenge-based learning (CBL). In this model, curriculum and pedagogy are necessarily worked through simultaneously and they cover, among other issues, the impacts on the learner of marrying elements of problem-based learning (sometimes termed "inquiry") with CSL. Finally, in Chapter 11, the geographical lens is again refocused through the "glocal" example Reach

Alliance: global network infrastructure of academics and institutions that is leveraged to support local EL and the learner's leadership development.

Finally, the Afterword reflects on the themes, arguments, and evidence across the contributions in this volume. It brings forth salient questions and issues to be confronted by the university in the Global North: how, with the expansion and diversification of EL, the university will continue to develop an engaged citizenry and democracy and support the learner's quest for professionalization. To do so, the university itself must examine its own teaching and learning content and processes and, equally, confront its local accountabilities for EL to work for all concerned.

REFERENCES

Advisory Committee (2021). *Igniting Change: Final Report and Recommendations.* Ottawa: Federation for the Humanities and Social Sciences of Canada, Advisory Committee on Equity, Diversity, Inclusion, and Decolonization. https://www.federationhss.ca/en/programs-policy/edi-and-decolonization/igniting-change

Asmelash, L. (2022, March 27). *What a UC Berkeley legal battle says about college housing affordability.* CNN. https://www.cnn.com/2022/03/27/us/uc-berkeley-lawsuit-student-enrollment-housing-costs-cec/index.html

Axelrod, P. (2002). *Values in conflict: The university, the marketplace and the trials of liberal education.* McGill-Queen's University Press.

Axelrod, P., Trilokekar, R. D., Shanahan, T., & Wellen, R. (Eds.). (2013). *Making Policy in Turbulent Times: Challenges and Prospects for Higher Education.* McGill-Queen's University Press.

Baldwin, D. (2021) *In the shadow of the ivory tower: How universities are plundering our cities.* Bold Type Books.s

Billett, S. (2009). Realising the educational worth of integrating work experiences in higher education. *Studies in Higher Education, 34*(7), 827–43.

Brabazon, H., Esmail, J., Locklin, R., & Stirling, A. (2019). Beyond employability: Defamiliarizing work-integrated learning with community-engaged learning. *Engaged Scholar Journal, 5*(2), 21–41.

Buzzelli, M., & Allison, D. J. (2017). Proposed strategic mandates for Ontario universities: An organizational theory perspective. *Canadian Journal of Higher Education, 47*(3), 170–91.

Buzzelli, M., & Asafo-Adjei, E. (2022). Experiential learning and the university's host community: Rapid growth, contested mission and policy challenge. *Higher Education,* 85: 521-38, https://doi.org/10.1007/s10734-022-00849-1

Collini, S. (2012) *What are universities for?* Penguin Books.

Curran, D. L., Owens, C., Thorson, H., & Vibert, E. (Eds.). (2018). *Out There Learning: Critical Reflections on Off-Campus Study Programs.* University of Toronto Press.

Fallis, G. (2007). *Multiversities, ideas and democracy.* University of Toronto Press.

Galarneau, D., Kinack, M., & Marshall, G. (2020, May 25). *Work-integrated learning during postsecondary studies, 2015 graduates.* Statistics Canada. https://www150.statcan.gc.ca/n1/pub/75-006-x/2020001/article/00003-eng.htm

Gaudry, A. & Lorenz, D. (2018). Indigenization as Inclusion, Reconciliation, and Decolonization: Navigating the Different Visions for Indigenizing the Canadian Academy. *AlterNative: An International Journal of Indigenous Peoples, 14,* 3, 218–27.Gavazzi, S. M. (2015). *The optimal town-gown marriage: Taking campus-community outreach and engagement to the next level.* CreateSpace Independent Publishing Platform.

Hearn, J. C. (1996). Transforming US higher education: An organizational perspective. *Innovative Higher Education, 21*(2), 141–54.

Hemstrom, K., Simon, D., & Palmer, H. (2021). *Transdisciplinary knowledge co-production for sustainable cities: A guide for sustainable cities.* Practical Action Publishing.

HEQCO. (2016). *A practical guide for Work-Integrated Learning.* Higher Education Quality Council of Ontario. http://www.heqco.ca/SiteCollectionDocuments/HEQCO_WIL_Guide_ENG_ACC.pdf

Kerr, C. (1966). *The uses of the university.* Harvard Univ. Press.

Kolb, D. A. (1984). *Experience as the source of learning and development.* Prentice Hall.

Lazzeroni, M., & Piccaluga A. (2015). Beyond "town and gown": The role of the university in small and medium-sized cities. *Industry and Higher Education,* 29(1), 11–23.

Marrone, M. (2018, January 25–7). *L'economia del tirocinio. Tirocinio e informalizzazione del lavoro in Emilia-Romagna* [Conference presentation]. II Convegno annuale SISEC, Milano.

McCallum, B. A., & Wilson, J. C. (1988). They said it wouldn't work (A history of cooperative education in Canada). *Journal of Cooperative Education, 14*(2–3), 61–7.

Meusberger, P., Heffernan, M., & Suarsana, L. (Eds.). (2018). *Geographies of the university: An introduction.* Springer.

Nelles, J., Bramwell, A., & Wolfe, D. A. (2005). History, culture and path dependency: Origins of the Waterloo ICT cluster. *Global Networks and Local Linkages: The Paradox of Cluster Development in an Open Economy,* 227, 252. https://munkschool.utoronto.ca/downloads/ipl/publications/pdfdoc/2005/D.%20Wolfe_History,Culture&Path%20Dependency.pdf

Newfield, C. (2016). *The great mistake: How we wrecked public universities and how we can fix them.* Johns Hopkins University Press.

OECD (n.d.). *The geography of higher education.* OECD. https://www.oecd.org/cfe/smes/geo-higher-education.htm

Perkmann, M., V. Tartari, M. McKelvey, E. Autio, A. Broström, A., P. D'Este, Fini, R., Geuna, A., Grimaldi, R., Hughes, A., Krabel, S., Kitson, M., Llerena,

P., Lissoni, F., Salter, A., & Sobrero, M. (2013). Academic engagement and commercialisation: A review of the literature on university-industry relations. *Research Policy, 42*(2), 423–42.

Perlin, R. (2012). *Intern nation: How to earn nothing and learn little in the brave new economy.* Version Books.

Songsore, E. & Buzzelli, M. (2018). Diversity and inclusion in Ontario universities: A snapshot through the lens of institutional strategic mandates. In B. Blummer, J.M. Kenton & M. Wiatrowski (Eds.), *Promoting Ethnic Diversity and Multiculturalism in Higher Education.* IGI Global.

Tiessen, R., & Huish, R. (Eds.). (2014). *Globetrotting or global citizenship? Perils and potential of international experiential learning.* University of Toronto Press.

University of Western Ontario. (2019). *Experiential Learning.* University of Western Ontario. https://experience.uwo.ca/index.html.

Weingarten, H. (2021). *Nothing less than great: Reforming Canada's universities.* University of Toronto Press.

PART ONE

Learners and the Intra-Institutional Lens

2 Moving Beyond Simplistic Perspectives on Experiential Learning and Graduate Employability

VILLE BJÖRCK

University West, Sweden

Introduction

An increasing approach among higher education institutions (HEIs) globally is to try and foster "employable graduates" by offering students opportunities for "experiential learning" (EL) (Buzzelli & Asafo-Adjei, 2022). While established research has recognized the multi-dimensional nature of both EL and graduate employability (GE), there continues to be a body of higher education research concerned with simplistic perspectives on what EL and GE mean and how EL fosters GE. By "simplistic" perspectives I mean understandings that are so simplified that they portray EL and GE inaccurately and sometimes in polarizing ways. This chapter problematizes four such perspectives that are emphasized globally in research and discusses their over-simplification in discourse. Thereafter, the chapter discusses how HEIs can use more nuanced perspectives on EL and GE in their education to increase the possibility of fostering graduates who are not only *ready to operate within* but also *critical* and *creative* enough to *challenge* and *change* established work practices in a profession. Furthermore, a body of research claims that HEIs working with GE is altogether different from and/or detrimental to their mission of developing *engaged* and *democratic* citizens (Boden & Nedeva 2010; Mtawa et al., 2019). In the discussion, I will argue that there is a key dimension of GE that fits well within the scope of developing engaged and democratic citizens but that GE is often understood from a perspective where this dimension is absent. Before this chapter moves on to the existing literature section, I want to clarify that the focus of this chapter is to problematize four simplistic perspectives on EL and GE that recur globally in higher education research, *not* to problematize experiential learning theory (ELT) as such.

Existing Literature

This section focuses primarily on how EL and GE are discussed in contemporary higher education research[1] and research that discusses one of these concepts from a more general perspective. The section begins by outlining research about EL, and thereafter it presents research about GE. Finally, the section outlines higher education research about the relationship between EL and GE.

Experiential Learning: A Concept That Is Depicted in Both Similar and Diverse Ways

Fenwick (2000) stated that there are myriad perspectives on what constitutes EL, and Illeris (2007) similarly underlined that the concept of EL is used in different ways and with different meanings. Two perspectives that are not new (Fenwick, 2000) but continue to appear globally in research give different pictures of what EL is. The first perspective is that EL *differs* from the scholastic learning taking place in formal education institutions and occurs *outside* such institutions, typically at workplaces (Björck, 2020a; Fenwick, 2000). The second perspective is that EL takes place in all spheres of society and thus also within formal education institutions because people learn from experience everywhere (Fenwick, 2000; Morris, 2020). This perspective is founded on the proposition that all learning is *experiential* since learning is always *based on* and/or *involves* some kind of experience (Kolb et al., 2014). This proposition forms a key basis of the *experiential learning theory* (ELT) proposed by Kolb (1984, p. 38) who accentuated that "learning is the process whereby knowledge is created through the transformation of experience."

While some research recognizes that all learning is experiential in the stated sense, there is a body of higher education research that implies otherwise by emphasizing that it is on work placements outside HEIs that students encounter EL (see e.g., Björck, 2020a; Buzzelli & Asafo-Adjei, 2022 who discussed this research). The learning occurring within off-campus placements is also referred to as Work-integrated Learning (WIL), Learning by doing, Work-based Learning (WBL), Practice-based Learning, Workplace Learning (WPL) and on-the-job learning (Sattler & Peters, 2013). This means that the EL term is often used interchangeably with these types of terms. EL and WIL are also often used as labels for the educational approach whereby students are offered opportunities to learn from work-based experiences (Billett & Valencia-Forrester, 2020; Björck, 2020b; Buzzelli & Asafo-Adjei, 2022; Jackson, 2017). Billett and Valencia-Forrester (2020) stated that the term "education" rather than the term "learning" should be used to refer to an educational approach. They exemplified their argument by declaring that Work-integrated Education (WIE) rather than WIL is the correct term for said educational approach (Billett & Valencia-Forester, 2020; see also Billett, 2022; Björck & Willermark, 2024, who underlined the importance of distinguishing between WIE and WIL). WIL and EL have also been used as labels for the *integration process* whereby campus-based and work-based learning experiences are "interweaved" (Jackson, 2017).

Furthermore, while there is a trend in higher education research to refer to EL as a form of learning that occurs outside HEIs and differs from scholastic learning, there is also research that has questioned this trend. Fenwick (2000, p. 245) problematized that portraying EL as a *unique* form of learning suggests "an absurd proposition," namely that there exist forms of learning that are neither based on nor involve any kind of experience. The concept of *classroom-based* EL has been put forward to acknowledge that EL takes place both inside and outside of formal education institutions (Lee et al., 2022; Lewis & Williams, 1994; Sattler, 2018).

Research has also problematized that when terms such as EL and WIL are used as labels for the learning occurring on work placements off-campus, there is a tendency to create polarized distinctions between campus-based learning and placement-based learning (Björck & Johansson, 2019). Björck (2021) noted that a popularized trend is to praise the off-campus learning for providing the *experience* that "actually" prepares students for a profession and criticizing on-campus learning for mainly providing students with knowledge in abstract theories rather than a tangible professional preparation (Björck, 2021).

Björck (2020b; 2021) further noted that this criticism is founded on a general skepticism of formal schooling that has long been directed towards accredited education institutions (Masschelein & Simons (2013). The skepticism suggests that these institutions tend to teach educational content that is not sufficiently preparing students for life "outside of school" (Dewey, 1904; Masschelein & Simons, 2013). Herrington and Herrington (2007) echoed this and stated that employers critique campus-based learning for lacking a clear "real-world" connection, which indicates insufficient preparation of students for working life. Higher education research that voices the said skepticism of scholastic learning tends to romanticize how the working-life domain outside HEIs provides a "realistic" learning environment for students (Björck, 2020a; Boud, 2000). This romanticization is founded on the belief that knowledge acquired in EL is more reality-based than knowledge acquired through campus-based training (Björck, 2020a). An argument that supports this way of thinking is that students cannot learn a profession simply by attending class but also require concrete work experiences in the practices of the profession (Mintzberg, 2005; Wilton, 2012). Some research, such as that by Raelin (2016), has argued that learning experiences from work rather than scholastic learning experiences provide the best preparation for the daily work of a profession. Furthermore, the narrative that the working-life domain outside HEIs provides a realistic learning setting (Jackson & Edgar, 2019; Wilson, 2012) is not only found in research but also in the marketing discourse of HEIs (Björck, 2020b). Both this research and marketing discourse tend to use labels such as EL and WIL to point out that learning experiences from this domain are key to become so-called *employable graduates* (Björck, 2021; Buzzelli & Asafo-Adjei, 2022).

Graduate Employability: A Concept That Is Both Simplified and Nuanced in Research

It is important to note that the employability concept is not only studied in relation to higher education, but it is also studied in a labour market policy context (Gazier, 1998; McQuaid & Lindsay, 2005). In higher education, it has become common to use the label *graduate employability* (GE) to denote this research topic (Tomlinson, 2012). The GE concept is both promoted and problematized in higher education research (Björck, 2021). Research promoting GE often emphasizes that a key agenda of HEIs is to foster employable graduates, an idea that has come to be known as *the employability agenda* (Crisp et al., 2019). While there are different perspectives on what employable graduates mean (Crisp et al., 2019), research has emphasized that a *work readiness* perspective continues to be common in a higher education context. According to this perspective, employable graduates simply mean *work ready* graduates (Björck, 2021; Lau et al., 2018; Trede & McEwen, 2012). Work ready indicates graduates who are *ready* to deal effectively with the work practices, work situations and work trends that they will encounter in a profession (Björck, 2021). A focus in higher education research that promotes GE focuses on how students can be taught so-called *employability skills* (also referred to as *job readiness skills)*, which ensure that they become work ready upon graduation (Jackson, 2014). Employability skills are often divided into *soft skills*, such as communication and teamwork, and *technical skills*, such as writing and information literacy (Coll et al., 2009; Freudenberg et al., 2011).

Higher education research that problematizes the GE-concept focuses on various relevant topics. First, GE is not only about fostering *work ready* but also *work changing* graduates (Björck et al., 2025; Crisp et al., 2019;

Trede & McEwen, 2012). In this critique, work changing graduates means those who are *critical* and *creative* enough to challenge and change established work practices and trends in a profession and in working life in general (Björck, 2021). Crisp, Higgs and Letts (2019) called for research that considers both the work readiness and the work changing dimension of GE, rather than one *or* the other. Another key topic in research that critiques GE is to challenge the simplified notion that the purpose of the employability agenda for HEIs is to merely foster graduates with the skills that employers demand and deem as crucial for graduates' work-readiness (Clarke, 2018; Crisp et al., 2019). Clarke (2018) underlined the importance of moving beyond this notion and the simplistic rhetoric it supports. Björck (2021) argued that underlying both this notion and the work-readiness perspective on GE in general is the simplistic perspective that the "real world" exists outside of HEIs.

Higher education research problematizing the GE-concept have also argued that the mission to foster employable graduates is difficult to reconcile with the mission of HEIs; namely to give students a *liberal education* to ensure that they graduate as *engaged* and *democratic* citizens (Buzzelli & Asafo-Adjei, 2022; Crisp et al., 2019;). Researchers like Boden and Nedeva (2010) argued that the employability agenda encourages HEIs to foster work ready graduates rather than graduates who are engaged and democratic citizens. In this chapter, I will point to an argument that tends to be overlooked in research. The argument is that there is a dominant perspective on GE which encourages us (people) to *not* see that there is a dimension of GE that fits well with HEIs mission of fostering engaged and democratic citizens. Which GE-perspective I refer to and which dimension of GE that fits well with this mission are clarified in the discussion.

Key Portrayals of the Relationship Between Experiential Learning and Graduate Employability

GE is a common topic in higher education research that portrays EL as a *form of learning* that students get to experience through work placements or an *educational approach* that provides students with work-based learning experiences through various forms of placements. When conceptualized in these ways, EL is often promoted as a key to ensuring that students become employable upon graduation (see e.g., Björck, 2021; Buzzelli & Asafo-Adjei, 2022; Davies, 2000; Jackson, 2015; Valencia-Forrester, 2022). In this context, EL is often said to be a *form of learning* that is founded on or an *educational approach* that provides the *actual work experiences* that make students ready for a profession (Jackson 2015, 2017). Björck

(2021) discussed the assumption that it is through work experiences that students actually learn a profession or field of work. Another common portrayal of why EL fosters GE is to state that it is through EL as a learning process that students integrate campus-based and work-based experiences and learn *how* to apply disciplinary knowledge in a workplace context. This ability to apply learning has been portrayed as a prerequisite for becoming ready for occupational work (Jackson, 2017), to ensure that graduates are not only well-educated in disciplinary knowledge but, in addition, can use this knowledge at work (Björck, 2021).

Experiential Learning and Graduate Employability: Four Simplistic Perspectives

The first and the second perspectives outlined are about EL, the third concerns GE, and the fourth is a perspective on how EL fosters GE. Each perspective will be presented separately but also linked to one or more of the others. This section also focuses on what is simplistic about each perspective and the research that reinforces them.

Learning From Experience Is Something Students Do *Outside* HEIs

This perspective supports the narrative that students learn from experience outside but *not* inside HEIs. This perspective has not emerged during the most recent times but has been identified before, notably by Fenwick (2000). What makes the perspective simplistic is that it fails to acknowledge that experience is involved in students' learning on campus as well. While the experiences they learn from campus can be both similar and different from their work placement-based learning experiences, it is in the words of Fenwick (2000, p. 245) "absurd" to suggest that learning from experience is something students merely do outside HEIs. However, this perspective continues to be kept alive by the research trend to indicate that work placements outside HEIs represent the *default site* for engaging in EL. A key example is research that specifically identifies such placements as *forms of EL* or more generally refers to the learning that students engage in on placements as EL. Buzzelli and Asafo-Adjei (2022) declared that placements are often described as forms of EL while Sattler and Peters (2013) and Björck (2020a) stated that EL is one of several labels that are often used to refer to the learning taking place on work placements outside HEIs. While there is research seeking to underline that EL also takes place on campuses (Lee et al., 2022; Lewis & Williams, 1994; Sattler, 2018), the stated perspective continues to be reinforced by the above-mentioned research trend. The perspective that learning from experience is something students do *outside* HEIs is connected to the second simplistic perspective on EL that this chapter problematizes.

EL Is Something *Other* Than On-Campus Learning

This perspective posits that EL has a unique feature that distinguishes it from on-campus learning, specifically that EL is about learning from doing whereas on-campus learning is "theoretical" in nature. Here, the term theoretical[2] implies that student learning on campus lacks experiential features and is derived from reading and discussing theories. What makes this perspective simplistic is the inherent assumption that experience is a feature that is unique to *one* form of learning called EL and that on-campus learning is purely "theoretical" in nature. However, research and experience demonstrate that there is not one exclusive form of learning where experience is involved. Rather, experience plays a part in all learning processes (Kolb et al., 2014; Morris, 2020). Secondly, this perspective is simplistic because students learning from reading and discussing theories on campus is accompanied by on-and off-campus experiences. Experiences from work placement-based training, among others, are often involved in the process of the student's learning of the theories they are introduced to through their courses. Indeed, students learn how to participate in seminars, lectures, and laboratory/clinical work by *experiencing* these learning activities on campus. Furthermore, the experiences of reading and discussing different research and theories ensure that students become informed of specific theories in their disciplines.

The perspective that EL is something *other* than on-campus learning also has a specific feature in common with the perspective that learning from experience is something students do *outside* HEIs. The common denominator is that the latter perspective is also founded on the assumption that on-campus learning is strictly "theoretical" in nature and thereby lacks experiential features. This is why this perspective emphasizes that students learn from experience *outside* HEIs. By being tacitly founded on the assumption that on-campus learning is strictly "theoretical" in nature, both of the previously stated perspectives allude to a message that polarizes on-campus training and the working-life domain outside HEIs for students. The message is that on-campus training is too focused on teaching students *abstract* and *idealistic* theories that are neither *concrete* nor *realistic* enough to be of proper use in the work being conducted outside HEIs. This message encourages students to believe that on-campus training lacks relevance for work and calls for students to embrace an inaccurate description of theory, namely that theory is a form of knowledge that is too abstract and/or idealistic to be of concrete use for professionals operating outside HEIs. This description also implies that students do not really need to acquire knowledge in theory to become graduates who are useful at work. This cannot be further from the truth because professionals purposively apply and routinely follow specific theories in the form of principles, explanatory models, ideas, and concepts, et cetera, in their daily work.

Moreover, it is vital to note how research reinforces the perspective that EL is something *other* than on-campus learning and the assumption that *EL is about learning from experience whereas on-campus learning is strictly "theoretical" in nature.* This perspective and assumption are reinforced by the research trend to emphasize that work placement-based learning is *experiential* (Björck, 2020a; Buzzelli & Asafo-Adjei, 2022; Fenwick, 2000) and that on-campus learning is *theory-based* (Björck & Johansson, 2019). Emphasizing this dichotomy implies that on-campus learning and work placement-based learning are in opposition. This implication is simplistic because students can acquire learning experiences on- and off-campus that together help them understand and apply theories.

An *Employable* Graduate: A *Work-Ready* Graduate

This *work readiness perspective* underlines that GE is all about graduates being ready to deal effectively with the work practices, situations and trends that are established in a profession and in working life in general (see e.g., Björck, 2021; Crisp et al., 2019; Trede & McEwen, 2012, who stated that an established trend in higher education research is to merely conceptualize GE in terms of work readiness). The critique of this perspective is that it fails to acknowledge that there is more to GE than work readiness. Specifically, this perspective fails to recognize that GE is also about fostering *work changing* graduates (Crisp et al., 2019). This means graduates who are *critical* and *creative* enough to *challenge* and *change* established work practices and work trends in a profession or in working life in general. Research has highlighted the need to move beyond the trend of merely conceptualizing GE in terms of work readiness (Clarke, 2018) by instead focusing on both of the stated dimensions of GE (Crisp et al., 2019; Trede & McEwen, 2012). However, research has also shown that this trend continues to be dominant (Björck, 2021) and reinforces the perspective that an *employable* graduate means a *work ready* graduate. A specific feature of this trend is that researchers use terms such as *work readiness* or *work ready* interchangeably with GE (Lau et al., 2018), which implies that GE is all about work readiness. The work readiness-perspective problematized above is also related to the following perspective on how EL fosters GE.

Learning Experience From the *Real-World* Is What *Really* Makes Students Employable Upon Graduation

This perspective underlines that it is experiences of learning in the so-called "real world" (here meaning the working-life domain outside HEIs) rather than on-campus learning, which really ensures that students become employable (work ready) upon graduation. A key characteristic of this perspective is that it abides by the work readiness-perspective that an *employable graduate* means a *work ready* graduate. Thus, this perspective supports the one-sided view that GE is about work readiness. The perspective that it is "real-world" learning experiences that really make students employable is also based on the assumption that this working life domain provides the relevant learning that on-campus training cannot provide (see Björck, 2020a; Orr, 2002, who discussed that a common assumption is that on-campus learning tends to lack proper realistic features).

Firstly, what makes this perspective simplistic is that it takes for granted that the working-life domain outside HEIs represents the *one* real world. This implies that HEIs and the education taking place there are not part of the real world. Secondly, it is simplistic to assume that there is *one* real world. Rather, students and people in general encounter both the same and different *realities* in formal education institutions, in work settings, and during their leisure time. Furthermore, taking for granted that the working-life domain outside HEIs represents the realistic learning environment that on-campus training cannot really provide is also simplistic. This is because it is arguably not true that students are generally taught knowledge on campus that provides inaccurate representations of the profession or field work they study for. Rather, what could be argued is that that learning experiences from work placement-based training could in many instances be more *hands-on*[3] than on-campus learning experiences. However, this does not mean that on-campus learning experiences lack realistic features. It could also be argued that some concepts or principles taught on campus are "unrealistic" in the sense that they can be very difficult and sometimes even impossible to apply in certain work settings. Nevertheless, the same can be said about the concepts, ideas, or missions, et cetera, that companies and organizations create themselves, for example, that professionals can find it very difficult or even impossible to apply them in their daily work.

The perspective that learning experience from the "real world" is what really makes students employable (i.e., work ready) upon graduation is also simplistic because it provides an inaccurate picture. It is arguably a mix of on- and off-campus learning rather than so-called "real-world" learning that fosters work readiness. Furthermore, it is vital to pinpoint the type of research that actually reinforces this perspective. It is reinforced by research which *idealizes* working life outside HEIs as the "real-world" learning environment that prepares students for work (see e.g., Kruger et al., 2015). The perspective is also reinforced by research which highlights that it is learning experience from working life outside HEIs rather than on-campus learning experiences that prepare students for work (see e.g., Björck 2020b, who discussed this body of research). An example of such research is that by Raelin (2016) who stated that "real-world" learning experiences rather than classroom learning provides an apt preparation for management work.

The perspective is also reinforced by research which underpins the assumption that on-campus learning lacks the proper realistic features that working life outside HEIs is understood to provide to students. Masschelein and Simons (2013) stated that research has not only directed this criticism towards HEIs but also towards formal educational institutions in general. Björck (2020a) problematized research that on the basis of this assumption ranks work placement-based learning higher than on-campus learning. A final remark I will make before this chapter moves on to the discussion is that all four of the outlined perspectives are not always voiced in an explicit manner, but often implied in research.

Nuanced Perspectives On Experiential Learning and Graduate Employability and How They Can Help Foster Work Ready and Work Changing Graduates

Nuanced perspectives on EL and GE are perspectives that provide multifaceted rather than one-sided descriptions. A nuanced perspective on EL is to underline that EL does not merely occur outside HEIs but that students and people in general learn from experience in all domains of society, although the experiences they learn from can be very different in different contexts. For instance, when students engage in local community projects, they can encounter specific environments and communities where they get the opportunity to learn from quite unique experiences that they have not experienced before and which can really enrich their learning. However, while local environments can provide rather unique learning experiences, it is arguably the case that students learn from experiences in all of the different environments they engage in on- and off-campus. Furthermore, based on the above-stated perspective that experience plays a vital part in all learning, it is problematic to use the EL label. This is because the EL label falsely implies that there exists *one* specific form of learning that is founded on experience and that experience is not involved in other forms of learning. What Kolb (1984) declared was not that there is *one* form of learning that is *experiential* but that experience is *the source* of learning. This means that the EL label is inherently problematic because it fails to recognize the role that experience plays in learning in general.

Moving on to GE, I argue that to constitute a nuanced perspective on GE, a perspective needs to acknowledge two aspects which illustrate that GE is a multi-dimensional phenomenon. The first aspect is that GE has both a work readiness and work changing dimension, which are both equally important and include different features (see e.g., Björck, 2021; Crisp et al., 2019 who discussed these two dimensions of GE). The second feature is that both dimensions of GE are acquired on- and off-campus through students integrating their on- and off-campus learning experiences. Emphasizing that GE has two equally important dimensions that are acquired both on- and off-campus is a more nuanced perspective than the simplistic perspective that *learning experience from the real world is what really makes students employable upon graduation.* Drawing on this nuanced perspective on GE, HEIs can work to create an education that places equal emphasis on both the work readiness and the work changing dimension of GE responding to the calls from researchers (Crisp et al., 2019). Abiding by this perspective, HEIs can also work to create an education where on- and off-campus learning experiences are treated as equally important and together help students become both work ready and work changing graduates. By doing so, the education provided by HEIs can for instance avoid perpetuating the common assumption that it is only through off-campus work placements that students get *the experience* that makes them work ready (Björck, 2021). However, providing an education that gives equal status to on- and off-campus learning experiences is arguably not easy. Research (Carr, 2006, Schön, 1987, Korthagen & Kessels, 1999, and Björck, 2020b) has claimed that on-campus learning experiences are in a formal education context often given higher status than off-campus learning experiences. To avoid this, there is arguably a need to provide an education that places emphasis on students integrating on- and off-campus learning experiences in such a way that they reinforce each other. For this to occur, on-campus educators must be interested in using students' off-campus learning experiences on campus, and off-campus educators must be interested in what students learn on campus. While there are certainly on- and off-campus educators that show this interest, research has illustrated that on- and off-campus learning can be rather disconnected (Crisp et al., 2019) and thereby difficult to integrate (Björck, 2020b; Nguyen, 2019).

Moreover, applying the nuanced perspective that students learn from experience both *on- and off-campus* can help HEIs to not give students a false impression that off-campus work placements provide the opportunity to *learn from experience* whereas on-campus training provides students with a form of learning that is strictly "theoretical" in nature. If students get this impression, they can easily embrace a common skepticism of HEIs, namely that on-campus training is generally too focused on abstract and idealistic theories to be of proper use to them in the working-life domain (Björck, 2021). In turn, if students embrace this skepticism, they are likely to view on-campus training as not really being key to their development into good professionals. Students with this view would arguably not be inclined to learn as much as they can from on-campus experiences. This would be detrimental to their development into work ready and work changing graduates. This is because on-campus learning experiences are key to becoming both a work ready and a work changing graduate. For instance, sharing learning experiences with educators and fellow students on campus can help students learn more about and become more prepared for established work practices in the profession or field of work they study for. When students share and discuss learning experiences, they can also become more critical of established work practices and more aware of how they could possibly be changed.

To be able to offer an education where the work readiness and the work changing dimension of GE are given equal focus, there is arguably a need for further discussions about what learning experiences students need to become both work ready and work changing graduates. It is vital that researchers, on-campus and off-campus educators are involved in these discussions. If off-campus educators are left out of discussions they could contribute to, they might feel that it is only on-campus educators who decide which learning experiences are vital to become work ready and work changing graduates. These discussions can help bring the work changing dimension more into the light of the established work readiness dimension of GE. In addition, making the work changing dimension more visible can shed light on an argument that tends to be missing from debates about whether HEIs work with GE is altogether different from and/or harmful to their mission of developing *engaged* and *democratic* citizens (Boden & Nedeva 2010; Mtawa et al., 2019, who questioned how compatible HEIs work with GE actually is with this mission). The argument is that because GE is often merely viewed from a work readiness perspective, it tends to be overlooked that GE has a work changing dimension that fits well with HEIs mission of developing engaged and democratic citizens. More specifically, this work aligns by fostering graduates who are critical and creative enough to bring about change in working life and society in general. While it may not fit according to the work readiness priority, GE as a concept is not different or detrimental to HEI's mission. The disregard without acknowledging nuance and potential benefits can be problematized.

Furthermore, as the GE concept is here to stay for the foreseeable future, I suggest that it is better to try and expand how this concept is usually understood than to criticize it for being inherently harmful to the HEIs mission of developing engaged and democratic citizens. Finally, I want to reiterate that what I find inherently problematic is the EL label and its simplistic implication that there exists a specific form of learning whose unique feature is that it is founded on experience. To actually move beyond simplistic perspectives, there is arguably a need to avoid using the EL label altogether. However, this is unlikely to happen because this label already has a dominant position in both research and the marketing discourse of HEIs. The current popularity of EL is also discussed by LaCroix in Chapter 3 and by Buzzelli in Chapter 4. More specifically, Lacroix discusses whether EL will "endure beyond a pedagogical fad" and Buzzelli discusses that HEIs has become increasingly oriented towards offering students an education that includes opportunities for EL.

NOTES

1 This means research that studies one or more aspects of higher education.
2 I am aware the fact that the term theoretical have different meanings and can be understood in both different and similar ways in different academic disciplines. What I problematize here is the assumption that experience does not play a part in students' on-campus learning but is only present in a form of learning commonly referred to as EL.
3 By hands-on, I mean learning experiences from being directly involved in and undertaking certain work assignments.

REFERENCES

Billett, S. (2022). Promoting graduate employability: Key goals, and curriculum and pedagogic practices for higher education. In B. Ng Ling, (Ed.), *Graduate Employability and Workplace-Based Learning Development* (pp. 11–29). Springer.

Billett, S., & Valencia-Forrester, F. (2020). Post-practicum project: Its educational purposes, importance, and roles. In S. Billett, J. Orrell, D. Jackson, & F. Valencia-Forrester (Eds.), *Enriching Higher Education Students' Learning through Post-work Placement Interventions* (pp. 3–23). Springer.

Björck, V. (2020a). The idea of academia and the real world and its ironic role in the discourse on Work-Integrated Learning. *Studies in Continuing Education, 42*(1), 1–16.

– (2020b). *Learning "theory" at university and "practice" in the workplace – A problematisation of the theory-practice terminology that the dualistic design of Work-integrated Learning institutionalises* [Doctoral dissertation, University West]. https://urn.kb.se/resolve?urn=urn:nbn:se:hv:diva-16063

– (2021). Taking issue with how the Work-Integrated Learning discourse ascribes a dualistic meaning to graduate employability. *Higher Education, 82*(2), 307–22.

Björck, V., Hedman Ahlström, B., & Kerekes, N. (2025). Work readiness and work-changing ability: Exploring the employability profiles of a social psychiatric care graduate programme's alumni. *Higher Education, Skills and Work-Based Learning, 15*(7), 96–109. https://doi.org/10.1108/HESWBL-07-2024-0186

Björck, V., & Johansson, K. (2019). Problematising the theory – practice terminology: A discourse analysis of students' statements on Work-Integrated Learning. *Journal of Further and Higher Education, 43*(10), 1363–75.

Björck, V., & Willermark, S. (2024). Where is the "WIL" in Work-Integrated Learning research? *Studies in Continuing Education*, 1–15.

Boden, R., & Nedeva, M. (2010). Employing discourse: universities and graduate "employability." *Journal of Education Policy, 25*(1), 37–54.

Boud, D. (2012). Problematising practice-based education. In J. Higgs, R. Barnett, S. Billett, M. Hutchings & F. Trede (Eds.), *Practice-Based Education: Perspectives and strategies* (pp. 55–68). Sense Publishers.

Buzzelli, M., & Asafo-Adjei, E. (2023). Experiential learning and the university's host community: Rapid growth, contested mission and policy challenge. *Higher Education*, 85(3), 521–38.

Carr, W. (2006). Education without theory. *British Journal of Educational Studies, 54*(2), 136–59.

Clarke, M. (2018). Rethinking graduate employability: The role of capital, individual attributes and context. *Studies in Higher Education, 43*(11), 1923–37.

Coll, R. K., Eames, C., Paku, L. K., Lay, M., Ayling, D., Hodges, D., Ram, S., Bhat, R., Fleming, J., Ferkins, L., Wiersma, C., & Martin, A. (2009, April). *An exploration of the pedagogies employed to integrate knowledge in work-integrated learning in New Zealand higher education institutions.* Teaching & Learning Research Institute. http://www.tlri.org.nz/sites/default/files/projects/9263-Finalreport.pdf

Crisp, G., Higgs, J., & Letts, W. (2019). The employability agenda. In J. Higgs, G. Crisp & W. Letts (Eds.), *Education for Employability (Volume 2): Learning for Future Possibilities* (pp. 3–12). Brill Sense.

Davies, L. (2000). Why kick the "L" out of "LEarning"? The development of students' employability skills through part-time working. *Education + Training, 42*(8), 436–44.

Dewey, J. (1904). The relation of theory to practice in education. *Teachers College Record, 5*(6), 9–30.

Fenwick, T. J. (2000). Expanding conceptions of experiential learning: A review of the five contemporary perspectives on cognition. *Adult Education Quarterly, 50*(4), 243–72.

Freudenberg, B., Brimble, M., & Cameron, C. (2011). WIL and generic skill development: The development of business students' generic skills through work-integrated learning. *Asia-Pacific Journal of Cooperative Education, 12*(2), 79–93.

Gazier, B. (1998). Employability: Definitions and trends. In Gazier, B. (Ed.), *Employability: Concepts and Policies* (pp. 37–71). European Employment Observatory.

Herrington, A. J. & Herrington, J. A. (2007). What is an authentic learning environment? In L. A. Tomei (Ed.), *Online and distance learning: Concepts, methodologies, tools, and applications* (pp. 68–77). Information Science Reference.

Illeris, K. (2007). What do we actually mean by experiential learning? *Human Resource Development Review, 6*(1), 84–95.

Jackson, D. (2014). Testing a model of undergraduate competence in employability skills and its implications for stakeholders. *Journal of Education and Work, 27*(2), 220–42.

– (2015). Employability skill development in work-integrated learning: Barriers and best practice. *Studies in Higher Education, 40*(2), 350–67.

– (2017). Developing pre-professional identity in undergraduates through work-integrated learning. *Higher Education, 74*(5), 833–53.

Jackson, D. A., & Edgar, S. (2019). Encouraging students to draw on work experiences when articulating achievements and capabilities to enhance employability. *Australian Journal of Career Development, 28*(1), 39–50.

Kolb, D. A. (1984). *Experiential learning: Experience as the source of learning and development.* Prentice Hall, Inc.

Kolb, D. A., Boyatzis, R. E., & Mainemelis, C. (2014). Experiential learning theory: Previous research and new directions. In J. Sternberg, L. Zhang (Eds.), *Perspectives on thinking, learning, and cognitive styles* (pp. 227–248). Routledge.

Korthagen, F. A., & Kessels, J. P. (1999). Linking theory and practice: Changing the pedagogy of teacher education. *Educational Researcher 28*(4), 4–17.

Kruger, J. S., Kruger, D. J., & Suzuki, R. (2015). Assessing the effectiveness of experiential learning in a student-run free clinic. *Pedagogy in Health Promotion, 1*(2), 91–4.

Lau, P. L., Baranovich, D. L., & Leong, K. E. (2018). Enhancing work readiness: A review of career development of adolescents in Malaysia. *International Journal of Education, 3*(8), 13–20.

Lee, J., Kobia, C., & Son, J. (2022). Improving global competence in classroom-based experiential learning activities. *Journal of Global Education and Research, 7*(2), 131–145.

Lewis, L. H., & Williams, C. J. (1994). Experiential learning: Past and present. *New Directions for Adult and Continuing Education, 1994*(62), 5–16.

Masschelein, J., & Simons, M. (2013). *In defence of the school: A public issue.* Education, Culture and Society Publishers.

McQuaid, R. W., & Lindsay, C. (2005). The concept of employability. *Urban studies, 42*(2), 197–219.

Mintzberg, H. (2005). How inspiring. How sad. Comment on Sumantra Ghoshal's paper. *Australian Universities Review, 4*(1), 108.

Morris, T. H. (2020). Experiential learning – A systematic review and revision of Kolb's model. *Interactive Learning Environments, 28*(8), 1064–77.

Mtawa, N., Fongwa, S., & Wilson-Strydom, M. (2021). Enhancing graduate employability attributes and capabilities formation: A service-learning approach. *Teaching in Higher Education, 26*(5), 679–95.

Nguyen, N. (2019). *Key factors affecting work-integrated learning in language teacher education: A multisite case study* [Dissertation, Western Sydney University]. http://hdl.handle.net/1959.7/uws:53270

Orr, C.M. (2002). Challenging the "academic/real world" divide. In N. A. Naples & K. Bojar (Eds.), *Teaching Feminist Activism: Strategies from the Field* (pp. 36–53). Routledge

Raelin, J. A. (2016). Work-based (not classroom) learning as the apt preparation for the practice of management. *Management Teaching Review, 1*(1), 43–51.

Sattler, L. A. (2018). From classroom to courtside: An examination of the experiential learning practices of sport management faculty. *Journal of Hospitality, Leisure, Sport & Tourism Education*, 22, 52–62.

Sattler, P., & Peters, J. (2013). *Work-Integrated Learning in Ontario's postsecondary sector: The experience of Ontario graduates.* Academica Group, Inc. https://heqco.ca/wp-content/uploads/2020/03/WIL_Experience_ON_Graduates_ENG.pdf

Schön, D. A. (1987). *Educating the reflective practitioner: Toward a new design for teaching and learning in the professions.* Jossey-Bass.

Tomlinson, M. (2012). Graduate employability: A review of conceptual and empirical themes. *Higher Education Policy, 25*(4), 407–31.

Trede, F., & McEwen, C. (2012). Developing a critical professional identity: Engaging self in practice. In J. Higgs, R. Barnett, S. Billett, M. Hutchings & F. Trede (Eds.), *Practice-Based Education: Perspectives and strategies* (pp. 27–40). Sense Publishers.

Valencia-Forrester, F. (2022). Beyond the hospital and entrepreneurial models of journalism education: Case studies of Work-Integrated Learning models in wise practice. *Graduate Employability Across Contexts,* 207–25.

Wilton, N. (2012). The impact of work placements on skill development and career outcomes for business and management graduates. *Studies in Higher Education, 37*(5), 603–20.

3 When Logics Collide: Experiential Learning and Intra-Institutional Dynamics

EMERSON LACROIX

University of Waterloo, Canada

Introduction

Experiential education is often discussed in pedagogical terms, as a student-centred approach to enhancing learning outcomes (Eyler, 2009; Schwartz, 2012). Framed within a curricular context, this discussion is useful for disseminating emerging practices, how-to guides, as well as considering challenges and solutions for implementing experiential learning practices into university courses (Donovan & Hood, 2021; Mantai & Huber, 2021). Experiential learning literature is ripe with examples of implementation across a wide variety of disciplines, and scholars have been successful in demonstrating some of the inherent value-added learning outcomes associated with experiential learning (Burch et al., 2019; Henderson, 2018). The pedagogical foundations of experiential learning are certainly important considerations to supply students with valuable learning experiences and allow them to continue developing into well-rounded students and democratic citizens. As Björck (Chapter 2 of this volume) points out, arguments are still unfolding about the connection between graduate employability, a democratic citizenry, and experiential learning. These benefits are not confined to university campuses but are enjoyed and nurtured in various local contexts (Collins-Nelsen and others at Chapter 8 of this volume; see also Bringle et al., 2009; Bringle & Hatcher, 2000). At the same time, curricular forms of experiential learning are becoming overshadowed by the obsession in Canadian universities with work-integrated learning (WIL) and its capacity to equip students with the skills and knowledge employers are looking for. What's more, introducing co-curricular forms of experiential learning (e.g., conference presentations, campus volunteering) quickly highlights the relative complexity of the term "experiential learning," and demonstrates that it is certainly not monolithic.

Curricular, co-curricular, and work-integrated experiential learning[1] each contribute distinct educational benefits to students and are embraced to varying degrees across the organizational mosaic of Canadian higher education. Recently, the province of Ontario incorporated experiential learning as a core funding metric for colleges and universities (Ministry of Training, Colleges, and Universities, 2021). Presented as a skill and job outcome, this development means that colleges and universities are required to report the proportion of graduates in programs who have participated in at least one course with an experiential learning component and is aligned with broader policy calls for guaranteed experiential learning opportunities for post-secondary students (The Premier's Highly Skilled Workforce Expert Panel, 2016). Eventually, upwards of 60% of the public money they receive from government will be tied to these funding metrics (Government of Ontario, 2019). To be sure, other provinces are following suit on accountability metrics and system transformation for their higher education sectors. Alberta has launched an Alberta 2030 strategy for transforming its post-secondary sector (Government of Alberta, 2021) and has recently created the Minister's Advisory Council on Higher Education and Skills (MACHES) (Government of Alberta, 2022). Manitoba has begun engaging in system-wide consultations for a new Post-Secondary Accountability Framework (Government of Manitoba, 2022), which has been met with tense responses from provincial constituents (Froese, 2022). Experience and skills training are at the heart of these initiatives and demonstrate provincial interest in experiential learning. Nonetheless, Ontario's recent funding updates provide a good institutional context to unpack the dynamics of experiential learning in the contemporary state of Canadian higher education.

What these developments demonstrate is that there is increasing institutional incentives to foster experiential learning across the post-secondary landscape. Here, discussions on experiential learning are moving beyond pedagogy and into the realm of organizational dynamics. It is in this realm that this chapter contributes an organizational perspective to account for the complexities of experiential learning and the implications for its future as an organizational goal. This understanding is critical for analyzing how experiential learning has risen as a provincial priority and the ways in which this priority reverberates within universities themselves. At play are intra-institutional dynamics – or the internal interactions between different organizational units – with respect to experiential learning. Despite some recent theorizing (see LaCroix, 2021), the intra-institutional dynamics of experiential learning remains under-analyzed. The chapter begins by outlining some foundational ideas of institutional theorizing in higher education and then discusses the relative connections to experiential learning with respect to organizational structure, reward systems, and academic employment patterns. Together, these factors have implications as to how deeply experiential learning will be institutionalized into the core institutional practices of Canadian universities and whether experiential learning will endure beyond a pedagogical fad.

Understanding Universities as Organizations: Sites of Multiple Logics

Institutional theorizing operates under the auspice of the open-systems perspective and forwards the notion that organizational structure is influenced by the environment that is external to organizations, as opposed to being internally driven. Organizations are situated within broader environments that influence their internal functions and behaviour (Tolbert & Hall, 2009). Contrary to earlier organizational perspectives which were more inward looking (e.g., closed-system), an open-systems approach acknowledges that both inter- and intra-organizational relations have implications for the technical functions of organizations and that organizations are not autonomous blobs, devoid of external influences (see Thompson, 2008). Put another way, organizations exist within an organizational field, or "those organizations that, in aggregate, constitute a recognized area of institutional life" (DiMaggio & Powell, 1983, p. 148). Universities, for example, are not autonomous sites of teaching, learning, and research that operate in an unbounded fashion. Rather, they are situated within a field in which they relate to one another and are subject to external pressures such as government and industry demands. In fact, it is the external environment that puts pressure on organizations that makes it more likely for organizations to have greater complexity in their structure (Meyer & Rowan, 1977; Tolbert & Hall, 2009). Ontario's new provincial funding metrics highlight this institutional dynamic, where particular priorities are placed onto universities, and these institutions must find ways to respond to them in a way that satisfies the government. In exchange, their provincial funding is undisturbed and allows them to carry on in a "business as usual" fashion.

A second feature of institutional theory is that, as a result of organizational pressures, organizations within the same field tend to become isomorphic over time (DiMaggio & Powell, 1983). When organizations inhabit the same environment, they are largely subject to similar pressures, and thereby develop similar responses to those pressures. As a result, organizations tend to resemble one another in terms of their formal structures and operations. When thinking of higher education, regardless of where one goes universities tend to resemble one another. In terms of structure, universities have similar administrative levels (e.g., board of governors, senate, executive positions) that liaise between the university and its external environment. Universities are largely comprised of similar faculties which accomplish the research and teaching functions of the institution, and these functions are supported by a variety of services and offices across campus that are staffed with knowledgeable professionals (e.g., libraries, counselling offices, information services).

These structural discussions highlight that universities do not operate completely independent from one another but rather inhabit an institutional field that has great influence on the way universities organize themselves. Across these institutions, organizational actors inhabit universities and are guided by various logics that influence the actions they take and what they perceive to be legitimate (for recent theoretical developments on inhabited institutions, see Hallett & Hawbaker, 2021). Institutional logics are, thus, sets of principles that prescribe "how to interpret organizational reality, what constitutes appropriate behaviour, and how to succeed" and are critical for understanding how institutions change over time and how organizational actors make sense of change-making forces (Thornton, 2004, p. 70). These logics are essentially the "rules of the game" when it comes to how elements of a particular institution are achieved (Thornton et al., 2012). At the same time, universities are not influenced by one single logic. Organizations are constantly subjected to a mosaic of logics that have varying degrees of impact on their goals, structure, behaviour, and processes (Greenwood et al., 2011; Thornton et al., 2012). Competing or multiple institutional logics can contribute to organizational change over time (Shields & Watermeyer, 2020). With respect to higher education, two prominent logics are the managerial and academic logics, which each have their own relevance to experiential education and direct how experiential learning, as part of the larger educative mission of the university, should be done.

The Managerial Institutional Logic

The managerial logic is emblematic of a New Public Management or neoliberal approach to university operations. Instead of traditional bureaucratic controls, alternative means are used to regulate the goals and operations of universities, such as accountability measures, funding metrics, and various incentive structures (Bleiklie, 2018; Bleiklie et al., 2017). The classic university structure is bottom-heavy, meaning that those working within various disciplines and offices are able to conduct their activities with relatively free enterprise and little administrative oversight or interference. While this model is characterized by loose-coupling (i.e., relatively loose organizational linkages between units) (Weick, 1976), the market logic creates tighter structural coupling (Canhilal et al., 2016). With a tighter organizational structure, messages and direction are more efficiently driven from the top, as the managerial logic is based on "strong leadership of the academic leaders, the hierarchical structures of the university authorities, as well as an emphasis on efficiency, standardization, and accountability" (Urbanek, 2021, p. 6). Along with a tighter organizational structure, the managerial logic situates universities in competition with one another, in which legitimacy and rewards are based on efficiency and responses to environmental pressure. Ontario universities have recently been placed in a greater degree of contrast with one another through the Strategic Mandate Agreement process, in which experiential learning is now a mandated part of government funding, and universities are now required to articulate both how they are fostering experiential education, as well as provide program metrics about where experiential learning is happening across their campuses. Managerially, this means that institutions must undergo scoping searches within their programs and courses to not only show where experiential learning is happening but also how they are innovating and creating new opportunities for students to learn actively within and outside academic programs. This process highlights the top-down nature of organizational behaviour, where external pressure reverberates throughout the university as a matter of tighter institutional control over the goals and operations of universities.

The Academic Institutional Logic

There is never one prevailing logic within organizations. While there may be *dominant* logics, organizations liaise a plethora of logics which seek to influence goals and actions. Another prominent logic within the university systems is the academic logic. The academic logic is rooted in the medieval foundations of the university system itself and the historic mission to impart knowledge on learners (Côté & Allahar, 2007; Urbanek, 2021). Contrary to the tight coupling of the managerial logic, the academic logic views the overall structure of the university to be a republic of scholars, valuing academic freedom and collegial decision making (Bleiklie, 2018). Indeed, faculty have considerable leeway to perform their research and teaching duties as they see fit (i.e., "academic freedom"). This logic also does not differentiate between academic freedom and institutional autonomy, lending itself to the bottom-heavy organizational structure that was noted above. In this case, while there is an administrative structure to the institution, it is the job of this structure of buffer the technical operations of the universities from external influences (i.e., environmental pressures) and allow the technical functions of the institution to continue on without the need to constantly be reorganizing and reorienting how teaching and research are done. The knowledge-foundations of the institution are primary, and the behaviour and decision-making of technical-level organizational actors are based off disciplinary professional knowledge as opposed to tight organizational goals. In this case, academic freedom has a significant impact on whether faculty members choose to implement experiential learning. The decision is based on their pedagogical rationale and whether the mode of instruction fits with their disciplinary teaching goals. Essentially, it is an entrepreneurial decision made by an organizational actor, as opposed to one based on organizational pressure. Under the academic logic, faculty have the freedom to choose which method of instruction is best, based on their expertise in the subject area and teaching strategies amassed over their career.[2]

A Note on Hybridity of Logics

The above subsections outline two particular logics at play within the university system. These logics are excellent heuristics for understanding the opposing forces at play within universities and which are often discussed (though perhaps not in name) in reference to neoliberal influences and mission ambiguity in universities (e.g., Côté & Allahar, 2007; Gooch, 2019). At the same time, the institutional logics perspective acknowledges that organizations are sites of hybridity, meaning that logics do not come with an either-or ultimatum. Universities are examples of hybrid institutions (Lepori, 2016) where different institutional principles engage with one another and have resonance with different constituent groups (Greenwood et al., 2011). This has significant implications for the intra-institutional dynamics of organizational goals and values. Where there is overlap between the two logics, opposing sides will seek to redefine organizational goals in ways that align with their particular values and technological priorities. In the case of experiential education, there is a great deal of intra-institutional logic work required to instantiate it as a core organizational practice, one which is able to resonate and reflect managerial and academic logics and appease tensions where there is contrast between the two.

Experiential Education and Logic Work

The managerial and academic logics each have their own relative implications for how experiential learning is being institutionalized within Canadian universities. Institutionalization is essentially an organizational process whereby a particular idea or practice becomes sedimented within and organization to the point that it becomes taken for granted (Tolbert & Zucker, 1996). From an organizational perspective, institutionalization of experiential learning would allow universities to demonstrate that there has been actual effort to foster and develop the pedagogy, as opposed to responding more ceremonially to external funding pressures (e.g., rebranding existing initiatives instead of developing new ones) (for a classic review of this process, see Meyer & Rowan, 1977). Although experiential learning has been entrenched in the Strategic Mandate funding metrics, this says nothing about the ways in which universities have responded and the intra-institutional dynamics at play. The intra-institutional dynamics that I will discuss include the ways in which experiential learning has impacted the organizational structure of universities, the particular considerations for existing reward structures, and the extent to which current employment trends are incommensurate with the general institutional goal to expand experiential learning opportunities for students.

Experiential Learning and Organizational Structure

Experiential learning continues to be a topic of interest for government and industry to prepare the next generation of workers (Macpherson & Rizk, 2022; Munro et al., 2014). As universities operate in an open system, current asks by government and industry have implications for how experiential learning is fostered and supported. Coupled with pedagogical interests in experiential learning, many institutions have made changes to their organizational structure over time to support experiential learning efforts. Structural changes to universities typically have two components to them: an administrative component which steers organizational efforts and the development of organizational infrastructure to help implement the steering initiatives. In Table 3.1, cursory examples suggest that across the spectrum of Canadian universities, experiential learning is being highlighted as an administrative priority that will steer future planning initiatives to embed experiential learning into the fabric of the institution.

These administrative statements signal to university constituents and external stakeholders that experiential learning is an administrative

Table 3.1. Administrative Steering of Experiential Learning

University of British Columbia, *Strategy 13: Practical Learning*	We are working with external partners and alumni to increase experiential learning – "learning by doing" – across academic programs, and to enhance career services. Where these connections extend beyond the province, they create scope for UBC to broaden its perspective and capacity for influence.
University of Calgary, *Experiential Learning Plan (2020–25)*	UCalgary's bold commitment to experiential learning will make learning-by-doing a cornerstone of our student experience and positions our university to become a leader among Canadian post-secondary institutions.
University of Waterloo, *Strategic Plan: 2020–25*	We will build on our global leadership in co–operative education with a commitment to provide every undergraduate and graduate student with expanded options in experiential learning by 2025. We are also committed to empowering students to create more flexible learning pathways aligned with the future of work and learning.
University of Prince Edward Island, *Strategic Plan: 2018–23*	UPEI will be a leader in providing outstanding programs and experiential learning opportunities that enable our students to develop to their full potential in both the classroom and the community, ensuring our students emerge from their studies ready to excel and contribute to the betterment of our world.

priority and that the university's administration is working to steer experiential learning as a core element of the institution. While these statements work to signal priorities, they also give rise to intra-institutional structural changes to support them. Each of these institutions has worked to create institutional infrastructure to support the expansion efforts of experiential learning. Commonly referred to as "hubs" or "offices" of experiential learning, Canadian universities have made changes to their organizational structure to help foster experiential learning and provide support and resourcing for its development across curricular, co-curricular, and work-integrated avenues. Critical to the theme of this volume, these hubs help broker new town-gown relationships and foster existing partnerships. A confounding factor, of course, is institutional size. Not all institutions have the same capacity to foster and resource new innovations to the same scale. Smaller institutions may mirror their larger counterparts with respect to expressing the value of experiential learning, but their capacity to foster and resource it will be to a lesser degree given existing capacities (e.g., budget, physical space, personnel). A second consideration is the extent to which these processes have resulted in anything "new" to the institution or whether they are more ceremonial and are examples of institutional rebranding and recoupling initiatives under new banners.

From an organizational standpoint, these offices and infrastructure operate as a "third space" (Whitchurch, 2013), as they lay outside of the managerial structure of universities but are also not housed or blended within the academic logic. If the administrative level of universities is more aligned with the managerial logic, and faculty are more aligned with the academic logic, it is in this third space that there is an opportunity for hybridity between the two. Along with the structural and administrative developments, within the third space, there has been a growth of specialized professionals whose positions are tailored to supporting the development and implementation of experiential learning. Friedson (2001) suggests that the key factor in establishing a profession is the cordoning-off of certain work that is so specialized those lacking particular training and knowledge could not perform it. For example, experiential learning coordinators help to develop resourcing and faculty aides. They are also instrumental for helping faculty find community partners and ensuring these relationships are nurtured within the academic environment. Co-op advisors help to build institutional partnerships with industry and community and place students in jobs, among other tasks. In some instances, such as the University of Waterloo, experiential learning is present in the senior administration with the Associate Provost, Co-operative and Experiential Education (University of Waterloo, n.d.). These positions are equipped with the specialized knowledge to help diffuse experiential learning throughout the university. By fostering these institutional resources, universities are helping to alleviate common troubles experienced by faculty such as the time it takes to meaningfully implement experiential learning in their courses and, more overtly, a lack of understanding of how to "do" experiential learning (LaCroix, 2021). Still, these resources are only helpful to the extent that faculty are aware they exist and have the capacity to engage with them. While the third space is valuable for bridging the divide between logics, it is in no way a perfect system that will result in a precipitous upswing of experiential learning programming in universities. Contributing to this process is faculty buy-in for curricular forms of experiential learning and the compatibility between experiential learning and the existing academic reward structures influencing faculty decision making.

Institutional Reward Systems

As a meta-theoretical perspective, classic arguments of institutional logics sought to first understand societal-level institutional structures (see Friedland & Alford, 1991). This macro starting point has paved the way to examining the micro-foundations of institutional logics and the impact that logics have on the sense-making and behavioural decisions of organizational actors. Much of the existing literature on implementing experiential learning frames this process as one of pedagogical entrepreneurialism, meaning that faculty have made conscious decisions to include different forms of experiential learning in their teaching practices (e.g., Holtzman & Menning, 2015; Lund Dean & Wright, 2017; Windsor & Carroll, 2015). While valuable, these pedagogical foundations do not consider the intra-institutional complexities of experiential learning and a critical component about institutional reward structures.

Institutional reward systems play a critical role in understanding why some organizational processes become embedded in organizations and others do not. To the extent that institutional innovations are incommensurate with the normative culture and practices of the organization, there is a barrier to how institutionalized that innovation will become. Classic organizational theorizing suggests that organizational actors have a variety of response options to such institutional pressure. Oliver (1991) and more recently Coburn (2004) have proposed typologies of possible responses by organizational actors to influences from their institutional environment, bridging macro-micro divides in organizations. Each suggests that organizational actors have several ways in which to respond to external pressure on the way they perform their roles and responsibilities within organizations. Ultimately, the more persistent and congruent institutional messages are with how actors already understand and view their roles, the more likely they will acquiesce and integrate these ideas into their professional practices. These perspectives have great resonance for the durability of experiential learning strategies within institutions. With hybrid institutions, the employees working within universities are influenced by their own professional norms and understanding of their roles. The academic logic is grounded in historical cultural norms about knowledge transmission and professional standards of knowledge production. These norms continue to be transmitted in the way knowledge production is evaluated and legitimated within the professoriate and have been relatively durable over time. Indeed, university policies exist with respect to tenure and promotion and are often reflective of knowledge-production logics.

While new innovations can certainly be spurred from the ground level through an entrepreneurial spirit, recent developments such as funding metrics and shifting administrative priorities means that there may be more top-down pressure on the professoriate to develop experiential learning. Though universities have expanded their institutional resourcing to support the institutionalization of experiential learning across their programs, there will also need to be work done to formally recognize and reward faculty who include experiential learning in their pedagogical practice. For example, recognizing experiential learning in the tenure and promotion process would bring experiential learning formally into the normative reward structure of the academic logic, that is, the way in which organizational practices are rewarded within this particular institutional logic. This would help address noted professional obstacles that stand in the way of faculty buy-in and make experiential learning more congruent with pre-existing elements of knowledge production (Skaggs & Graybeal, 2019). When coupled with the expanded institutional resourcing, moving experiential learning into the academic reward structure would help to hybridize the administrative (i.e., managerial) desire to foster experiential learning with the faculty (i.e., academic) normative professional practices. Essentially, doing so would help hybridize institutional desires to expand experiential learning without alienating faculty interest and reinforcing top-down managerial tensions. While there is a high degree of "bean counting" happening right now within institutions to identify where experiential learning is already taking place, these considerations will be forefront to the next phase of fostering experiential learning and the development of new learning opportunities and modalities. This is certainly not an uncomplicated process, and university administrators and other experiential learning stakeholders will need to consider the changing nature of the professoriate, specifically, the institutional reliance on precarious employment.

Implications of the Precariat for Experiential Learning

The intra-institutional dynamics of experiential learning faces further complexities when one considers the changing nature of the professoriate. Especially in the case of curricular, and to a lesser extent co-curricular and work-integrated learning, experiential learning relies on the professoriate to become integrated and offered in Canadian university degrees. However, the nature of the professoriate continues to change due to the reliance on part-time or sessional faculty members (Rose, 2020). Some estimates suggest that one-in-three academic staff in Canada work on a contract-to-contract basis (Canadian Association of University Teachers, n.d.), and this precarious working situation has negative impacts on their ability to engage with students and contribute to knowledge production (Foster & Bauer, 2018). Due to the neoliberalization of the university (Cannella & Koro-Ljungberg, 2017; Troiani & Dutson, 2021), there is increasing reliance on this small majority to perform a high degree of the teaching tasks in academic disciplines.

The transformation of the professoriate from full-time permanent workers to predominantly precarious workers has negative implications for the institutional capacity to foster enduring experiential learning opportunities for Canadian university students. Namely, the challenges and barriers tenured/tenure-track faculty may feel towards experiential learning are amplified for sessional instructors who often have less institutional resources and lower pay. For example, it has been demonstrated that student-evaluations of teaching have a disproportionate impact on sessional instructors, especially those of equity-deserving backgrounds (Smele et al., 2021). While there has been a slow culture shift away from these evaluations for assessments of teaching, sessional instructors may be less likely to take on advanced pedagogical practices at the risk of them impacting their teaching evaluations. This is one potential impact on experiential learning, though there is scant empirical data on sessional faculty use on experiential learning. Another consideration is that the revolving-door model on course delivery is incommensurate with the time it takes to foster meaningful relationships for modes of experiential learning like community-engaged projects. Given that a foundation of community-engaged scholarship is knowledge exchange and mutual benefit between academic and community partners (Bringle et al., 2009), these relationships and projects require a considerable amount of advanced planning and these projects are unlikely to take-off when the course may be taught by a different instructor the next time it is offered.

There is an over-reliance on sessional faculty in the current academic system, and this employment pattern is incommensurate with administrative priorities to foster experiential learning. If institutions are serious about fostering experiential learning and providing at least one (or multiple) experiential learning opportunities for every student, further consideration will be needed as to how this will be accomplished with a workforce largely comprised of contingent workers. Potentially, this will require further logic work to hybridize academic resources and reward structures to include precariously employed faculty and rely less on assessments which reflect a broader marketized logic toward higher education. Providing additional resourcing and recognizing/rewarding the enhanced workload required for curricular forms of experiential learning will be critical for this large subset of academic workers to consider taking on an advanced pedagogy. Simply put, if there are existing barriers faced by tenured faculty with respect to fostering experiential learning (LaCroix, 2021; Skaggs & Graybeal, 2019), these difficulties will be more acute for contingent faculty members who also face their own unique professional challenges in universities.

Conclusion

This chapter has focused on experiential learning from an institutional perspective. Rather than a pedagogical focus, exploring the intra-institutional dynamics highlights that experiential learning is more than a pedagogical fad: it is an institutionally complex process. Adopting an institutional approach is valuable for researchers and policy makers to consider how a new institutional priority diffuses throughout organizations and the internal dynamics of such a process. As experiential learning continues to be discussed within university administrative priorities, further research is needed to analyze the organizational complexities of this process, the relative implications for different organizational constituents, and what it means for fostering town-gown relations. Two particular logics that are at play are the managerial and academic logics, which are often compared and contrasted in institutional research on higher education (Canhilal et al., 2016; Lepori, 2016). While these logics are distinct, universities are hybrid organizations and are sites of institutional collisions. Experiential learning is not removed from this process and is subject to the influence of both logics. This chapter has shown that the enduring potential of experiential learning requires a great deal of intra-institutional logic-work within universities to balance the managerial desire of institutional accountability with the normative culture and reward structure of the professoriate. We should also not overlook the importance of "third space" professionals who are often middle-workers to these institutional dynamics and who may be most important for translating opposing perspectives to either side. Currently, experiential learning is present in administrative steering documents, and this has affected the structure of universities in some ways. While these developments may steer the institution toward a more concerted effort to foster experiential learning, this may prove to be a null exercise if it is not acknowledged within traditional academic reward structures. This becomes more complex with the understanding that efforts to expand experiential learning may land in the lap of precariously employed faculty members. Further research is needed on the role these faculty members play in this process and their relative capacity to assist or challenge the institutionalization of experiential learning.

NOTES

1 In conjunction with the Introduction to this volume, I separate these terms for the sake of clarity. Readers may well come across these terms used interchangeably or grouped in different fashions.

2 The constellation of pedagogical strategies and preferred teaching methods are what Everitt (2012) refers to as "arsenals of practice" (p. 203).

REFERENCES

Bleiklie, I. (2018). New public management or neoliberalism, higher education. In J. C. Shin & P. Teixeira (Eds.), *Encyclopedia of International Higher Education Systems and Institutions* (pp. 1–6). Springer Dordrecht.

Bleiklie, I., Enders, J., & Lepori, B. (2017). Organizational configurations of modern universities, institutional logics and public policies – towards an integrative framework. In I. Bleiklie, J. Enders & B. Lepori (Eds.), *Managing universities: Policy and organizational change from a western European comparative perspective.* (pp. 303–26). Palgrave Macmillan.

Bringle, R., & Hatcher, J. (2000). Institutionalization of service learning in higher education. *The Journal of Higher Education, 71*(3), 273–90. https://doi.org/10.1080/00221546.2000.11780823

Bringle, R. G., Clayton, P. H., & Price, M. (2009). Partnerships in service learning and civic engagement. *Journal of Service-Learning and Civic Engagement, 1*(1), 1–20.

Burch, G. F., Giambatista, R., Batchelor, J. H., Burch, J. J., Hoover, J. D., & Heller, N. A. (2019). A meta-analysis of the relationship between experiential learning and learning outcomes. *Decision Sciences Journal of Innovative Education, 17*(3), 239–73. https://doi.org/10.1111/dsji.12188

Canadian Association of University Teachers. (n.d.). *Precarious labour in our academic institutions.* https://ourfuture.caut.ca/brief_precarity

Canhilal, S. K., Lepori, B., & Seeber, M. (2016). Decision-making power and institutional logic in higher education institutions: A comparative analysis of European universities. In R. Pinheiro, L. Geschwind, F. O. Ramirez & K. Vrangbæk (Eds.), *Research in the Sociology of Organizations* (Vol. 45, pp. 169–94). Emerald Group Publishing Limited. https://doi.org/10.1108/S0733-558X20150000045019

Cannella, G. S., & Koro-Ljungberg, M. (2017). Neoliberalism in higher education: Can we understand? Can we resist and survive? Can we become without neoliberalism? *Cultural Studies ↔ Critical Methodologies, 17*(3), 155–16. https://doi.org/10.1177/1532708617706117

Coburn, C. (2004). Beyond Decoupling: Rethinking the relationship between the institutional environment and the classroom. *Sociology of Education, 77*(3), 211–44. https://doi.org/10.1177/003804070407700302

Côté, J., & Allahar, A. (2007). *Ivory tower blues: A university system in crisis.* University of Toronto Press.

DiMaggio, P., & Powell, W. (1983). The iron cage revisited: Institutional isomorphism and collective rationality. *American Sociological Review, 42*(2), 147–60. https://doi.org/10.2307/2095101

Donovan, P., & Hood, A. (2021). Experiential learning in the large classroom using performative pedagogy. *Journal of Management Education, 45*(3), 344–59. https://doi.org/10.1177/1052562920965625

Everitt, J. G. (2012). Teacher careers and inhabited institutions: Sense-making and arsenals of teaching practice in educational institutions. *Symbolic Interaction, 35*(2), 203–20. https://doi.org/10.1002/symb.16

Eyler, J. (2009). The power of experiential education. *Liberal Education, 95*(4), 24–31.

Foster, K., & Bauer, L. B. (2018 September). *Out of the shadows: Experiences of contract academic staff.* Canadian Association of University Teachers. https://www.caut.ca/sites/default/files/cas_report.pdf

Friedland, R., & Alford, R. (1991). Bringing society back in: Symbols, practices, and institutional contradictions. In P. DiMaggio & W. Powell (Eds.), *The New Institutionalism in Organizational Analysis* (pp. 232–63). University of Chicago Press.

Friedson, E. (2001). *Professionalism: The third logic: on the practice of knowledge.* The University of Chicago Press.

Froese, I. (2022). "Not really a consultation": Faculty walk out on Manitoba government meeting, say proposed model flawed. *CBC News.* https://www.cbc.ca/news/canada/manitoba/faculty-walks-out-university-winnipeg-performance-based-model-manitoba-1.6487410?cmp=rss&mc_cid=9e141164c0&mc_eid=003d30813f

Gooch, P. (2019). *Course correction: A map for the distracted university.* University of Toronto Press.

Government of Alberta. (2021). *Alberta 2030: Building skills for jobs.* https://open.alberta.ca/dataset/2bd41938-8100-4987-996d-b73d888cdbdc/resource/f897376a-95a9-4fe0-bfa7-9900ab815cd8/download/ae-alberta-2030-building-skills-for-jobs-strategy-summary-2021-04.pdf

– (2022). *Alberta 2030: New advisory council launches.* https://www.alberta.ca/release.cfm?xID=830490CE556AD-F4B9-9405-49DC21C67A66D1DA

Government of Manitoba. (2022). *Manitoba government launches substantive, system-wide consultation process on the new post-secondary accountability framework.* https://news.gov.mb.ca/news/index.html?item=54379

Government of Ontario. (2019). *2019 Ontario budget: Protecting what matters most.* https://budget.ontario.ca/pdf/2019/2019-ontario-budget-en.pdf

Greenwood, R., Raynard, M., Kodeih, F., Micelotta, E. R., & Lounsbury, M. (2011). Institutional complexity and organizational responses. *Academy of Management Annals, 5*(1), 317–71. https://doi.org/10.5465/19416520.2011.590299

Hallett, T., & Hawbaker, A. (2021). The case for an inhabited institutionalism in organizational research: Interaction, coupling, and change reconsidered. *Theory and Society, 50*(1), 1–32. https://doi.org/10.1007/s11186-020-09412-2

Henderson, A. (2018). Leveraging the power of experiential learning to achieve higher-order proficiencies. *Journal of Economic Education, 49*(1), 59–71. https://doi.org/10.1080/00220485.2017.1397576

Holtzman, M., & Menning, C. (2015). Integrating experiential learning and applied sociology to promote student learning and faculty research. *College Teaching, 63*(3), 112–18. https://doi.org/10.1080/87567555.2015.1019825

LaCroix, E. (2021). Organizational complexities of experiential education: Institutionalization and logic work in higher education. *Journal of Experiential Education, 45*(2), 157–71. https://doi.org/10.1177/10538259211028987

Lepori, B. (2016). Universities as hybrids: Applications of institutional logics theory to higher education. In J. Huisman & M. Tight (Eds.), *Theory and Method in Higher Education Research* (Vol. 2, pp. 245–64). Emerald Group Publishing Limited. https://doi.org/10.1108/S2056-375220160000002013

Lund Dean, K., & Wright, S. (2017). Embedding engaged learning in high enrollment lecture-based classes. *Higher Education, 74*(4), 651–68. https://doi.org/10.1007/s10734-016-0070-4

Macpherson, E., & Rizk, J. (2022). Essential skills for learning and working: Perspectives from education and employment leaders across Canada. *Conference Board of Canada*, 18.

Mantai, L., & Huber, E. (2021). Networked teaching: Overcoming the barriers to teaching experiential learning in large classes. *Journal of Management Education, 45*(5), 715–38. https://doi.org/10.1177/1052562920984506

Meyer, J., & Rowan, B. (1977). Institutionalized organizations: Formal structure as myth and ceremony. *American Journal of Sociology, 83*(2), 340–63.

Ministry of Training, Colleges, and Universities. (2021). *College and university Strategic Mandate Agreements*. https://www.ontario.ca/page/all-college-and-university-strategic-mandate-agreements

Munro, D., MacLaine, C., & Stuckey, J. (2014). *Skills – Where are we today? The state of skills and PSE in Canada*. The Conference Board of Canada.

Oliver, C. (1991). Strategic responses to institutional processes. *Academy of Management Review, 16*(1), 145–79. https://doi.org/doi:10.5465/AMR.1991.4279002

The Premier's Highly Skilled Workforce Expert Panel. (2016). *Building the Workforce of Tomorrow: A Shared Responsibility*. https://files.ontario.ca/hsw_rev_engaoda_webfinal_july6.pdf

Rose, D. (2020). A snapshot of precarious academic work in Canada. *New Proposals: Journal of Marxism and Interdisciplinary Inquiry, 11*(1), 7–17.

Schwartz, M. (2012). *Best practices in Experiential Learning*. The Learning and Teaching Office. https://www.mcgill.ca/eln/files/eln/doc_ryerson_bestpracticesryerson.pdf

Shields, R., & Watermeyer, R. (2020). Competing institutional logics in universities in the United Kingdom: Schism in the church of reason. *Studies in Higher Education, 45*(1), 3–17. https://doi.org/10.1080/03075079.2018.1504910

Skaggs, S. L., & Graybeal, L. (2019). Service-learning and experiential learning in criminal justice education: An exploratory examination of faculty perspectives. *Journal of Criminal Justice Education, 30*(2), 296–312. https://doi.org/10.1080/10511253.2018.1488983

Smele, S., Quinlan, A., & LaCroix, E. (2021). Engendering inequities: Precariously employed academic women's experiences of student evaluations of teaching. *Gender and Education*, 1–17. https://doi.org/10.1080/09540253.2021.1884194

Thompson, J. (2008). *Organizations in action: Social science bases of administrative theory*. Transaction Publishers.

Thornton, P. (2004). *Markets from culture: Institutional logics and organizational decisions in higher education publishing*. Stanford University Press.

Thornton, P., Ocasio, W., & Loundsbury, M. (2012). *The institutional logics perspective: A new approach to culture, structure, and process*. Oxford University Press.

Tolbert, P. S., & Hall, R. (2009). *Organizations: Structures, Processes, and Outcomes* (10th ed.). Pearson Education Inc.

Tolbert, P. S., & Zucker, L. G. (1996). The institutionalization of institutional theory. In C. C. Hardy & W. Nord (Eds.), *Handbook of Organization Studies* (pp. 175–90). SAGE Publications Ltd. http://sk.sagepub.com/books/studying-organization/n6.xml

Troiani, I., & Dutson, C. (2021). The neoliberal university as a space to learn/think/work in higher education. *Architecture and Culture, 9*(1), 5–23. https://doi.org/10.1080/20507828.2021.1898836

University of Waterloo. (n.d.). *Office of the associate provost, co-operative and experiential education*. https://uwaterloo.ca/associate-provost-co-operative-and-experiential-education/

Urbanek, P. (2021). Institutional logic in a higher education system under reform: Evidence from Polish public universities. *International Journal of Leadership in Education*, 1–21. https://doi.org/10.1080/13603124.2021.2006796

Weick, K. (1976). Educational organizations as loosely coupled systems. *Administrative Science Quarterly, 21*(1), 1–19. https://doi.org/10.2307/2391875

Whitchurch, C. (2013). *Reconstructing identities in higher education: The rise of "third space" professionals*. Routledge.

Windsor, E., & Carroll, A. (2015). The bourgeoisie dream factory: Teaching Marx's theory of alienation through an experiential activity. *Teaching Sociology, 43*(1), 61–7. https://doi.org/10.1177/0092055X14547824

4 Mission on the Fly? Experiential Learning in Search of Principles and Ethics

MICHAEL BUZZELLI

University of Western Ontario, Canada

Introduction

The Uses of the University, by Clark Kerr (1966), former Chancellor of UC Berkeley, marks a rich tradition of debate on the nature, purpose, and roles of the American university (e.g., Newfield, 2016). This tradition is evident in Canada, too, where investment and expansion in higher education in earlier post-WWII decades has given way to ever more scrutiny of institutions and systems (e.g., Fallis, 2007). Reflecting perhaps the placid policy environment of earlier postwar decades, the late scholar of Canadian higher education, John Dennison, once remarked that universities want "to be funded and to be left alone" (Skolnik, 2005, p. 8). Recent decades by contrast have seen ever more scrutiny including intensifying calls for public accountability and responsiveness from higher education. Local accountability and community engagement is one such pressure: a frontier now being charged up by the growth and expansion of experiential learning (EL).

Not without precedent, such as in professions with a history of work-integrated learning (e.g., social work and psychology practica, medical internships, etc.), the rapid expansion of EL in recent years has enfolded disciplines with less formal history in this regard, across the arts, humanities, and social sciences as well as basic sciences. EL is used broadly here to include the full range of outside-of-classroom arrangements, whether paid or unpaid; these may be work-integrated, field- and research-based, as well as in service to community. For a variety of reasons including responses to external pressures (e.g., institutional mandates, performance-based funding), universities have demonstrated their readiness to offer EL. Indeed, across disciplines, programs and institutions are increasingly guaranteeing and requiring EL experiences for credentialling. As shown in Chapters 2 and 3, one outcome of these trends is a reconfiguration of the intra-institutional logics that deliver EL. Another outcome, the focus of this chapter, is a reshaping of the university's educative mission itself.

The expansion and diversification of EL creates new and different societal engagement for the university. Unlike international arrangements (Curran et al., 2018; Tiessen & Huish, 2018), local community connections are the most apparent and ready to handle this function for the university. Yet the so-called town-gown relationship is complex, involving alternative needs, dependencies, and power relations (Baldwin, 2021; McNeil et al., 2022; Gavazzi, 2015). Does the university recognize the complexity of these relationships and base its EL development on guiding principles and ethics?

This chapter provides a novel picture of selected Canadian universities' understanding of the development of EL through the lens of senate meeting minutes. Alternative university "types" (e.g., research-intensive and primarily undergraduate) are examined to document and interpret senate proceedings on EL and community engagement.[1] We conclude with discussion of institutional mission and ethics for policy on meaningful societal engagement via EL.

Institutions and Local Governance

With the rapid growth of EL, there is a pressing need – and a matching opportunity – to understand and to develop policy on the evolution of the educative mission and, with it, the nature and roles of the university within its local community. We situate this imperative in the broad theoretical frame of regional political economy (Harvey, 2001; Keating & Loughlin, 1997; Logan & Molotch, 1987) and its rich vein of inquiry into the institutional bases of local governance (Storper, 2013; Amin, 1999; Harvey, 1989).

The place of the university in its local community is often approached through the prism of research-related activities and economic relations. *The Second Industrial Divide* (Piore & Sabel, 1984) set the stage for renewed inquiry into regional (re)development. Case studies have proliferated (Storper, 1997), some, for example, highlighting the role of the university in regional innovation systems and the geographies of industrial parks (Gunasekara, 2006; Asheim & Gertler, 2005; Mowery & Sampat, 2005; Cooke, 2001). The case of Kitchener-Waterloo (KW), Canada, is one such exemplar and is instructive in several respects (Bramwell & Wolfe, 2008; Howitt, 2019). Blackberry (now RIM) "spun" out of 1980s collaboration with the University of Waterloo to generate a lauded industrial cluster of high-tech firms. Unsurprisingly, the "Waterloo way" attracts attention for its potential to inform development elsewhere (e.g., Ornston & Camargo, 2021; Leibovitz, 2003).

Equally important, the case of KW mirrors salient themes in research on the university's societal engagement: first, scholarship tends to focus on economic (re)development, often narrowly circumscribed (Compagnucci & Spigarelli, 2020; Lazzeroni & Piccaluga, 2015). Ongoing debate over the mission and adaptability of the university, however, suggests more textured contributions to regional renewal. At one extreme, civic boosters (Jonas & Wilson, 1999) promote the so-called "triple helix" partnership of universities, industry, and the state for jobs and investment (Etzkowitz, 2008). By contrast, critical social scientists insist on unfettered research and teaching free from the ephemera and influence of political cycles and labour market needs (e.g., McKinney, 2019; Giroux, 2007). With respect to EL, we might ask whether the university will take its place in the triple helix or assert its autonomy and independence.

Beyond economic development, scholars agree that collaboration among key regional agents can be generative by creating associative forms of governance needed for prosperity in whatever path it follows (Wolfe & Gertler, 2016; Gertler & Wolfe, 2002; Leibovitz, 2003; Taylor, 2019). A further insight indicated by the KW experience, then, is that the preponderance of scholarship on the university's place in its community concerns research-related activities, typically in connection with STEM disciplines of science, technology, engineering and maths (Perkmann et al., 2013). In contrast to research- and STEM- based associations, EL resides in the teaching and learning mission and enfolds a fuller representation of curricula and disciplines. The following examples are suggestive of teaching- and learner-based societal engagement. In Montreal, the specialized École nationale de cirque is a cultural-economic intermediary playing an important role in the development of a distinct local circus arts cluster in the 1990s and 2000s (Rantisi & Leslie, 2013). In Kingston, Canada, Massey et al. (2014) draw on the notion of the creative class to demonstrate the importance of university-community relations (with Queen's University) to foster students' sense of community, openness and inclusion. A benefit is greater post-graduation student retention. Broader still, Katz & Nowak (2018) trace Pittsburgh's renaissance after the decline of steel manufacturing in which higher education is providing expertise and leadership on local priorities and community challenges (e.g., social exclusion). Acknowledging historical and geographical contingency, they label Pittsburgh's rebirth a "new localism." The EL window on the university in its region affords an opportunity to examine collaborations growing out of teaching and learning across the whole of campus. Expansion of co-ops, internships and community-engaged/-service learning, among other EL pedagogies, afford a richer view of the university's place in the networked society (Jones III et al., 2007; Castells, 1996).

Taken together, the rapid expansion of EL and its impact on curriculum and pedagogy lead us to consider internal institutional reforms. Institution-(re)building is central to regional governance and relies upon – even necessitates – adaptations by constituent organizations (Taylor, 2019). The university is but one agent within regional networks, certainly, yet it is also a complex organization. It bears asking how the university (or types of universities; see Rantisi & Leslie, 2013) experiences reforms to meet demands for societal engagement (Buzzelli & Allison, 2017). Broad public sector reforms in the West arrived belatedly to Canada and to its universities (Le Grand, 2003; Jones, 2004; Scheutze & Bruneau, 2004). Strategic plans and policy making are now *de rigueur* in contrast to more placid policy commitments of earlier post-WWII decades (Axelrod et al., 2013). For example, influenced by the new public policy of transparency and accountability, there is a growing expectation that universities develop and report on their local impacts (Buzzelli & Songsore, 2022). Problematically, municipalities and regional authorities are not stakeholders of resident universities (i.e., not base funders; see Jones, 1997) yet the "multiversity" is called upon to be responsive and accountable beyond its traditional principal missions of scholarship and education (Fallis, 2007).

Two decades of organizational research suggest the university will struggle with community engagement for EL (Crain, 2008; Milian et al, 2017; LaCroix, 2021). The university is characterized by its high degree of formal autonomy and devolved conglomerate administration of academic units (Buzzelli & Allison, 2017). Invoking the classic "garbage can model" of decision-making (Cohen et al., 1972), administration and reform in the USA research university is described this way: "rather unclear and sometimes contradictory [goals], poorly understood techniques and systems for achieving those goals, questionable methods for assessing success in meeting those goals, distributed and often decentralized responsibility for decision making, and fluctuating participation in governance activities" (Hearn, 1996, p. 145). One can surmise how this translates in the rapidly developing terrain of EL.

Mission on the Fly

EL pedagogy relies upon community connections, new linkages in which the learner is the connective tissue attending the workplace-as-classroom. Following earlier work (Buzzelli & Asafo-Adjei, 2022; Buzzelli & Songsore, 2022) in the province of Ontario, Canada, this chapter seeks to answer: does the university recognize the complexity of these relationships and base its EL development on guiding principles and ethics? Internally, the answer to this question includes consideration of the organizational adaptations necessary to deliver and succeed. For example, is EL administration centralized or dispersed among units and courses? Externally, the answer begs evidence of the university's understanding of associative governance with the community partners needed to "host" the suite of EL pedagogies. Who initiates partnerships, how are they governed, and is evaluation of EL in-built? In the broadest terms, having asked and addressed these questions prior to EL implementation would suggest the institution has charted a path and that the development of EL is understood, stewarded, and evaluated.

In Canada, academic senate, or simply, senate, is usually the charter (i.e., legislated) governing body charged with oversight of the institution's academic mission (Eastman et al., 2022). Growing out of a series of developments over the 20th century, the bi-cameral governance model of most Canadian universities emerged with senate nominally equal to the university's Board of Governor (variously titled) (Cameron, 1991; Jones, 1996). Whereas the latter typically oversees fiduciary and financial operation of the university and is composed of members primarily appointed by provincial stakeholders, senates are substantially populated by academic staff elected and appointed from within the institution. Ongoing debate in the literature questions the relative status and authority of senates (Bradshaw & Fredette, 2009; CAUT, 2009; Hurtibise, 2019; MacKinnon, 2014). While,

> [a]cademic decision-making ... tends to be bottom-up ... [with consensus built in at each level of the university, it is broadly true that] "Senates are responsible for matters such as admissions policy, academic programs and curriculum, academic quality, scholarships and awards, student appeals, and granting of degrees [and further] strategic academic direction, policy, approvals, and oversight (Eastman et al., 2022, 79; see also Pennock et al., 2015).

Thus, one can expect senate to provide a visible hand on such matters. At the least, with consensus as the hallmark of university decision-making, one could expect senate to be a forum that reflects and debates bottom-up developments such as the ground-shifting pedagogies of EL.

On these grounds, monthly senate meeting minute documents were sampled from six recognized Canadian universities in three institutional categories: (1) two "medical-doctoral," incorporating universities with a medical school and a research profile (McGill University and University of Toronto); (2) two "comprehensive" institutions, those with a balance of research and teaching, including graduate teaching (Simon Fraser University and University of Victoria); (3) two "primarily undergraduate" institutions with a primarily teaching focus (University of Northern British Columbia and Mount Allison University). These categories and the placement of the universities within them are drawn from Canada's annual university rankings by Maclean's magazine in 2022 (similar to Carnegie classifications in the US). The Maclean's ranking is helpful because it incorporates teaching-related metrics that speak directly to the development of EL and the senate's oversight role in facing and stewarding changes within the teaching domain. The institutions used here are the lead-ranked universities in each of the three Maclean's categories.

Senate documents were drawn from these institutions for the ten years from January 2012 forward and, additionally, up to the most recent meeting minutes available at the selected institutions (i.e., into 2022). In most instances the public documents (i.e., excludes *in camera* deliberations) are available on institutional senate/governing web sites ("Governing Council" in the case of the University of Toronto). For Mount Allison University, senate documents were not publicly available until September 2017 (prior records were requested but unavailable). Table 4.1 provides an example of the coverage of the documents collected. For coding, the approach was to be as inclusive as possible, guided by both common terms (e.g., "internship") and inductively incorporating terms as they arose from within the documents (e.g., "practicum"). Document coding involved comprehensive reading of all meeting minutes (n = 472) to determine if EL and community (both broadly defined) were noted or discussed, with respect to the latter, if community was discussed particularly in relation to EL. The coding approach was conservative and inclusive. For instance, at Simon Fraser University's April 2012 senate meeting, the Chair noted "new funding has been allocated for internships through Mitacs, a national, not-for-profit research organization." Finding no other mention of EL, this instance is nonetheless included but marked in the table as limited discussion. As demonstrated below, senate deliberations were often more substantive. The example serves to underscore the conservative/inclusive approach to coding which in turn aids in interpreting the quantity and texture of senate discussion of EL.

Turning to the individual institutional records, the example of Simon Fraser University is shown in Table 4.1 as it presented the highest proportion of EL coding (36% of 113 senate meetings). This is followed by UNBC (33% of ninety meetings); Toronto (28% of 64); McGill (25% of 93); Victoria (15% of 80). Table 4.1 exhibits near complete coverage of the fifteen coding terms used, a breadth evident across the set. Albeit data from a

Table 4.1. Senate Discussion of Experiential Learning at Simon Fraser University, Canada, 2012–22

	2012	2013	2014	2015	2016	2017	2018	2019	2020	2021	2022
January	o	o	C	o	F	o	o	o	o	o	H
February	o	o	o	o	o	o	o	o	C	o	H
March	o	o	J, L, H (l.d.)	o	o	F	A	F (l.d.)	*H,F	o	o
April	L (l.d.)	H, J, L	o	J	F, J, M	o	A, H	o	o	o	o
May	o	A, C	A	L	o	o	o	o	F, H	o	A
June	C (l.d.)	A	o	C, F, L	o	J, C (l.d.)	o	o	o	o	
July	F	C (l.d.)	FHJ	o	o	x	o	o	o	H	
August	x	x	x	x	x	x	x	x	x	o*	
September	C, O, F, H	C	C,M. H & J (l.d.)	J	o	o	o	L	o	o	
October	C	o	o	J	x	o	o	o	o	o	
November	H	C (l.d.)	M	o	o	o	M	o	A	o	
December	O	o	o	C	x	o	o	o	o	o	

Notes: "o" represents a meeting in which EL was not noted/discussed. "x" indicates no senate meeting held. * indicates a special or extraordinary meeting held. Document coding: A = experiential; B = learning; C = community; D = engage*; E = service; F = co-op; G = applied; H = field; I = experience; J = incubat;* K = industry; L = intern;* M = practice*; N = placement; O = work-study; P = non-traditional; Q = out of the classroom. "l.d." indicates limited method of the coded element nonetheless included. See text for further discussion.

small sample of six institutions, a particular point of interest is the relatively consistent proportion of EL coding amongst institutions of all types. Mount Allison University appears to support the view that those institutions characterized as more teaching-focused would deliberate EL more fulsomely. Its senate discussed EL at 53% of thirty-two meetings in evidence, however, direct comparisons are tenuous given the University's data gap noted above. On the other hand, if one were expecting medical/doctoral institutions to be less invested in developing EL within their educative mission vis-à-vis greater emphasis on research, it does not appear to be in evidence here. More generally, considering the conservative and inclusive coding strategy employed and the study period of rapid EL development, the mean 68% (unweighted) absence of EL discussion across these six lead-ranked institutions suggests that EL may be an emergent feature of teaching and learning with only limited senate discussion and guidance.

Table 4.2 recasts the institutional data for a composite picture by "overlaying" senate calendars across the sum total of 472 meetings at all

Table 4.2. Count of Senate Meetings and Discussion of Experiential Learning at Six Lead-Ranked Universities in Canada, 2012–22

	2012	2013	2014	2015	2016	2017	2018	2019	2020	2021	2022
January	5	4 (N)	5 (S,V,M,N)	5 (M)	5 (S,M)	5 (M,N)	5 (V,T,A)	6 (N)	5 (T)	6	4 (S)
February	4	5 (M,T)	4 (V)	2 (M)	4 (V)	4 (M,N)	4 (V,A)	5 (A)	5 (S,M,N,A)	5 (A)	4 (S,N)
March	5	5 (V)	5 (S,V)	5	5 (M)	4 (S)	6 (S,T)	5 (S,M)	4 (S,A)	6 (T)	5 (T)
April	5 (S,M)	4 (S,N)	4 (M)	5 (S)	5 (S,N)	4	6 (S,A)	4 (V,M,T)	5 (T,A)	5 (M)	4 (M,T)*
May	5 (T)	5 (S,M)	5 (S)	4 (S,N)	5	4	5	5 (A)	4 (S,N)	5	2 (S)**
June	2 (S)	3 (S,N)	3	3 (S,N)	2	1 (S)	2	2 (N)	3 (N)	2 (N)	
July	1 (S)	1 (S)	1 (S)	1	1	x	1	1	1	1 (S)	
August	1 (N)	1 (N)	1	1 (N)	1	1	x	1	1	2	
September	3 (S)	3 (S,N)	3 (S)	3 (S)	2	4 (A)	3 (N,A)	3 (S,M)	4	4	
October	5 (S)	5 (N)	5 (T,N)	5 (S)	3	6 (M,T,N,A)	6 (N)	6 (T)	6 (T,N)	5 (T,N)	
November	5 (S,M)	5 (S)	5 (S,M,T)	5	4 (M)	6 (M,N,A)	6 (S,A)	5	6 (S,V,M,N)	4	
December	3	4 (N)	3 (N)	4 (S,V)	2 (M)	4	4 (V,A)	4 (A)	4 (V)	3	

Notes: Counts indicate the combined total number of senate meetings across all institutions. "x" indicates no senate meeting held at any institution. S= Simon Fraser; V = Victoria; M = McGill; T = Toronto; N = UNBC; A = Mount Allison. Data for Mount Allison available only for the period of September 2017 through March 2021 (as outlined in table). *No data for UNBC. **No data for Victoria, McGill, and UNBC.

institutions. It bears noting here that it is common practice for senates to not meet in given block periods in the calendar (e.g., no August meetings at Simon Fraser as shown in Table 4.1). This explains much of the variation in cell counts. A first impression of Table 4.2 is again the broad representation of EL across the selected universities' senates. Eight months in this overlay (e.g., January 2014) included at least three senates noting or discussing EL. Upon closer examination, a more striking insight is the relative lack of discussion or mere mention of EL. Despite our inclusive coding strategy, most months at least three senates met (n=91) registered only one or two coded instances of EL. Notably, this silence occurs at least once in each year from 2012 to 2022. More extreme are the (n = 20) months in which at least three senates met yet did not register any discussion of EL (e.g., December 2021). In other words, when EL was gaining momentum in the sector as a whole, there were twenty instances over the 10-year sampling period when these senates met but were virtually silent on EL. This coding treatment of senate meetings at the six selected institutions indicates that EL was "on the radar" yet its nature and impact on the educative mission was perhaps not fully appreciated, internalized, and guided, at least from the perspective of senate deliberations.

Alongside this coding, the deliberative content of senate meetings also reveals mixed engagement with EL. Senate discussions evidence themes that reflect both meaningful engagement with this qualitatively different teaching and learning as well as uncertainty and even symbolic treatment. On the latter point, for example, UNBC's senate (December 2013) highlighted EL in noting its National Survey of Student Engagement (NSSE): "based on comments from first- and fourth-year students, UNBC provides a supportive environment for students. The snapshot indicates that UNBC is a university that values and provides experiential learning opportunities for students." Similarly, at Victoria's senate meeting in November 2020, it was noted: "The Maclean's ranking shows UVic as holding second-place among Canada's comprehensive schools with notable highlights on experiential learning " (pp. 2). Rankings and symbolic representation are a discourse unto themselves, but these highlights signal that senates were tuned to the emergence of EL early on. In June 2016, Simon Fraser's senate noted the 25% growth of its co-op education offerings over the prior four years. At its March 2018 meeting, its senate asked: "How can we on Senate facilitate, or reduce the barriers to, experiential programs/ways of teaching?"

The question motivates the present chapter and implicates, perhaps expectedly, resourcing and institutional planning. Unsurprisingly, senate discussions included several instances of EL deliberations around resourcing and budgeting, such as: (a) at Victoria in the context of strategic planning and lobbying with Universities Canada in federal budget submissions (February 2016, December 2018, January 2019); (b) weaving EL into academic planning at Toronto (2013 meetings; March 2021), Simon Fraser (June 2013, May 2014), and Mount Allison (September 2017), the latter including EL in its advancement plan as well. The timing of this content fits the ascent of EL as reinforced by the Mount Allison senate Chair's remarks that EL should be a focus of senate's work going forward (October 2017, September 2018). A particular curriculum theme connected to EL was environment and sustainability education, sometimes in the context of institutional strategic direction (Simon Fraser, June 2013 and April 2018; McGill, May 2013; Victoria, December 2018). Meeting minutes also included mention of organizational planning. Toronto's Governing Council noted in January 2020 (p. 7) that it had launched a central Experiential Learning Hub "as an entry point into experiential learning opportunities across the three campuses for students, faculty and staff, as well as external partners." It also noted its intent to incorporate EL into planning and development of new campus spaces (October 2019). At UNBC, senate noted its termination of a partnership (with UBC, Vancouver) for engineering EL in lieu of its own new Co-op Education program. Thematically, resourcing and planning with respect to EL provided the most consistent if variable content reflecting the impact of EL.

Another window on the impact of the rise of EL pertains to senate discussion of its aims and definition, particularly given the empirical meeting count and the inclusive coding approach. In this context, a distinct early thread was prompted by the Provost at UNBC, initiating (August 2013) a discussion over several meetings on the future of its Co-op Education program (declining enrolments) in light of the growth of internships and experiential learning in general. Also early on, other senates discussed opportunities for research-based experiences, thus strategically merging the research mission with EL development (Toronto, October 2014; Victoria, January 2014). By contrast, a distinction not recognized across the full suite of minutes is that of community-engaged or -service learning (CEL). Whereas work-integrated learning typically involves paid or unpaid co-ops and internships, often with a variety of partners including industry, CEL is usually unpaid and arranged with community groups and aimed at social justice (Brabazon et al., 2019). Despite EL's community basis and ample discussion of community engagement, one could reasonably expect to find these important pedagogical and substantive distinctions in the texts. Instead, meeting minutes indicate shared if often undefined understanding of myriad EL arrangements. In addition, minutes also exhibit their quite different implications for pedagogy and curricula and, indeed, understandings of the nature and role of the university in its local community.

The related question of community engagement also furnishes a variety of evidence. Mount Allison's senate often discussed EL and community engagement including a raft of new courses in February of 2020 that would foster local connections. In May 2015, UNBC's senate noted the following with respect to regional engagement and advancement: "The revamped Office of Regional Programs is reviewing and implementing various course delivery options to enhance the availability of Academic and Continuing Studies courses. UNBC has been working with the Northern Development Initiative Trust to foster opportunities for internships in local government, planning, and economic development" (p. 20). A remarkable exception here is Simon Fraser's experience where both the community engagement and EL themes were ample but scarcely linked. In February 2020, its senate discussed the opening of various facilities in the region for CEL. Otherwise, across the full sample, the EL and community engagement themes were each in evidence but often running in parallel.

This brings us to what is arguably the *raison d'etre* of EL: the learners' pathways and experiences. A common thread from 2020 forward was consternation over the impact of the COVID-19 pandemic on institutions' ability to offer in-community EL placements and students' ability to satisfy placements and complete their degrees. In various ways, in fact, these concerns were evident from 2012 as senates confronted the qualitatively different challenges posed by EL. For example, we find such discussions as: (a) how to include EL in recruitment and retention (UNBC, September 2018); (b) whether local or farther afield, ensuring EL is inclusive and available to all students (Victoria, March 2013 and January 2014); (c) how to ensure timely degree completion when EL is in place (Simon Fraser, March 2017; Victoria, January 2019; Toronto, October 2021); (d) and the possibility of requiring students to withdraw if they do not make timely progress on completion in their EL placements (UNBC, January 2017). That senates would be concerned with these core questions is entirely reasonable and expected. The senates of Mount Allison (May 2019), McGill (April 2021), and, in particular, UNBC (June 2020) discussed how to adjust student grading and credentialling in order to incorporate the many forms of EL and community engagement. Simon Fraser went further in March 2014, discussing whether to cancel a study abroad program given unresolved debate over its academic rigour. For the university as a whole, it would seem prudent for senate to have addressed these fundamental questions in the EL development phase or at least to have acted as a "lighthouse" when EL came calling to port.

Flexible Policy, "Flexiversity"?

The tabular data and text content of senate meetings provide a rich but variable picture of institutions facing the advent of EL. Hard-nosed resourcing questions were most abundant and even included affirmation of EL-dedicated campus spaces, student supports, and budget priorities. Following Chapters 2 and 3, one could expect these responses to hold primacy in senate deliberations given the immediacy of the impact of EL on the university's educative mission. Senate discussions were otherwise general and aspirational at best. Evident also in the themes of community engagement, students/learning, and indeed the very definition of EL itself, senates appeared to be in a reactionary posture. In this respect, the tenor of reacting to and "dealing with" the advent of EL was similar to the remarkable scramble to respond to the onset of the COVID-19 pandemic, finding change in response to externally generated pressures and priorities rather than internal goal- and priority-setting (Rochet et al., 2008).

Interspersed sparingly in the foregoing discussion is the experience at McGill. Although our dual foci of EL and community registered in only 25% of its meetings, its senate's engagement with these themes is both more comprehensive and critical, such as: (a) articulation of the place of EL in institutional strategy and goals (May 2013, February 2017), including how EL aligns with the University's aspirations toward the UN's Sustainable Development Goals (SDGs) (January 2016); (b) a tighter weaving of EL and community (April 2012, November 2014), including initiatives to bridge via CEL specifically (January 2012 and 2017), and via dedicated spaces and resources such as the McGill University Business Engagement Centre (MUBEC; November 2012) and the Quartier de l'Innovation (April 2014); (c) stewardship over credentials and curriculum, such as environment and sustainability noted above, Arts students opportunities vis-à-vis EL's focus on industry partnerships (November 2012), and discussion of the role of EL in the Master's degree (April 2019); (d) and finally, ample discussion of students' learning and welfare, including regulating unpaid internships (November 2016), equitable access to EL opportunities (December 2016), and the implications of EL in McGill's charter of student rights.

There is more occurring on campus than senate discussions, of course, a proviso that is also the core argument here. One could expect senate meetings to at least reflect the surfacing of EL if not leading or stewarding it. If this minimum bar is true, the mixed evidence documented here may underscore the view that senates have diminished status and importance in Canadian university governance. Yet the high-relief example of

McGill is a valuable exception: despite its status tied more to its research profile and international reach, its unmatched deliberation over EL and community is rather more proactive and, we would argue, generative if imperfect (Bouma, 1998; Zucker, 1987). Like Toronto (April 2022), McGill (April 2014) indicated its intent to develop performance indicators for its community outreach and CEL activities. Policy observers might rightly wonder what would be measured and how performance could be assessed when the EL impacts on student welfare, learning outcomes, curriculum and resourcing are still being discussed; at some institutions, it is hardly noted at senate. Nevertheless, the McGill example, and perhaps Mount Allison, demonstrate how "plugged-in" senate can be.

In this context, we are led back to our overarching question: whether the university recognizes and guides EL development and works collaboratively with the community. Internally, if senate is where we expect to find the articulation of guiding principles, goals and ethics, the answer to our question is at most only a faint affirmative. Based on these cases, Hearn's (1996) invocation of the often-cited garbage can model for research universities seems to translate to EL: unclear goals, underdeveloped monitoring, and loose governance. The tabular and discursive evidence documents emergent and unresolved EL considerations with respect to students, disciplines, learning outcomes and assessment, partnerships, and program evaluation. In embracing EL so fulsomely, is the multiversity exhibiting sector normative behaviour? In the absence of the guiding hand of senate academic leadership, is it investing in EL via executive concentration instead of shared governance? Whatever the reason for this breadth of implementation, the experience of the six selected institutions signals a reactive approach to the arrival of EL as opposed to fundamental discussion of whether, how, and why it should be adopted.

Externally, innumerable partners and arrangements are involved in connecting learners, professors, courses, and programs. What organizational-ethical dilemmas will emerge from the rapid and flexible approach to community governance exhibited by institutions implementing EL? Perlin (2012) provided an early glimpse of a variety of failures and perverse effects of disjointed governance in internships and similar arrangements in the US university sector. The nexus of arrangements will almost certainly deliver reminders in the years ahead that planning and development should precede implementation. The Presidents of McGill University and Université de Montréal, Suzanne Fortier and Daniel Jutras, recently urged "Let's use universities to restart Montreal" (*Montreal Gazette* and *La Presse* 30 October 2020) (Fortier and Jutras, 2020). The spirit is laudable. When it concerns EL, the goals, principles and ethics of

EL should be articulated *prima facie* for the sake of learners, learning, and community partners, among others. The alternative may amount to academic mission drift via relationships and metrics consecrated on the fly.

NOTE

1 This chapter represents an initial "pilot study" of six university cases. A subsequent paper based on twelve cases is currently being prepared for publication in an academic journal.

REFERENCES

Amin, A. (1999). An institutional perspective on regional economic development. *International Journal for Urban and Regional Research*, 23, 365–78.

Asheim, B. T., & Gertler M. S. (2005). The geography of innovation: regional innovation systems. In J. Fagerberg, D. Mowery & R. Nelson (Eds.), *The Oxford Handbook of Innovation* (pp. 291–317). Oxford University Press.

Axelrod, P., Trilokekar, R. D., Shanahan, T., & Wellen, R. (Eds.). (2013). *Making policy in turbulent times: Challenges and prospects for higher education.* McGill-Queen's University Press.

Baldwin (2021). *In the shadow of the ivory tower: How universities are plundering our cities.* Bold Type Books.

Bouma, G. (1998). Distinguishing institutions and organisations in social change. *Journal of Sociology, 34*(3), 232–45.

Brabazon, H., Esmail, J., Locklin, R., & Stirling, A. (2019). Beyond employability: Defamiliarizing Work-Integrated Learning with community-engaged learning. *Engaged Scholar Journal: Community-Engaged Research, Teaching and Learning, 5*(2), 21–41.

Bradshaw, P., & Fredette, C. (2009). Academic governance of universities: Reflections of a senate chair on moving from theory to practice and back. *Journal of Management Inquiry, 18*(2), 123–33.

Bramwell, A., & Wolfe, D.A. (2008). Universities and regional economic development: The entrepreneurial University of Waterloo. *Research Policy, 37*(8), 1175–87.

Buzzelli, M., & Allison, D. J. (2017). Proposed strategic mandates for Ontario universities: An organisational theory perspective. *Canadian Journal of Higher Education, 47*(3), 170–91.

Buzzelli, M. & Asafo-Adjei, E. (2022). Experiential learning and the university's host community: Rapid growth, contested mission and policy challenge. *Higher Education,* 85. https://doi.org/10.1007/s10734-022-00849-1

Buzzelli, M. & Songsore, E. (2022). Differentiated visions: How Ontario universities see and represent their futures. *Canadian Journal of Educational Administration and Policy,* 198, 111–23.

Cameron, D. (1991). *More than an academic question: Universities, government and public policy in Canada.* Institute for Research on Public Policy.

Castells, M. (1996). *The rise of the network society.* Blackwell.

CAUT. (2009). *Report of the CAUT ad hoc advisory committee on governance.*

Cohen, M. D., March, J. G., & Olsen, J. P. (1972). A garbage can model of organizational choice. *Administrative Science Quarterly, 17*(1), 1–25.

Compagnucci, L., & Spigarelli, F. (2020). The Third Mission of the university: A systematic literature review on potentials and constraints. *Technological Forecasting and Social Change,* 161, 1–30.

Cooke, P. (2001). Regional innovation systems, clusters, and the knowledge economy. *Industrial and Corporate Change, 10*(4), 945–74.

Crain, G. (2008). Managing change in dental education: Is there a method to the madness? *Journal of Dental Education, 72*(10), 1100–13.

Curran, D., Owens, C., Thorson, H., & Vibert, E. (Eds.). (2018). *Out there learning: Critical reflections on off-campus study programs.* University of Toronto Press.

Eastman, J., Jones, G.A., Trottier, C., & Begin-Caouette, O. (Eds.) (2022). *University governance in Canada: Navigating complexity.* McGill-Queen's University Press.

Etzkowitz, H. (2008). *The triple helix: University–industry–government innovation in action.* Routledge.

Fallis, G. (2007). *Multiversities, ideas and democracy.* University of Toronto Press.

Fortier, S. & Jutras, D. (2020, October 30). *Let's use universities to restart Montreal.* Universities Canada. https://univcan.ca/news/lets-use-universities-to-restart-montreal/

Gavazzi, S. M. (2015). *The optimal town-gown marriage: Taking campus-community outreach and engagement to the next level.* CreateSpace Independent Publishing.

Gertler, M., & Wolfe, D. (Eds.) (2002). *Innovation and social learning: Institutional adaptation in an era of technological change.* Palgrave Macmillan.

Giroux, H. A. (2007). *University in chains: Confronting the military-industrial-academic complex.* Routledge.

Gunasekara, C. (2006). Reframing the role of universities in the development of regional innovation systems. *The Journal of Technology Transfer, 31*(1), 101–13.

Harvey, D. (1989). From managerialism to entrepreneurialism: Transformation of governance in late capitalism. *Geografiska Annaler Series B-Human Geography, 71*(1), 145–58.

– (2001) *Spaces of capital: Toward a critical geography.* New York: Routledge.

Hearn, J. C. (1996). Transforming US higher education: An organizational perspective. *Innovative Higher Education, 21*(2), 141–54.

Howitt, C. (2019). *BlackBerry town: How high-tech success has played out for Canada's Kitchener-Waterloo.* James Lorimer and Company.

Hurtibise, D. (2019). Thirty years of scholarly literature on university governance in Canada (1988–2016). *Canadian Journal of Educational Administration and Policy,* 191, 106–17.

Jonas, A. E., & Wilson, D. (Eds.). (1999). *The urban growth machine: Critical perspectives two decades later.* SUNY Press.

Jones, G. A. (1996). Governments, governance and Canadian universities. In J. C. Smart, (Ed.), *Higher education: handbook of theory and research* (vol. 11, 337–71). Agathon Press.

– (1997). Preface. In G.A. Jones (Ed.), *Higher education in Canada: Different systems, different perspectives* (pp. ix–xi). Garland.

– (2004). Ontario higher education reform, 1995–2003: From modest modifications to policy reform. *The Canadian Journal of Higher Education, 34*(3), 39–54.

Jones III, J., Woodward, K., & Marston, S. (2007). Situating flatness. *Transactions Institute of British Geographers NS, 32,* 264–76

Katz, B., & Nowak, J. (2018). *The new localism: How cities can thrive in the age of populism.* Brookings Institution.

Keating, M., & Loughlin, J. (1997). *The political economy of regionalism.* Routledge.

Kerr, C. (1966). *The uses of the university.* Harvard University Press.

LaCroix, E. (2021). Organizational complexities of experiential education: Institutionalization and logic work in higher education. *Journal of Experiential Education, 45*(2), 157–71.

Lazzeroni, M., & Piccaluga, A. (2015). Beyond "town and gown": The role of the university in small and medium-sized cities. *Industry and Higher Education, 29*(1), 11–23.

Le Grand, J. (2003). *Motivation, agency and public policy: Of knights and knaves, pawns and queens.* Oxford University Press.

Leibovitz, J. (2003). Institutional barriers to associative city-region governance: The politics of institution-building and economic governance in "Canada's Technology Triangle." *Urban Studies, 40*(13), 2613–42.

Logan, J., & Molotch, H. (1987). *Urban fortunes: The political economy of place.* University of California Press.

MacKinnon, P. (2014). *Universities, leadership and public policy in the twenty-first century: A president's perspective.* University of Toronto Press.

Massey, J., Field, S., & Chan, Y. (2014). Partnering for economic development: How town-gown relations impact local economic development in small and medium cities. *Canadian Journal of Higher Education, 44*(2), 152–69.

Mckinney, K. (2019). "You cannot avoid all of this past, present, and future when it's everywhere around you": Reflecting relational thinking and field study experiences. In D. Curran, C. Owens, H. Thorson, & E. Vibert (Eds.),

Out there learning: Critical reflections on off-campus study programs (pp. 27–47). University of Toronto Press.

McNeil, D., Mossman, M., Rogers, D., & Tewdwr-Jones, M. (2022). The university and the city: Spaces of risk, decolonisation, and civic disruption. *Environment and Planning A, 54*(1), 204–12.

Milian, R. P., Davies, S., & Zarifa, D. (2016). Barriers to differentiation: Applying organizational studies to Ontario higher education. *Canadian Journal of Higher Education, 46*(1), 19–37.

Mowery, D. C., & Sampat, B. N. (2005). Universities in national innovation systems. In J. Fagerberg, D. Mowery & R. Nelson (Eds.), *The Oxford Handbook of Innovation* (pp. 209–39). Oxford University Press.

Newfield, C. (2016). *The great mistake: How we wrecked public universities and how we can fix them.* Johns Hopkins University Press.

Ornston, D., & Camargo, L. (2021). *The benefits of an apathetic anchor: Why Waterloo adjusted faster than Ottawa.* Innovation Policy Lab Working Paper 2021-01, Munk School of Global Affairs and Public Policy.

Pennock, L., Jones, G. A., Leclerc, J. M., & Li, S. X. (2015). Assessing the role and structure of academic senates in Canadian universities, 2000–2012. *Higher Education, 70*(3), 503–18.

Perkmann, M., Tartari, V., McKelvey, M., Autio, E., Broström, A., & D'Este P., Fini, R., Geuna, A., Grimaldi, R., Hughes, A., Krabel, S., Kitson, M., Llerena, P., Lissoni, F., Salter, A., & Sobrero, M. (2013). Academic engagement and commercialisation: A review of the literature on university-industry relations. *Research Policy, 42*(2), 423–42.

Perlin, R. (2012). *Intern nation: How to earn nothing and learn little in the brave new economy.* Version Books.

Piore, M., & Sabel, C. F. (1984). *The second industrial divide.* Basic Books.

Rantisi, N., & Leslie, D. (2015). Significance of higher educational institutions as cultural intermediaries: The case of the École nationale de cirque in Montreal, Canada. *Regional Studies, 49*(3), 404–17.

Rochet, C., Keramidas, O., & Bout, L. (2008). Crisis as change strategy in public organizations. *International Review of Administrative Sciences, 74*(1), 65–77.

Scheutze, H., & Bruneau, W. (2004). Less state, more market: University reform in Canada and abroad. *The Canadian Journal of Higher Education, 34*(3), 1–12.

Skolnik, M. (2005). The Rae review and the structure of postsecondary education in Ontario. In C. M. Beach (Ed.), *A challenge for higher education in Ontario* (pp. 7–26). John Deutsch Institute for the Study of Economic Policy, Queen's University.

Storper, M. (1997). *The regional world: Territorial development in a global economy.* Guilford.

– (2013). *The keys to the city: How economics, institutions, social interaction and politics shape development.* Princeton University Press.

Taylor, Z. (2019). *Shaping the metropolis: Institutions and urbanization in the United States and Canada.* McGill-Queen's University Press.

Tiessen, R., & Huish, R. (Eds.). (2018). *Globetrotting or global citizenship? Perils and potential of international experiential learning.* University of Toronto Press.

Wolfe, D. A., & Gertler M. S. (Eds.). (2016). *Growing urban economies: Innovation, creativity, and governance in Canadian city-regions.* University of Toronto Press.

Zucker, L. G. (1987). Institutional theories of organization. *Annual Review of Sociology*, 13, 443–64.

PART TWO

Partners and Networks in the Community

5 On Experiential Learning Through Social Innovation, Social Enterprise, and Social Entrepreneurship in Canadian Universities: An Institutional Complexity Perspective

PETER MILLEY

University of Ottawa, Canada

Introduction

For more than fifty years, groups of actors in Canadian universities have worked to promote various local community-campus interactions (CCI) as avenues for experiential learning (EL) that literally occurs "in town".[1] Through these efforts, EL has been constructed as "hands-on" or "authentic" experiences involving performance tasks that push learners to apply their existing knowledge, skills, and dispositions while simultaneously integrating new ones through their interactions with actors and organizations beyond "normal" or "conventional" environments for academic learning. CCI-based EL involves augmenting students' involvement in campus-based programs and classrooms, in which they learn through lectures, rote studying, and exams, with practical experiences in organizational and community settings off campus to address "real-life" problems and needs. These EL efforts aim to combine the first and third missions of the university by providing education and service to the local community. Over time, an array of modes matured for EL through CCI and these were woven into the institutional fabric of many universities. Among these modes are community volunteering and service learning, project-based learning, practicums, clinical placements, field placements, entrepreneurship development, co-operative education, internships, and other work experiences.[2]

After the start of the New Millennium, initiatives aimed at promoting social innovation (SI) and social enterprise and entrepreneurship (SEE) materialized on many Canadian university campuses (Milley et al., 2020; Scaled Purpose, 2015). Sometimes these were projects, hubs, centres, labs, and incubators associated with specific disciplines, departments or faculties that were designed to engage students as an internal audience in developing ideas and dispositions oriented to addressing social problems and needs, but, frequently, these initiatives encouraged interdisciplinary and intersectoral collaboration and served a general audience of students across the university communities. In both formats, they often sought to engage external audiences, such as members of vulnerable or marginalized groups, or organizations representing such groups, who have interests in addressing problems and needs. These initiatives emerged in light of increased expectations among stakeholders in higher education (HE) about the economic and social contributions that universities should make at local, regional, national, and international levels (Marginson, 2016). SI and SEE initiatives attracted attention because they promised to accelerate such positive impacts (McGowan & Westley, 2015; Nichols et al., 2013), thereby contributing to the legitimacy of universities. Such initiatives spread to become a new breed of CCI-based platforms for EL (Milley et al., 2020). Similar developments took place in university systems in countries in the Global North and South (Benneworth & Cunha, 2015; Giesecke & Schartinger, 2024; Göransson et al., 2021; Halsall et al., 2022; Pinheiro et al., 2015; Wu et al., 2023).

As Buzzelli points out in the introductory chapter to this volume, participants and stakeholders in HE hold a variety of views on what universities exist to do and achieve and what values should underpin thinking and action in university communities. Disagreements and debates about purposes and values in HE are not merely philosophical; they have economic, sociological, and political dimensions (Wiksten & Schugurensky, 2022) that affect educational goals and processes in universities. This is something LaCroix highlights in the third chapter of this volume, where misunderstandings between university administrators and academics about the "logics" associated with EL can lead to the university "missing the mark" educationally and in terms of its social contributions. In an example from my own research (Milley, 2016a; Milley 2016b), programs integrating work experiences as a form of CCI-based EL that do not seek to counteract well-known discriminatory practices in labour markets and workplaces may serve to reproduce discrimination. In other words, such programs do not value and pursue equality or equity. With these concerns in mind, this chapter explores what SI and SEE, as relatively new phenomena on the landscape of CCI-based EL, convey into university communities in terms of purposes, underlying values, and beliefs. As a complementary contribution to that of LaCroix, it draws on neo-institutional theory to describe the institutional logics reflected in SI and SEE initiatives as a function of the competing demands confronting actors in HE. This analysis concentrates on the publicly available descriptions of forty-three SI and SEE initiatives affiliated with one or more Canadian universities.[3] It focuses on how up to five macro-level logics (i.e., state, market, corporation, professions, and community) are reflected and conveyed in these descriptions and what this suggests in terms of how CCI-based EL is oriented with respect to underlying purposes and values.

The chapter begins by defining SI and SEE and how they reflect a new mode of CCI-based EL. It then outlines a theoretical framework that links neo-institutional theory with concerns about purposes, values, and beliefs in HE. The methodology is then described, followed by findings that offer an aggregate and granular view of the logics conveyed in the sample of initiatives. The chapter concludes with a discussion of findings, summary observations, and directions for future research.

SI and SEE as Sites for CCI-Based EL

Definitions of social innovation, social enterprise, and social entrepreneurship are manifold and contested. A brief introduction is offered here, recognizing it can only be a starting point.[4] SI is about fostering inclusive collaborations to co-create ways of addressing unmet social needs while enhancing society's capacity to act collectively (Adams & Hess, 2010; Mulgan, 2012a). Social entrepreneurship is about highly motivated individuals and organizations using business methods and innovative strategies to tackle social problems (Jackson & Harrison, 2011). The primary goal of social entrepreneurs is to create social value as opposed to, or in addition to, generating financial profits (Phillips et al., 2015). Social enterprise is about creating organizations that serve social goals. Such organizations can be based in market-oriented, charitable, or state-funded models. They can take on private for profit, communal not for profit, and state affiliated forms. And they can be hybridized in terms of these models and forms (Defourny & Nyssens, 2008). Some authors see SI and SEE as closely related conceptual and empirical phenomena, while others argue they can and should be distinguished in theory and practice (Cunha et al., 2015). These differences in opinion also exist among practitioners in HE. A recent description of the landscape of relevant initiatives in the Canadian university system revealed that some focus solely on SI, some on SEE, and some combine SI and SEE (Milley et al., 2020), and experienced practitioners in HE operate from a variety of perspectives in terms of their values and beliefs (Milley et al., 2020).

Despite their conceptual and valuational differences, most SI and SEE initiatives in HE integrate CCI-based EL as a central element in their design (Benneworth et al., 2020; Milley et al., 2020). Most concentrate on learning, development, and capacity building with an emphasis on experiential methods (Bayuo et al., 2020). A distinguishing feature of numerous SI and SEE initiatives is they combine conventional internal audiences (e.g., students enrolled in official programs) with non-traditional external audiences (e.g., community members experiencing vulnerable circumstances, experienced or budding social entrepreneurs). Some initiatives focus only on serving external audiences, such as those living in homeless shelters or experiencing other forms of deprivation. This approach is unconventional in the mainstream programs of most universities, which are almost always exclusionary in terms of clientele.[5]

The landscape of SI and SEE initiatives in HE is diverse in terms of organizational locations and forms, disciplines served, and foci regarding social problems and needs. For example, there are SI hubs and labs that bring internal audiences of students together with external audiences to engage in EL processes oriented to co-generating solutions to social problems and needs. Many of these serve multiple disciplines or academic programs, with some focusing on specific issues such as health, poverty, homelessness, or forced migration (Milley et al., 2020). Others take an "agnostic" approach and instead offer EL processes and methods that are applied to a variety of social issues and needs that different external audiences identify and work on with students. There are also social enterprise incubators that are positioned as institution-wide resources or within single organizational units like business schools. There are initiatives that operate between multiple HE institutions to provide CCI-based EL for students from all those institutions through partnerships with municipal governments and community organizations. The latter initiatives aim to address social, economic, and environmental issues on regional bases. And there are a multitude of other permutations and configurations (Milley et al., 2020).

Theoretical Framing

The purposes, content and means of "higher learning", including in and through CCI-based EL, are open to complex processes of contestation, adaptation, and change (Cantwell et al., 2018). Each mode of EL can be oriented to one or more goals, depending on the interests, values, beliefs, and practices of constituents (Moore, 2010), while broader institutional and cultural norms, policies and rules serve to structure constituents' agency (Sidhu & Gage, 2021). For example, a community service-learning (CSL) program, which provides volunteering opportunities with community organizations for university students, may be conceived and implemented as an EL opportunity for the students to (a) do something good while deepening their appreciation of aspects of communal life such as vulnerability, interdependence, and reciprocity,

(b) focus on developing dispositions to sustain healthy communities like active participation and citizenship, (c) emphasize the development of skills and other instrumental benefits that students can use when seeking future employment, or (d) attempt to integrate and balance these competing purposes (Taylor et al, 2015). Similarly, an SI or SEE initiative may aim to (a) help participants learn how to promote social goods through social means, such as co-creating and implementing solutions with members of vulnerable groups to meet the latter's unmet social needs, or (b) it may emphasize the development of leadership and entrepreneurship skills that participants can use to develop their own social and economic ventures or help them seek future employment, or (c) it may help participants develop an appreciation for the common good and the political and other processes needed to pursue it; or (d) it may attempt to clarify and balance these contrasting purposes (McBride & Mlyn, 2020).

Neo-institutional theorists have developed a framework to study complex institutional dynamics in HE-like contexts over the purposes, content and means of CCI-based EL. This framework sees such underlying forces as arising from competing demands based in multiple institutional logics (ILs) that inform and structure the sense-making and actions of organizational members and stakeholders (Thornton et al., 2012). ILs are symbolic systems constituted by sets of principles, norms, beliefs and aims that shape actors' understandings of organizational reality and practices. These ideations are socially constructed over time and often have a taken-for-granted character. ILs are, thus, macro-level rational structures that frame local understandings of organizational situations and how to act confidently in them (Hallett & Ventresca, 2006; Suddaby & Greenwood, 2005). Recent research shows that five ILs are relevant to understanding the institutional complexity of universities in and beyond Canada (Cai & Mountford, 2022a). These include logics of the state, market, corporation, professions, and community (Table 5.1).[6]

The definitions and dimensions outlined in Table 5.1 reveal that each IL carries a set of ideations that differentiate it from other ILs.[7] For example, members of a community legitimize their understandings and actions through references to their unity of will, secured through trust and reciprocity within a collective group. whereas participants in a market refer to economic advantage secured through competitive, transactional relations to justify their understandings and actions. Similarly, each IL has a distinctive basis of norms, attention, and strategies. For instance, in a community, norms arise from group membership, attention focuses on commitment to the group, and strategies aim to increase the standing of members and respect for their concerns, needs, values, and practices. In a market context, norms stem from self-interest,

Table 5.1. Institutional Logics: Definitions and Dimensions

Logic	Definition	Dimensions
State	Symbolic system associated with an institutional order that relies on the state's regulatory and/or redistributive powers for coordinating individual and organizational activities in a framework based in law, and state authority, tools and resources	Source of legitimacy: democratic participation Source of authority: law, regulation, policy, state bureaucracy Basis of norms: citizenship Basis of attention: status of interest groups Basis of strategy: increase community good (through state authority, tools, resources)
Market	Symbolic system associated with an institutional order that invokes the market as a transactional mechanism for coordinating individual and organizational activities in a neoliberal framework (competition, marketization)	Source of legitimacy: economic advantage (profit, value creation) Source of authority: activism of shareholders/stakeholders Basis of norms: self-interest Basis of attention: status in the market Basis of strategy: increase efficiency and value
Corporate	Symbolic system associated with an institutional order that relies on corporate entities as a mechanism for coordinating individual and organizational activities in a framework of role authority and an emphasis on market position/reputation of the entity	Source of legitimacy: market position of the entity Source of authority: centrality of role in the entity Basis of norms: employment (or formal membership) in the entity Basis of attention: status of role and entity Basis of strategy: growth and diversification
Professional	Symbolic system associated with an institutional order that invokes professional relational networks as a mechanism for coordinating individual and organizational activities in a framework based on distinctive expertise	Source of legitimacy: personal expertise Source of authority: professional association and/or network Basis of norms: membership in professional association and/or network Basis of attention: status in the profession Basis of strategy: increase personal and professional reputation
Community	Symbolic system associated with an institutional order that invokes communal mechanisms for coordinating individual and organizational activities based in a collective unity of will and a belief in trust and reciprocity, within a common boundary (geographic, group identity, shared values)	Source of legitimacy: unity of collective will through trust and reciprocity Source of authority: commitment to community values Basis of norms: membership in the community Basis of attention: commitment to the community Basis of strategy: increase standing and respect of members and their concerns, needs, values and practices

emphasis is placed on status in the market, and strategies aim to increase efficiency and economic value.

Following this framework, actors in universities think, decide, and act in the context of multiple logics being conveyed into their daily activities in the form of competing institutional demands (Oertel & Soll, 2017).[8] An ongoing challenge for organizational actors in HE is to seek a balance between these forces (Cai & Mountford, 2022b). In the case of CCI-based EL, the complexity of situations is also shaped by ongoing outreach and engagement with multiple stakeholders who convey different values and beliefs from their locations in the private, public, and community sectors. The convergence (or lack thereof) with the logics structuring the perspectives of key stakeholders can affect an EL initiative's reputation, perceived legitimacy, political support, and resourcing (Thornton et al., 2012).

It is important to note, however, that one IL may, at times, come to predominate in group or organizational settings, such that it serves to constrain actors' use of other logics (Lee & Lounsbury, 2015). For example, many scholars have observed that neoliberal ideologies have, over the last four decades, become central drivers of institutional strategy and practice in HE in Canada and globally (Lawrence & Rezai-Rashti, 2022; Marginson, 2011; Marginson, 2016; Roberts & Peters, 2019). Viewed through a neo-institutional lens, neoliberalism privileges the logic of markets (Lee & Lounsbury, 2015). Studies have revealed how the interests of powerful actors in the state and private sector converged to expand markets in HE, confronting university-based actors with demands to embrace marketization as a means of garnering reputation, resources, legitimacy, and support for their institutions (Kezar, 2009; Marginson, 2013). These dynamics have been observed in some CCI-based EL settings. For example, the prolific connections co-operative education programs forge between employers and students have been seen to result in participants fixating on economic advantage and their status in labour markets to the detriment of socially progressive learning (Milley, 2016a; Milley 2016b), and the emergence of SEE initiatives has been analyzed as a neoliberal sociopolitical movement that converts strategies of community organizing to market based, profit oriented approaches (Spicer et al., 2019).

It is possible, however, for actors in HE to contest or counterbalance a prevailing IL. This requires having access to symbolic and material resources that convey other ILs. Here, CCI-based EL could play a role by encouraging interactions with external actors that influence internal sense-making and institutional change through the infusion of inputs from multiple sectors and perspectives (Fitzgerald et al., 2012; Hartley et al., 2010; Kezar, 2013). Viewed this way, the historical rise of SI and SEE initiatives as sites for CCI-based EL can be seen as a potential response to the process of disillusionment that neoliberal marketization in HE has produced with respect to deleterious effects like economic inequality, social exclusion, instrumentalization and commodification of education (Alajoutsijärvi et al., 2021; Mintz, 2021; Velayutham, 2021). This is producing internal and external pressures on universities to address negative impacts of widespread marketization. So, instead of conveying pronounced market logics, SI and SEE initiatives may be conceived and activated to bring new symbolic and material resources into universities that convey alternative logics, such as those of the community.

The question, thus, arises as to what ILs – or mix of ILs – are conveyed in the symbolic and material inputs that SI and SEE, as sites for CCI-based EL, bring to universities and surrounding communities. This question is addressed using the foregoing theoretical framework and the methodology described next.

Methodology

This study relied on a document analysis research design incorporating a deductive-dominant content analysis method (Armat et al., 2018; Bowen, 2009).[9] It used a pre-determined data coding framework consisting of five categories of ILs derived from definitions from neo-institutional theory outlined in Table 5.1. This framework was used to code and analyze the texts of publicly available descriptions of forty-three CCI-based SI and SEE EL initiatives in Canadian universities (Table 5.2). The texts in the sample were ostensibly produced by key actors in the initiatives. They were systematically collected from university and university affiliated websites in the spring of 2018, following a method outlined in Milley et al. (2020).[10]

The coding framework was complemented with a classification schema for the identification of initiatives in terms of their focus on SI and/or SEE and whether they undertook EL with audiences internal (e.g., registered students) or external to the university.[11]

Considering the guiding research question for the study, the objective of data analysis was to identify the mix of ILs, as conveyed in the descriptive texts and relative to the classification profiles of the initiatives.

Procedure

The files containing descriptions of each of the forty-three initiatives were imported into NVivo 12, a qualitative data analysis software program. Each initiative's descriptive text was then "coded" relative to the

Table 5.2. List of Initiatives Included in the Sample

Initiative	University/Universities	Province/ Territory	Launch Year
Agility Idea Shop	University of Lethbridge	AB	2016
Centre for Social Enterprise	Memorial University	NL	2016
Centre for Social Innovation and Impact Investing (Sauder S3i)	University of British Columbia	BC	2009
CityLab	McMaster University	ON	2017
CityStudio Vancouver	Simon Fraser University, University of British Columbia, Emily Carr University of Art and Design	BC	2011
Change Lab Action Research Institute (CLARI)	Saint Mary's University, Université Sainte-Anne, Cape Breton University, St. Francis Xavier University, Mount Saint Vincent University, Acadia University	NS	2016
DESIS Lab	Emily Carr University of Art and Design	BC	2012
Discovery University	Saint Paul University, University of Ottawa, Carleton University	ON	2005
Extension Innovation and Enterprise Centre (EIEC)	Saint Francis Xavier University	NS	No date
Greenhouse	University of Waterloo	ON	2013
Guelph Lab	University of Guelph	ON	2015
Impact Collective	OCAD University	ON	2014
Innovate Calgary Social Enterprise Incubator Program	University of Calgary	AB	2018
Island Sandbox	Cape Breton University	NS	2014
L'Espace Lab	Université du Québec en Abitibi-Témiscamingue	QC	2018
Libro Social Innovation Program	University of Windsor	ON	2018
MacEwan Social Innovation Hub	MacEwan University	AB	2018
Maison de l'innovation sociale	HEC Montreal, Concordia University	QC	2017

(*continued*)

Table 5.2. (Continued)

Initiative	University/Universities	Province/ Territory	Launch Year
Making the Shift Youth Homelessness SI Lab	York University	ON	2017
MaRS Solutions Lab	University of Waterloo	ON	2013
Mauril-Bélanger Social Innovation Workshop	Saint Paul University	ON	2018
METIS (Entre Genie et Medecine)	Ecole Polytechnique Montréal	QC	2010
Northern Innovation Hub	University of Ottawa	ON	2014
NouLab	University of New Brunswick	NB	2015
Office of Social Innovation	Ryerson University	ON	2016
RADIUS	Simon Fraser University	BC	2013
Schlegel Centre for Entrepreneurship and SI	Wilfrid Laurier University	ON	2017
SHIFT	Concordia University, Université du Québec à Montréal	ON	2018
SIX	Carleton University	ON	2017
Skills Society Citizen Action Lab	University of Alberta	AB	2016
Social Enterprise and Entrepreneurship (SEE)	Algoma University	ON	2014
Social Innovators' Integration Lab	McGill University, Carleton University	QC, ON	2016
Social Learning for Social Impact GROOC	McGill University	QC	2015
Social Ventures Zone	Ryerson University	ON	2014
SparkZone	Saint Mary's University, Mount Saint Vincent University, NSCAD University	NS	2014
Strategic Innovation Lab	OCAD University	ON	2008
Sustain X	University of Alberta	AB	2016
Trico Changemakers Studio	Mount Royal University	AB	2018
Tswassen Farm School	Kwantlen Polytechnic University	BC	2015
Ulab Social Innovation Hub	Concordia University	QC	2016
Vancouver Island Social Innovation Zone (VISIZ)	Royal Roads University, University of Victoria	BC	2016
Vivacity	Mount Royal University, University of Calgary, University of Lethbridge	AB	2013

Winnipeg Boldness	University of Manitoba, University of Winnipeg	MB	2014
Waterloo Institute for Social Innovation and Resilience (WISIR)	University of Waterloo	ON	2010

framework of ILs and the classificatory schema. This was an iterative process that involved continually interpreting the meaning of texts against coding definitions and classifications. Exemplary segments were eventually identified to serve as "touchstones" to support decision making about what other segments to code and to which code or classification. This sometimes required the use of contextual cues that existed in data that was available beyond the descriptive texts, such as who were the partners or what were the funding sources of an initiative.

Data Analysis

Coded data were analyzed in two interrelated ways. First, the classification categories were used to create a typology of eight possible types of initiatives. Next, matrices were created to display the prevalence of ILs coded for each of the forty-three initiatives. Data in these matrices were then converted into the graphs.

Findings

Types of Initiatives and Their Audiences

An overall view of initiatives and their audience types reveals that, in those focused on SI, approximately 60 percent of the audience are internal to the university and 40 percent are external. A similar finding exists for initiatives that concentrate on SEE (see Figure 5.1). Internal audiences are students enrolled in university programs and who have access to CCI-based EL. External audiences are varied across initiatives. They include representatives from vulnerable populations or community stakeholder groups to budding or experienced social entrepreneurs and actors interested in investing in potential social start-ups.

Based on the study's classification schema, eight types of initiatives were identified in the sample. Between one and eight initiatives are associated with each type, with six typological categories containing five or more (Table 5.3).

Figure 5.1. Focus of Initiative and Type of Audience for Experiential Learning

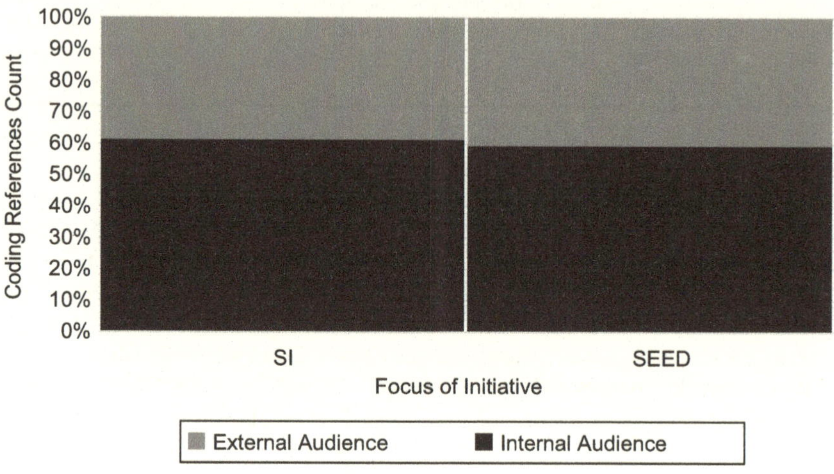

Table 5.3. Typology and Count of Initiatives Based on Classification Schema

	Focus of Initiative		Audience for EL		
Type	SI	SEE	Internal	External	Count in sample
1	✓	✓	✓	✓	8
2	✓	✓	✓		8
3	✓	✓		✓	6
4		✓	✓	✓	5
5	✓		✓		8
6	✓			✓	5
7		✓	✓		1
8		✓		✓	2

Looking across the typology, numerous initiatives offer a combined focus on SI and SEE (n=16 of 43), and/or combine internal and external audiences in their approach to EL (n=19 of 43). More than half (n=27 of 43) address three or more of these classification categories. Eight initiatives categorized as type 1 stand-out in addressing all four dimensions. Another notable pattern is that more initiatives include a focus on SI rather than on SEE. This is apparent when comparing those with a sole focus on SI (n=13 (i.e., total for types 5, 6)) versus those concentrating only on SEE (n=3 (i.e., total for types 7, 8)).

Individual Initiatives and Their Associated Institutional Logics

Based on the application of the study's coding framework of ILs to the sample of descriptive texts, it is possible to depict the ILs conveyed in each of the forty-three initiatives (Figure 5.2).

The findings in Figure 5.2 reveal a kaleidoscopic mix of ILs conveyed across the sample, indicating heterogeneity across the landscape of SI and SEE initiatives in the Canadian university system. A granular view reveals that just over half of the initiatives (n=22 of 43) express four or five ILs, nearly a third (n=13 of 43) convey three ILs, and about one-fifth (n=8 of 43) impart two.

Of the group that impart two ILs, the majority (n=5 of 8) express the logics of community and profession. These initiatives tend to be grassroots and small scale. For example, St. Paul University's Discovery U aims to provide "people living on low incomes to participate in ... Humanities and Social Sciences courses [delivered by professors] at not cost ... to encourage a commitment to learning [and help] develop critical thinking and problem-solving skills." This initiative is offered in partnership with a local church community and shelter supporting persons living in conditions of homelessness. It reflects a professional logic in the involvement of academics as a professional group turned towards community purposes, and, simultaneously, a community logic is expressed in the strategy of improving the standing of community members. Another example is Emily Carr University of Art and Design's DESIS Lab[12] that engages students in organizing events to help develop their skills in design (imparting a professional logic) to advance social engagement, social innovation, and sustainability to change how people "design, live, imagine, feel and be" (reflecting a community logic).

The middle group that reflects three ILs emphasizes two combinations of logics: (a) community, professional and corporate (n=6 of 13), and (b) community, professional and state (n=5 of 13). Those expressing the first combination tend to be hubs encouraging SI and/or SEE through collaboration with community members, reflecting a community logic. In these cases, the logic of profession was conveyed through claims about the existence and development of expertise and resources in SI or SEE as unique fields of endeavour, and corporate logic was imparted through statements about the unique status of the hub as an organization. An example is Ontario College of Art & Design (OCAD) University's Strategic Innovation Lab.[13] It is described as "a centre of excellence in design thinking, strategic foresight and social innovation" (reflecting a corporate logic) that "brings an understanding of complex systems and futures

Figure 5.2. Institutional Logics Conveyed in Descriptive Texts of Initiatives

studies, through techniques such as environmental scanning, emergent signal analysis, scenario learning, and technology assessment … to develop creative insights" (conveying a professional logic) through "a growing community of scholars and practitioners, design, business and policy professionals, teachers and students" (expressing a community logic). The initiatives communicating the other combination of logics are an eclectic mix of entities for EL related to SI or SEE. Key features they have in common are their commitments to using CCI (reflecting a community logic) as a basis for developing and applying specific expertise (conveying a professional logic) to social problems and needs in collaboration with state actors (expressing a state logic). One example is the Guelph Lab. It describes itself as building on the history of CCI (reflecting a professional logic of expertise in CCI) at the University of Guelph to enable open government at the City of Guelph (expressing a state logic) while supporting innovation to address the "complex challenges facing the community" (reflecting a community logic).[14] Another example is the Tsawwassen Farm School. It is a collaboration between the Tsawwassen First Nation and Kwantlen Polytechnic University that brings together "knowledge in sustainable agriculture and traditional indigenous food systems … to build community and create dialogue around land stewardship." It offers EL on a certified organic farm that is "open to all with curiosity on how to feed a growing population while restoring the land." This case is unique in the sample in that it incorporates a First Nation as both a state actor and community. In it, a professional logic is reflected in the fusion and promotion of knowledge traditions, a state logic is imparted in the regulative goal of restorative land stewardship from within a First Nations perspective, and a community logic is expressed through focus on building community through open dialogue.

In the final group, there are eleven initiatives that reflect four ILs and eleven that express all five ILs. Of those imparting four, a majority (n=6 of 11) do not feature a market logic, and, of this majority, most (n=5 of 6) are hubs that focus on SI and not on SEE. They include initiatives that provide experiences for students in multiple regional HE institutions in partnership with municipal governments and in collaboration with community organizations. CityStudio Vancouver is an example. It is "an innovation hub where City staff, students, and community co-create experimental projects to make Vancouver more sustainable, liveable and joyful." CityStudio "aims to build trust relationships in the community" (reflecting a community logic) by having students work "directly with City staff" (revealing a state logic) to develop skills, experience, and networks for "inspiring action in the community and government" (positioning changemaking within a professional logic). CityStudio observes it is "the first of its kind in Canada and unique around the world" and that it coaches other cities in adopting its model (reflecting two elements of corporate logic: it's unique status as an organization and having a growth strategy). Another pattern in the subgroup of initiatives reflecting four ILs is that a sub-subgroup (n=3 of 11) does not feature a corporate logic, instead, they signal aspects of market logic. In one case, this was related to the initiative's tie to social impact investing, a market mechanism for obtaining financial resources. In the other two cases, a market logic was signaled in their work in developing social entrepreneurship. For example, Island Sandbox is a "collision space for ideas and innovation." Set up between Cape Breton University and Nova Scotia Community College, the Sandbox "bring[s] students together with communities' entrepreneurs, innovators, investors and academia to ... experiment and to see the world through the eyes of an entrepreneur." Here, the reliance on engaging community members reflects a community logic, the emphasis on building expertise in entrepreneurship signals a professional logic, and the emphasis on entrepreneurial thinking, including with respect to attracting investment, reflects market logic. Beyond this, the initiative is tied to a state logic in its aim to "move Cape Breton forward" by helping entrepreneurs access provincial government funding.

In the subgroup of eleven initiatives that express all five ILs, almost all (n=9) focus on SEE exclusively or with attention also paid to SI. Five of these are affiliated with schools of business or enterprise development. An example is Simon Fraser University's RADIUS, a "social innovation hub for thoughtful changemakers" which has aims, activities, and strategies reflecting a complicated mix of ILs. Launched in 2013, RADIUS is a physical hub located on the edge of the corporate district of Vancouver. It is near the "downtown east side," a community of long standing, complex social needs including poverty, homelessness, racism, and mental health and addiction issues. It features educational and research programs related to SI and changemaking, labs focused on the co-creation of solutions to a variety of social needs (e.g., local economic development, refugee livelihoods, health promotion) and a "social venture" accelerator program. Its support and resources come from internal sources like the business school that hosts it, the central administration, other faculties that access EL through its labs, and from external sources like the governments, charitable foundations, NGOs, and corporations. RADIUS is a multi-dimensional initiative with an assortment of audiences and stakeholders. Its mission of improving the standing of members of the local community (a community logic) is informed, filtered, and counterbalanced with other ILs. It represents an "ideal type" (in Max Weber's (2012) sense) of a multifaceted CCI-based EL SI/SEE initiative. Such

Figure 5.3. SI and SEE Initiatives and Aggregated Associated Institutional Logics

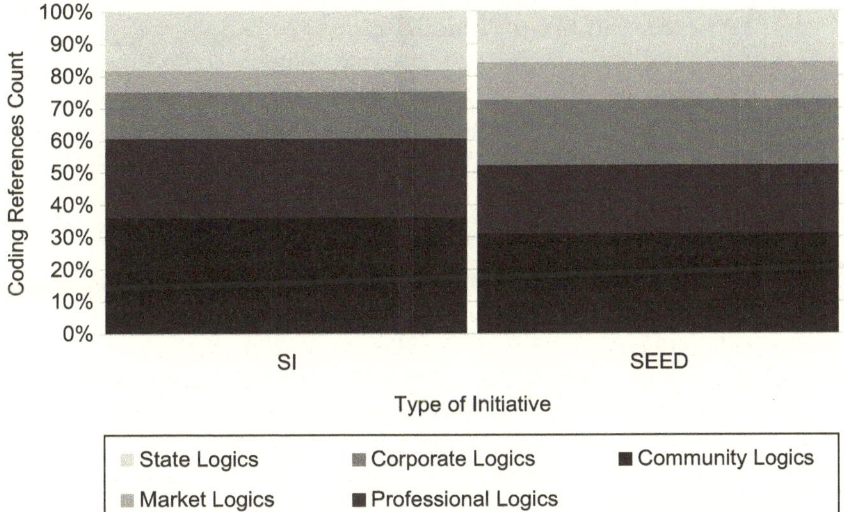

initiatives pay attention to markets to help social entrepreneurs launch and scale their ideas through social enterprises, including through the sourcing of financial support, reflecting a market IL. They focus on their distinctive position and status on the landscape of initiatives to continue garnering legitimacy and support, while gestating SEE as part of their operations. Additionally, they pursue avenues for growth and diversification to ensure their viability as initiatives. These three aspects are based in corporate logic. They pay attention to the application of expertise in SI and SEE and to the development of skills and dispositions suited to SI and SEE as fields of professional opportunity and identity. This reflects professional logic. Finally, they do this working in collaboration or partnership with state institutions, such as municipal and provincial governments, signifying that state logic infuses their operations.

Aggregate View of Initiatives and Associated Institutional Logics

During the preceding granular analysis, a pattern emerged in which initiatives focused on SI appeared to reflect more community logic and less market and corporate logic than initiatives oriented to SEE, and vice versa. An aggregated analysis corroborates this finding. Figure 5.3 compares the prevalence of ILs associated with initiatives focusing on SI or SEE. These data reveal the incidence of community logic to be 36 percent in SI versus 31 percent in SEE, while the commonness of market and corporate logics are 6.5 percent and 14.5 percent respectively in SI versus 11.5 percent and 20 percent in SEE.

Figure 5.3 also reveals that professional logic is slightly more pronounced in SI versus SEE contexts, with the frequency in SI being 24.5 percent in contrast to 21 percent in SEE. The prevalence of state logic is similar in SI and SEE contexts, at 18 percent and 16 percent respectively.

Discussion

The professed aim of SI and SEE initiatives to contribute to social good, in part through CCI-based EL, suggests the logic of community should be substantially reflected in their aims, values, foci, and strategies. The findings from this study support this expectation. However, the prevalence of community logic varies considerably between individual initiatives, and it is less present in aggregate than one might anticipate. This is because a variety of other ILs shape and are conveyed by such initiatives. As seen, the majority express four or five ILs, a minority convey two, and none are exclusively oriented by a community IL. Those conveying the fewest ILs tend to be small, grassroots, and focused on SI. Those conveying the most ILs tend to be organizationally established and focused on a combination of SI and SEE. They also tend to combine multiple internal and external audiences for EL and have a variety of internal and external stakeholders. These patterns suggest that as SI and SEE initiatives become organizationally established, they get exposed to an increasing number and variety of competing demands. In short, they become exposed to and imbricated in institutional complexity (Thornton et al., 2012).

Insights can be gained about this complexity by looking at what the variegated mix of ILs expressed in such initiatives represents to actors and stakeholders. For example, this study reveals the logic of profession to have a substantial presence across the sample. It is found in almost all the initiatives, where it is frequently reflected in claims to distinctive expertise being applied in or developed by the initiatives. This speaks to the convention in universities that actors require coherent academic identities for their practices to be viewed and accepted as legitimate. For instance, actors in SI and SEE claim expertise in forging unconventional forms of CCI through new practices while consolidating identities such as "social innovator", "changemaker" and "social entrepreneur". In their recent study on SI in universities, Cinar and Benneworth (2021) argue this promulgation of professional identity is a necessary step in the legitimization of SI practices in HE. In another example, the findings revealed corporate logic to have a meaningful presence in more than half the initiatives. In many cases, this logic is indicated by claims made about the unique status of such initiatives as organizational entities. These assertions emphasize the contributions of initiatives as social impact organizations or what distinguishes them qualitatively from other organizations. These expressions appear to be related to establishing the legitimacy of initiatives, something that Cinar and Benneworth (2021) observed SI actors need to attend to in university settings.[15] These two examples reveal how additional demands based in additional ILs can draw SI and SEE actors' attention away from pursuing their primary aims, actions, values, and outcomes.

Similar observations can be made about how the logics of state and market inform the work of setting direction and steering such initiatives. The findings reveal a state IL to be present in many initiatives. This logic is often indicated in strategies of pursuing community good through some degree of reliance on the authority, tools, or resources of state entities. This reliance is revealed through references to affiliations with state entities, such as having access to dedicated funding or partnerships with state actors and organizations.[16] State entities work within laws, regulations, policies, and specified or conventional procedures (Thornton et al., 2012). Forming affiliations with them entails conforming with these institutional features, which can present additional demands like complicated project proposal processes, unfamiliar rules and conventions, and laborious reporting requirements (Bourgon, 2011). With respect to the logic of the market, it is less prevalent in the findings than anticipated given concerns addressed earlier about the increased marketization of HE, with SEE seen as a conduit of this trend. Nonetheless, a market IL appears to inform a plurality of cases in the sample. This logic is indicated through a focus on increasing status in the market. Examples include claims about helping social entrepreneurs prepare and position themselves, their ideas, and enterprises in markets and about helping participants develop skills to participate in labour markets as employees but with an updated mindset oriented to social issues and the need for change in organizations, communities, and societies. A market logic is also reflected in activities geared to helping participants compete for financing from governments or other "social finance" sources (Langley, 2020). The work involved in addressing demands conveying state and market ILs may, again, pull actors' attention in directions that do not correspond with their original aims, values, and beliefs for pursuing SI and SEE as sites for CCI-based EL.

An array of potentially competing institutional demands can, thus, be seen to convey a mix of ILs into SI and SEE initiatives. These demands may be institutionally desired, but they can also serve to distort, drain, or disrupt initiatives from their primary purposes. Actors responsible for these initiatives are, thus, confronted with a delicate balancing act in terms of setting direction and staying or changing the course. Theirs is conceptually, relationally, morally, and strategically demanding work (Milley et al., 2020). But this search for balance likely differs depending on the type of initiative. As the findings here reveal, those focused on SI may feature fewer demands framed within market and corporate logics than do those concentrating on SEE, but SI initiatives may be confronted with higher expectations from community groups and state entities. The audiences for EL also play into these dynamics: A complicated mix also appears to increase the institutional complexity surrounding such initiatives.

Closing Thoughts

As Buzzelli pointed out in the introductory chapter to this volume, universities, and the actors in them, are confronted with competing interests, demands, and pressures that require a constant renegotiation of their "social contract" with their host community and "town." Given widespread concerns about the deleterious effects of marketization as a globally ascendant logic in HE institutions, it may be heartening to see the prevailing IL in most SI and SEE initiatives based in and promoting CCI-based EL to be that of community. Importantly, the initiatives in this study reveal it is a logic pertaining to the *local* community. Moreover, this latter emphasis suggests that other demands, such as preparing audiences for participation in labour or finance markets or serving university administrations in instrumentalizing CCI and EL to enhance institutional reputations, may not be predominating. This suggests there may be less distortion than one might expect in the orientation towards social betterment in the CCI-based EL opportunities offered through SI and SEE initiatives. In other words, the explicit or implied social contract of SI and SEE initiatives may be holding, at least based on the data and analysis provided here.

Some caveats need to be placed around such cautious optimism, and these provisos provide direction for future research. The data used here are self-reported and of only one type – i.e., public descriptions taken from one point in time. This means it is not possible to know if what the descriptions say is what plays out in practice. In addition, the production and circulation of symbolic and material resources in organizations is an ongoing process. Their conveyance of logics is, thus, dynamic. The data used here provide insights about the variegated mix of ILs informing and expressed by initiatives, but they offer a static view taken from a slice in time. The current study cannot provide insights on the micro-level dynamics by which actors draw on and promulgate "field level logics" (Cai & Mountford, 2022a; Cai & Mountford, 2022b) that hybridize or instantiate ILs as part of the ongoing process of making sense of and responding to competing institutional demands. Here, readers may gain insights from LaCroix's chapter in the current volume that examines the competing "logics" at an intra-institutional level between university administrators and academics involved in EL programs and how these generate misunderstandings that deleteriously affect EL. Nonetheless, further investigation through other methods could help assess, for example, whether such initiatives convey in practice field level logics that contain a neoliberal vision of a reduced influence of the state and communities and an increased appetite for market-oriented thinking and action.

The design of future studies addressing these caveats could be informed by the work that Cai and Mountford (2022a) have done to review, synthesize and classify five-dozen empirical studies in HE that draw on neo-institutional theory. They argue that the potential of neo-institutional theory can be unlocked in HE research by operationalizing the concept of ILs to examine the "tangible influence of macro-logical structure observed in meso- and micro-logical behaviour, routines and artefacts" (p. 1640). This implies research designs, such as case studies (e.g., Blaschke et al., 2014), that include the requisite methods and instruments to amass longitudinal data to identify field level logics and the dynamics by which they serve to instantiate or hybridize societal-level logics or contribute to the formation of new societal logics (Mountford & Cai, 2022). Cai and Mountford (2022a) observe that designs featuring inductive and deductive combinations could lead to better results in IL-informed studies of HE. Following their classification, the current study follows a "societal level deduction" design in that the ILs examined here were derived from the pre-existing and well-accepted model articulated by Thornton et al. (2012). This would be enhanced by a design featuring societal level deduction and field level induction, with the former identifying societal level logics reflected at the field level, and the latter identifying "new" logics at the field level (Cai & Mountford, 2022a).

NOTES

1 CCI has also been pursued in Canadian universities for other activities such as community-based research (CBR) and community economic development (CED).

2 In Canadian higher education, a prominent professional association of EL practitioners has encapsulated and rebranded numerous of these modes for EL based in CCI as work integrated learning (see CEWIL Canada, 2021).

3 These data were collected through a systematic search of the websites of Canada's ninety-six public universities (see Milley et al., 2020).

4 The current study is descriptive-analytical not conceptual or definitional when it comes to SI and SEE. For robust insights on concepts and definitions, see Cunha et al. (2015), Dawson and Daniel (2010), Edwards-Schachter and Wallace (2017), Howaldt and Schwarz (2010), McGowan and Westley (2015), Moulaert et al. (2017), Mulgan (2012a; 2012b), and Nicholls et al. (2015).

5 A notable exception regarding learning services to external audiences are continuing studies departments or institutes that offer professional development or non-credit workshops, courses and certificates on a cost recovery, revenue generating, or charitable basis.

6 Thornton et al. (2012) produced a typology of seven ILs. The decision to use five of these is based on Mountford and Cai's (2022) meta-analysis that found those five were present in the knowledge base of ILs research in HE, but two – religion and family – were rarely present.

7 Table 5.1 adapts conceptual inputs from Thornton et al. (2012), Greenwood et al. (2010), and Lee and Lounsbury (2022).

8 This institutional complexity is amplified because of the different levels present in HE systems, such as the system, central administration, faculty, school or department levels, and the individual professor or researcher level. The institutional demands and balance of logics may be different depending on where an actor is in this multi-level system.

9 According to Armat et al. (2018), deductive-dominant content analysis is when the researcher begins the analysis using pre-defined categories developed from a theoretical framework or extant research findings but remains open to developing new categories or revisiting the definitions of categories considering meaningful segments of text that do not "fit" the original analytical schema.

10 The Milley et al. (2020) study identified forty-six SI/SEE initiatives operating in Canadian universities, using a detailed set of criteria for inclusion/exclusion based, in part, on definitions of SI and SEE. The sample of forty-three initiatives in the current study was derived from their sample by applying additional criterial related to the definition of EL provided in the introduction of this chapter. The application of these criteria resulted in three initiatives from the Milley et al. (2020) sample being excluded in the current study.

11 Data collection in the Milley et al. (2020) study included references to the stated purposes, foci and activities undertaken in that study's sample

of initiatives. Those data included explicit references to the initiatives' engagement in SI and SEE, making it possible to distinguish which initiatives included in the current study's sample engaged in SI, SEE or both.

12 https://www.ecuad.ca/academics/research-area/centres-lab/desis.

13 https://slab.ocadu.ca/.

14 The Guelph Lab further describes its mission as (a) convening interdisciplinary teams of policy makers, funders, citizens, service providers, business, and labour, (b) enabling those with first-hand experience and knowledge of social problems to help share and lead discussions, (c) testing proposals that emerge from the process and assessing their impact.

15 Cinar and Benneworth (2021) argue that SI may sit uncomfortably in universities because SI may point to how other disciplines and organizations may be structurally implicated in producing unfair outcomes and that those structures need changing. Here, the interdisciplinary and intersectoral approach of many SI initiatives may be seen as a threat, hence, the push among SI and SEE actors to establish their professional and organizational legitimacy.

16 In numerous cases the reliance on state authority and resources was indicated only through symbolic means, such as claims that initiatives were serving a named city or region, connoting service to a defined political jurisdiction as a state entity.

REFERENCES

Adams, D., & Hess, M. (2010). Social innovation and why it has policy significance. *The Economic and Labour Relations Review, 21*(2), 139–55.

Alajoutsijärvi, K., Alon, I., & Pinheiro, R. (2021). The marketisation of higher education: Antecedents, processes, and outcomes. In J. D. Branch, B. Christiansen (Eds.), *The marketisation of higher education: Concepts, cases, and criticisms* (pp. 17–45). Springer International Publishing.

Armat, M. R., Assarroudi, A., Rad, M., Sharifi, H., & Heydari, A. (2018). Inductive and deductive: Ambiguous labels in qualitative content analysis. *The Qualitative Report, 23*(1), 219–21.

Bayuo, B. B., Chaminade, C., & Göransson, B. (2020). Unpacking the role of universities in the emergence, development and impact of social innovations: A systematic review of the literature. *Technological Forecasting and Social Change,* 155

Benneworth, P., & Cunha, J. (2015). Universities' contributions to social innovation: Reflections in theory & practice. *European Journal of Innovation Management, 18*(4), 508–27.

Benneworth, P., Cunha, J., & Cinar, R. (2020). Between good intentions and enthusiastic professors: The missing middle of university social innovation structures in the Quadruple Helix. *Regional Helix Ecosystems and Sustainable Growth: The Interaction of Innovation, Entrepreneurship and Technology Transfer*, 31–44.

Blaschke, S., Frost, J., & Hattke, F. (2014). Towards a micro foundation of leadership, governance, and management in universities. *Higher Education*, 68, 711–32.

Bourgon, J. (2011). *A new synthesis of public administration: Serving in the 21st century*. McGill-Queen's Press-MQUP.

Bowen, G. A. (2009). Document analysis as a qualitative research method. *Qualitative research journal*, *9*(2), 27–40.

Cai, Y., & Mountford, N. (2022a). Institutional logics analysis in higher education research. *Studies in Higher Education*, *47*(8), 1–25.

– (2022b). *Institutional logics in higher education: What we learn from the existing research and suggestions for future research*. Research findings, No. 8, June. Centre for Global Higher Education.

Cantwell, B., Coates, H., & King, R. (2018). Introduction. In B. Cantwell, H. Coates, & R. King (Eds.), *Handbook on the politics of higher education* (pp. 1–8). Edward Elgar Publishing.

CEWIL Canada. (2021). *What is work integrated learning (WIL)?* https://cewilcanada.ca/CEWIL/CEWIL/About-Us/Work-Integrated-Learning.aspx

Cinar, R., & Benneworth, P. (2021). Why do universities have little systemic impact with social innovation? An institutional logics perspective. *Growth and Change*, *52*(2), 751–69.

Cunha, J., Benneworth, P., & Oliveira, P. (2015) Social entrepreneurship and social innovation: A conceptual distinction. In L. M. Carmo Farinha (Ed.), *Handbook of research on global competitive advantage through innovation and entrepreneurship*. IGI global.

Dawson, P., & Daniel, L. (2010). Understanding social innovation: a provisional framework. *International Journal of Technology Management*, *51*(1), 9–21.

Defourny, J., & Nyssens, M. (2008). Social enterprise in Europe: Recent trends and developments. *Social Enterprise Journal*, *4*(3), 202–28.

Edwards-Schachter, M., & Wallace, M. L. (2017). "Shaken, but not stirred": Sixty years of defining social innovation. *Technological Forecasting and Social Change*, 119, 64–79.

Fitzgerald, H. E., Bruns, K., Sonka, S. T., Furco, A., & Swanson, L. (2012). The centrality of engagement in higher education. *Journal of Higher Education Outreach and Engagement*, *16*(3), 7–28.

Giesecke, S., & Schartinger, D. (2024). The transformative potential of social innovation for, in and by education. *Journal of Social Entrepreneurship*, *15*(1), 140–60.

Göransson, B., Donati, L., & Wigren-Kristoferson, C. (2021). Introduction to the special issue on universities and social innovation. *Technological Forecasting and Social Change*, 173, 121186.

Greenwood, R., Magan Díaz, A., Xiao Li, S., & Cespedes Lorente, J. (2010). The multiplicity of institutional logics and the heterogeneity of organizational responses. *Organization Science*, 21, 521–39.

Hallett, T., & Ventresca, M. J. (2006). Inhabited institutions: Social interactions and organizational forms in Gouldner's Patterns of Industrial Bureaucracy. *Theory and Society*, 35, 213–36.

Halsall, J. P., Snowden, M., Clegg, P., Mswaka, W., Alderson, M., Hyams-Ssekasi, D., Oberoi, R., & Winful, E. C. (2022). Social enterprise as a model for change: mapping a global cross-disciplinary framework. *Entrepreneurship Education, 5*, 1–22.

Hartley, M., Saltmarsh, J., & Clayton, P. (2010). Is the civic engagement movement changing higher education? *British Journal of Educational Studies, 58*(4), 391–406.

Howaldt, J., & Schwarz, M. (2010). *Social Innovation: Concepts, research fields and international trends.* Sozialforschungsstelle Dortmund.

Jackson, S. J., & Harrison, G. J. (2011). Social entrepreneurship: concepts and implications for problem solving. *Social Entrepreneurship*, 1–24.

Kezar, A. (2009). Change in higher education: Not enough, or too much? *Change: The Magazine of Higher Learning, 41*(6), 18–23.

– (2013). Understanding sensemaking/sensegiving in transformational change processes from the bottom up. *Higher Education*, 65, 761–80.

Langley, P. (2020). The folds of social finance: Making markets, remaking the social. *Environment and Planning A: Economy and Space, 52*(1), 130–47.

Lawrence, M., & Rezai-Rashti, G. M. (2022). Pursuing neoliberal performativity? Performance-based funding and accountability in higher education in Ontario, Canada. In J. Zajda (Ed.), *Discourses of Globalisation and Higher Education Reforms: Emerging Paradigms* (pp. 149–67). Cham: Springer International Publishing.

Lee, M. D., & Lounsbury, M. (2015). Filtering institutional logics: Community logic variation and differential responses to the institutional complexity of toxic waste. *Organization Science, 26*(3), 847–66.

Marginson, S. (2011). Higher education and public good. *Higher Education Quarterly, 65*(4), 411–33.

– (2013). The impossibility of capitalist markets in higher education. *Journal of Education Policy, 28*(3), 353–70.

– (2016). *Higher education and the common good.* Melbourne University Publishing.

McBride, A. M., & Mlyn, E. (Eds.). (2020). *Connecting Civic Engagement and Social Innovation: Toward Higher Education's Democratic Promise.* Campus Compact.

McGowan, K., & Westley, F. (2015). At the root of change: The history of social innovation. *New Frontiers in Social Innovation Research*, 52–68.

Milley, P. (2016a). Commercializing higher learning through the discourse of skills in university co-operative education: Tensions and contradictions. *Canadian Journal of Educational Administration and Policy*, 180, 99-134.

– (2016b). The ideology of skills and its implications for socially progressive learning in university co-operative education. In E. Samier (Ed.) *Ideologies in educational administration and leadership* (pp. 19–34). Routledge.

Milley, P., Szijarto, B., & Bennett, K. (2020). The landscape of social innovation in Canadian universities: An empirical analysis. *Canadian Journal of Nonprofit and Social Economy Research, 11*(1), 21–41.

Mintz, B. (2021). Neoliberalism and the crisis in higher education: The cost of ideology. *American Journal of Economics and Sociology, 80*(1), 79–112.

Moore, D. T. (2010). Forms and issues in experiential learning. *New Directions for Teaching and Learning, 2010*(124), 3–13.

Moulaert, F., MacCallum, D., Mehmood, A., & Leubolt, B. (2017). *Social innovation as a trigger for transformations.* European Commission. https://lirias.kuleuven.be/retrieve/498034

Mountford, N., & Cai, Y. (2022). Towards a flatter ontology of institutional logics: How logics relate in situations of institutional complexity. *International Journal of Management Reviews, 25*(2), 363–83.

Mulgan, G. (2012a). The theoretical foundations of social innovation. In A. Nicholls & A. Murdock (Eds.), *Social innovation: Blurring boundaries to reconfigure markets* (pp. 33–65). Palgrave Macmillan.

Mulgan, G. (2012b). Social innovation theories: Can theory catch up with practice? In H. W. Franz, J. Hochgerner, & J. Howaldt (Eds.), *Challenge social innovation: potentials for business, social entrepreneurship, welfare and civil society* (pp. 19–42). Springer.

Nicholls, A., Simon, J., & Gabriel, M. (2015). Introduction: Dimensions of social innovation. In A. Nicholls, J. Simon, & M. Gabriel (Eds.), *New frontiers in social innovation research* (pp. 1–26). Palgrave Macmillan.

Nichols N., Phipps D., Provencal, J., & Hewitt, A. (2013). Knowledge mobilization, collaboration and social innovation: Leveraging investments in higher education. *Canadian Journal of Nonprofit and Social Economy Research, 4*(1), 25–42.

Oertel, S., & Soll, M. (2017). Universities between traditional forces and modern demands: The role of imprinting on the missions of German universities. *Higher Education, 73*(1), 1–18.

Phillips, W., Lee, H., Ghobadian, A., O'Regan, N., & James, P. (2015). Social innovation and social entrepreneurship: A systematic review. *Group & Organization Management, 40*(3), 428–61.

Pinheiro, R., Wangenge-Ouma, G., Balbachevsky, E., & Cai, Y. (2015). The role of higher education in society and the changing institutionalized features in higher education. *The Palgrave International Handbook of Higher Education Policy and Governance,* 225–42.

Roberts, P., & Peters, M. A. (2019). *Neoliberalism, higher education and research.* Brill.

Scaled Purpose Inc. (2015). *Where to begin: How social innovation is emerging across Canadian campuses.* https://static1.squarespace.com

/static/54989eb5e4b0148a61452d50/t/56a15a3c3b0be350f654045d/1453414972551/Where+To+Begin+-+Social+Innovation+Scan.pdf

Sidhu, R., & Gage, W. H. (2021). Enhancing the odds of adopting e-learning or community-focused experiential learning as a teaching practice amongst university faculty. *Heliyon, 7*(4), e06704.

Spicer, J., Kay, T., & Ganz, M. (2019). Social entrepreneurship as field encroachment: How a neoliberal social movement constructed a new field. *Socio-Economic Review, 17*(1), 195–227.

Suddaby, R., & Greenwood, R. (2005). Rhetorical strategies of legitimacy. *Administrative Science Quarterly, 50*(1), 35–67.

Taylor, A., Butterwick, S. J., Raykov, M., Glick, S., Peikazadi, N., & Mehrabi, S. (2015, October). *Community service-learning in Canadian higher education.* https://open.library.ubc.ca/soa/cIRcle/collections/facultyresearchandpublications/52383/items/1.0226035

Thornton, P. H., Ocasio, W., & Lounsbury, M. (2012). *The institutional logics perspective: A new approach to culture, structure and process.* OUP Oxford.

Velayutham, S. (2021). Understanding how the marketisation of higher education contributes to increased income inequality and decreased social mobility. In J. D. Branch & B. Christiansen (Eds.), *The Marketisation of Higher Education: Concepts, Cases, and Criticisms* (pp. 371–95). Springer International Publishing.

Weber, M. (2012). *Max Weber: collected methodological writings.* Routledge.

Wiksten, S., & Schugurensky, D. (2022). Between the state, society and global markets: Three roles of higher education. In C. A. Torres, R. F. Arnove, & L. I. Misiaszek (Eds.),*Comparative education: The dialectic of the global and the local* (5th ed., pp. 273–95). Rowman & Littlefield.

Wu, Y. J., Goh, M., & Mai, Y. (2023). Social innovation and higher education: evolution and future promise. *Humanities and Social Sciences Communications, 10*(1), 1–14.

6 Actively Involving Primary Stakeholders in Experiential Learning

CATHERINE M. GIROUX, KAYLEE EADY, AND KATHERINE A. MOREAU

University of Ottawa, Canada

Introduction

One goal of experiential learning (EL) is to provide students with opportunities to apply their learning in real world settings, thereby helping to ensure graduates are ready to join the workforce (Buzzelli & Asafo-Adjei, 2022). Governments may incentivize EL programs to ensure that graduates are equipped with the necessary skills to meet labour market demands (Barsukov et al., 2018; Waldner & McGorry, 2012). However well-intentioned this goal may be, EL can become ethically problematic and may reproduce undesirable outcomes if not planned thoughtfully and in collaboration with those who will likely be affected by the learning experiences (Grace et al., 2017; Logar et al., 2015; Meisel, 2008; Oldfield, 2008). For example, in 2020 the Government of Canada incentivized service-learning experiences by collaborating with a well-known volunteer sending organization as part of the Canada Student Service Grant (Government of Canada, 2020). Such organizations have been heavily problematized in the literature since they may perpetuate colonial power structures (Buchmeyer, 2017; Epprecht, 2004; Keehn, 2016; Tiessen & Kumar, 2013). Expecting students and higher education (HE) institutions – with no connection to local needs or experiences – to meaningfully contribute to a community can be deeply problematic. For more on the principles and ethics of EL, consult Chapter 4 of this volume. Evidence has shown that service-learning experiences are often conceptualized in practice as service provision or outreach. In such cases, communities are used as venues for learning and are situated within a problem-based lens and student learning is centred on solving the problems, reinforcing power structures, stereotypes, and inequalities (Hunt et al., 2011; Kline et al., 2018; refer to Chapter 7 to learn more about dismantling such power structures as colonialism). Involving the primary stakeholders (defined in the following section) who stand to lose or gain from EL as partners in the design, delivery, and evaluation of these experiences can help mitigate these ethical tensions.

Stakeholder involvement in EL is an emerging area of inquiry. Thus, the focus of this chapter is to conceptualize the term "stakeholders," with an emphasis on primary stakeholders, in the context of EL and provide strategies for actively involving them in designing, teaching, assessing, and evaluating EL activities. Throughout the chapter, we contend that the involvement of stakeholders is essential for improving EL and should become best practice in HE.

Conceptualizing the Term "Stakeholders" in Experiential Learning

Experiential learning is increasingly a core component of students' education and growth in HE, as they acquire in-demand skills and gain competencies to transition into the workforce. It can include such approaches as eService-learning, co-op, remote co-op, practicums, service-learning, and community-based projects. Diverse groups of stakeholders or interested parties may be involved in its design, delivery, and evaluation. The HE literature often labels these stakeholders as internal or external. Internal stakeholders are those who participate in the day-to-day activities of the HE institutions, including students, faculty members, and administrative staff (Marshall, 2018). Conversely, external stakeholders are groups or individuals that have an interest in HE but are not involved in day-to-day activities, including employers, community agencies, and government bodies (Marshall, 2018). However, this dichotomy between internal and external stakeholders is not always clear. Employers and community agencies often become actively involved in the daily activities of HE institutions when they welcome, train, and assess students in their application of skills as well as when they allow them to explore their understanding of topics in real-life contexts. As such, with respect to EL, it seems more appropriate to use the terms *primary* and *secondary stakeholders,* where primary stakeholders are those who stand to gain or lose something directly from EL, and secondary stakeholders are those who are indirectly affected, either positively or negatively (Alkin & Vo, 2017).

Who identifies as primary and secondary stakeholders may vary depending on the nature or context of the EL opportunity. Primary stakeholders can encompass students and faculty members, employers and community agencies who provide students with real-life contexts for the EL as well as clients/consumers/patients who receive services from students engaging in EL. In contrast, secondary stakeholders can include accreditation bodies that ensure HE programs offering EL are appropriate and align with the given standards, taxpayers, government bodies, and other funders who help sustain resources for EL. Given this conception of stakeholders, our focus in this chapter is on actively involving primary stakeholders in EL. In the sections that follow, we endeavour to provide practical guidance on how to involve primary stakeholders actively, collaboratively, and sustainably in EL.

Facilitating Primary Stakeholder Involvement Within the Higher Education Context

The inclusion of diverse perspectives in the design, delivery, instruction and evaluation of EL enhances learning and facilitates effective practice. While HE faculty members, who maintain their own community involvement through research and/or service activities, may have experience-based knowledge and expertise that they can share with students, other primary stakeholders, including employers and community agencies, can bring different perspectives to design, teaching, assessment, and evaluation that help meet the diverse learning needs of students and of communities (Chan, 2010). The gaps between the HE system and societal needs have been spotlighted in recent years; HE institutions are social institutions, but are not delivering in meeting societal needs (Horton, 2010). Thus, HE institutions have been called upon to improve their engagement with communities. The meaningful integration of societal perspectives through the active involvement of primary stakeholders in EL is an important strategy for effectively preparing students to enter the workforce because it facilitates the development of essential competencies that can only be developed through hands-on experience (Towle & Godolphin, 2011). Yet, the involvement of primary stakeholders in EL is limited and fragmented (Rowland & Kumagai, 2018; Towle et al., 2016).

This lack of primary stakeholder involvement may reflect that those leading EL in HE do not know how to effectively involve primary stakeholders. The active involvement of primary stakeholders can take various forms. Their first-hand understanding of how students can interact and work with primary stakeholders can inform the development of learning outcomes, structures, and processes, criteria to confer students' competencies, as well as the maintenance and improvement of EL (Inguva et al., 2018). Moreover, primary stakeholders can take on roles that involve collaboratively planning and designing EL opportunities, teaching and assessing students partaking in EL, and evaluating the process, impact, and efficiency of specific EL opportunities. In these roles, primary stakeholders should be involved as partners and as shared decision makers due to the positive effects that it can have on students' learning (Nghia, 2017; Steghöfer et al., 2018) as well as on enhancement of the relationships among HE and employers or community agencies involved in EL.

Developing Partnerships with Primary Stakeholders

Meaningful and active involvement of stakeholders in the design, delivery, and evaluation of EL is contingent on relationships. It requires HE institutions to share power and engage more widely. Higher education institutions that offer co-op programs are required to cultivate partnerships (i.e., respectful, reciprocal, long-term relationships) with workplaces such that workplaces have clear expectations of what it will mean to take on a student, HE institutions understand what competencies are required by workplaces, and students trust that they will attain sufficient educational outcomes during their placements (Broström et al., 2019; Choy & Delahaye, 2011). Relationship-building becomes especially important for those involved in EL activities that are not integrated or sustained at an institutional level, as co-ops are, such as those that may be faculty initiated and occur as part of discrete courses or those that immerse students in working with vulnerable populations (Oldfield, 2008; Prose et al., 2013). Project-based EL experiences, for example, can be demanding on employers and community agencies and may be unsustainable if relationships are not developed. If HE institutions are to improve their community engagement and integration of societal perspectives in HE through all forms of EL, Towle et al. (2016) argue, that "we must move from isolated initiatives to coordinated and sustained programmes that develop [stakeholder and interested parties'] involvement curricula and authentic partnerships at an institutional level" (p.71). The University of Toronto Medical Doctor (MD) program is working towards this level of change. It partners with Elders and community members to offer an Indigenous Health elective to medical students rooted in EL. Students participate in immersive experiences, community events, intensive readings, and a Blanket Exercise (in brief, involving Indigenous role-play) (Herzog, 2017; University of Toronto MD Program, 2018). Elders and community members facilitate the curriculum content and learning activities (University of Toronto MD Program, 2018). One goal of the curriculum is to train future physicians to provide appropriate and culturally sensitive care upon starting clinical practice by partnering with the communities to whom they will provide care. For more about Indigenous storytelling and EL, refer to Chapter 7 of this volume.

Key Considerations for Involving Stakeholders in the Design, Teaching, Assessment, and Evaluation of Experiential Learning

In the following sections, we critically discuss the roles of primary stakeholders in the design, teaching, assessment, and evaluation of EL.

Design Considerations

Primary stakeholders can be involved in the design of EL opportunities. Specifically, they may wish to be actively involved in the creation of learning outcomes, the design of assessment activities, and the design of learning activities and content. Primary stakeholders bring diverse perspectives and experiences to the design of EL, which can contribute to authentic learning experiences for students. In addition, primary stakeholder participation in the design of EL activities may result in more meaningful and appropriate learning experiences as stakeholders can identify their goals and priorities and plan with these in mind (Greenhouse et al., 2022). For example, Inguva and colleagues (2018) used a participatory design to involve primary stakeholders – namely students – in the design of chemical engineering lab sessions. Senior students and graduate teaching assistants helped to conceive a project that met the stated learning objectives within an authentic context. They also informed the design of the experiment and the construction of the resources required to conduct it. The students involved in the design of the lab assisted in launching the initiative; specifically, they acted in a train-the-trainer capacity to help others facilitate the sessions. The lab activity was evaluated during the three years following implementation, with student satisfaction scores increasing year over year.

Bilous and colleagues (2018) suggested that the integrity of relationships and clear lines of feedback between primary stakeholders and HE institutions is essential for the collaborative design of EL activities. Critical reflection on the roles and relationships between stakeholders is important; in some instances, the university may be construed as the leader in the relationship – being the "space" where expert knowledge resides (Kline et al., 2018). It is important to recognize that primary stakeholders bring specific knowledge and expertise to the partnership and, thus, collaborating with them in the design of EL shifts the learning experience away from top-down pedagogies, resulting in a sense of shared expertise and responsibility for learning (Bilous et al., 2018; Kline et al., 2018). As an example, early in the COVID-19 pandemic, clinical training opportunities for medical students were cancelled due to health and safety concerns. Similarly, clinic visits for patients were cancelled, thereby preventing patients from accessing healthcare services. To address these gaps, students and faculty members at a US-based medical school developed a volunteer opportunity wherein students reached out proactively to high-risk patients. Subsequently, students and faculty members worked collaboratively to develop a patient outreach curriculum, which was then included in the medical school's primary care clerkship (i.e., clinical experience for third year medical students) (Greenhouse et al., 2022). Students and faculty members in this case identified a learning gap and a health service delivery gap and collaborated to develop a curriculum that would help students achieve their learning goals (i.e., interdisciplinary education, public health, primary care, and patient outreach) while also helping meet a societal need (i.e., maintaining health services for those at risk of developing complications due to COVID-19 or inadequate access to other social determinants of health). Students who participated in the EL reported a deepened understanding of the barriers facing healthcare and valued further training in advocating for patients outside the hospital; patients reported that they found the program helpful for being connected with health and social supports and even for overcoming social isolation (Greenhouse et al., 2022). It should be noted that, in this example, students and faculty worked collaboratively, but patients did not appear to be involved as a stakeholder in the curriculum development process despite being the target of the healthcare intervention.

Considerations for Teaching and Assessment

Primary stakeholders' experiential knowledge and expertise are well-positioned to teach as well as assess students' competencies (knowledge, skills, and behaviors). The university's adult learners engage in learning from a real-life lens and for immediate real-world application (Chan, 2010). Thus, while discipline-specific knowledge is a foundation of andragogy, primary stakeholders can help bridge the theory-to-practice gap in teaching and learning, thereby enhancing student learning by drawing on their real-life experiences and context expertise to support the development of holistic competencies (Aničić & Divjak, 2022; Chan, 2022). Specifically, they can facilitate students' transition from classroom to practice with the teaching and assessment of intrinsic skills such as communication, active listening, collaboration, professionalism, leadership, amongst others, which are often challenging to practice in the classroom but essential to effective activities in workplaces (Chan, 2022; Henrich, 2016; McCale, 2008).

The current state of primary stakeholder involvement in the delivery of teaching and assessment in EL is difficult to ascertain as the published literature on these specific topics remains fragmented and limited to local efforts (Kline et al., 2018). It is also challenging to establish how these published efforts may translate to EL across disciplines and fields without a comprehensive analysis of the latter. Nevertheless, the literature characterises primary stakeholders' teaching practices as "the facilitation of active and enquiry-based learning from purposive (work) activity" (Lester & Costley, 2010). They are experts capable of sharing their knowledge, facilitating understanding, and mentoring in practice as well as capable of assessing students' performance and attainment of learning outcomes (Aničić & Divjak, 2022). Specifically, in their practices, primary stakeholders can share experiences, explain concepts, provide relevant, field-based examples, demonstrate expected performance, provide field-based tasks to apply learning, and provide supervision and guidance on student work. They can also participate in assessment activities, such as observation and the provision of formative feedback to students as well as the assessment of student learning evidenced through, for example, presentations, interviews, proposals, reports, projects, and portfolios (Aničić & Divjak, 2022; Brodie & Irving, 2007).

The interdisciplinary Health Mentors Program at the University of British Columbia is a promising example of a primary stakeholder led EL opportunity for students in the health professions (Towle et al., 2014). It occurs over a 16-month period and uses a small-group format. In this EL program, primary stakeholders (i.e., individuals living with chronic health conditions who interact with the healthcare system) become mentors to health professions students. The learning outcomes are thoughtfully broad to allow the mentors and students to tailor learning to their needs, but the program goals are to foster learning about living with chronic conditions from patients' perspectives. The learning activities, including rich discussions, storytelling, and observations are mentor-led and self-managed through the mentor-student partnership. Assessment is primarily formative, and learning is evidenced through reflective journaling as well as summary reflections and presentations during a program cohort symposium. Supervising faculty members then make judgements of learning based on this evidence to award academic credit for the students' professional programs.

To successfully deliver teaching and assessment in EL, primary stakeholders need various supports. Teaching and assessment practices will necessarily be diverse and reflect the diverse needs of workplaces and communities, students, HE institutions, and accrediting bodies, which also involve inherently complex decisions. Primary stakeholders need to have discussions among themselves about fostering a shared understanding of teaching and assessment responsibilities and expectations. They also need clear communication of policies and principles for, as well as mutual understandings of, processes and practices of teaching and assessment. The skills required to participate in teaching as well as assessment of and for learning, such as the ability to make judgements and provide constructive feedback, are of important consideration (Costley, 2007). Throughout all the above, there is a need for a common language to facilitate shared understanding among all primary stakeholders involved (Costley, 2007; Steghöfer et al., 2018).

Considerations for Evaluation

Experiential learning (EL) is resource intensive and individuals who are planning, designing, and implementing EL need to provide justifications as to why it is beneficial and worthy of continued resources (Chan, 2022). They also need to make evidence-based decisions on how to improve EL and appropriately allocate existing resources for it. With growing demands for data-informed justifications and decisions, the evaluations of EL's merit, value, and worth are important. Evaluators (i.e., those trained in evaluation) and stakeholders involved in EL need to collaboratively predetermine the standards that they will use to judge EL. These standards may be self-referenced (e.g., stakeholders' documented expectations for the EL), relative (e.g., comparisons between those participating in the EL and those who are not participating in it), or absolute (e.g., comparisons of the EL to an external benchmark established by the university or external funders) (Cousins & Shulha, 2008; Moreau, 2017). A central question for the evaluation of EL is: "how does it measure up against other learning opportunities or stakeholders' expectations of it?" (Moreau, 2017).

Gosenpud (1990) implied that the evaluation of EL should involve relative standards by comparing the EL with other andragogical/pedagogical methods or comparing changes in students' learning before and after the EL. However, such suggestions seem overly simplistic given the complexities of EL as well as the various primary stakeholders involved in it. They do not account for factors, interventions, and influences that may work together with the EL to bring about changes in specific outcomes (Moreau & Eady, 2015). Instead, we advocate for a participatory approach to the evaluation of EL that includes a mix of self-referenced, relative, and absolute comparisons. Cousins and Earl (1995) suggest that participatory evaluation is conducted as a partnership between trained evaluators and stakeholders who may or may not have evaluation training. Evaluators and stakeholders bring different knowledge and skills to the process. They bring expertise in evaluation logic and methods and an understanding of professional standards of practice as well as the above-mentioned comparisons. Stakeholders are familiar with the EL context because this is where they work, collaborate, or learn regularly. Cousins and Whitmore (1998) describe how there are two distinct streams of participatory evaluation – transformative participatory evaluation (T-PE) and practical participatory evaluation (P-PE). In T-PE, the focus is on the use of evaluation to empower community groups oppressed by dominating groups (Cousins & Whitmore, 1998), a stream which may be less relevant to EL because it leaves the evaluation responsibilities primarily in the hands of only one primary stakeholder group (i.e., community agencies) involved in EL. Conversely, in P-PE, the focus is to foster program decision-making and problem solving and the use of evaluation findings and processes (Cousins, 2005). This means that all those involved in the evaluation can share in the responsibility for it and use the evaluation findings and processes to improve EL, appropriately allocate existing resources, and determine its merit, value, and worth. With their vested interest in the EL and their involvement in the evaluation of it, primary stakeholders can use the evaluation to enact change in the design and delivery of EL. By being involved in the evaluation processes, primary stakeholders can also enhance their own evaluation skills, knowledge, and capacities. Such enhancements can aid in subsequent evaluations of the EL and, thus, be beneficial long-term as EL should undergo evaluation regularly to improve and evolve it.

When conducting a P-PE of EL, a trained evaluator would work with a team of primary stakeholders to develop the evaluation questions, indicators, data collection methods, data analyses, utilization plan for the evaluation findings and processes, the evaluation dissemination activities, and standards to judge the merit, value, and worth of the EL. As a team, they would draw on the three fundamental dimensions in participatory evaluation that Cousins and Whitmore (1998) developed and Daigneault and Jacob (2009) validated. The first dimension, control of decision-making, refers to the individuals who control the technical decision-making about evaluation processes and conduct: evaluators, stakeholders, or a balanced mix of the two (Cousins & Whitmore, 1998). Within a P-PE of EL, the evaluator(s) and primary stakeholders would share this decision-making and, thus, jointly decide on the evaluation plan, the data collection methods and instruments used, the best way to analyze the data, and disseminate the findings (Cousins & Chouinard, 2012). The second dimension, stakeholder diversity, refers

Figure 6.1. Continua of Control, Stakeholder Selection, and Participation for a P-PE of EL

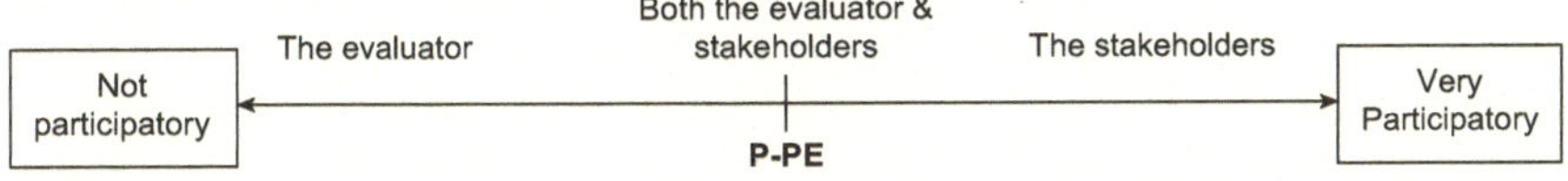

2. Stakeholder Selection:
What is the level of diversity among the stakeholders who are involved in the P-PE of the EL?

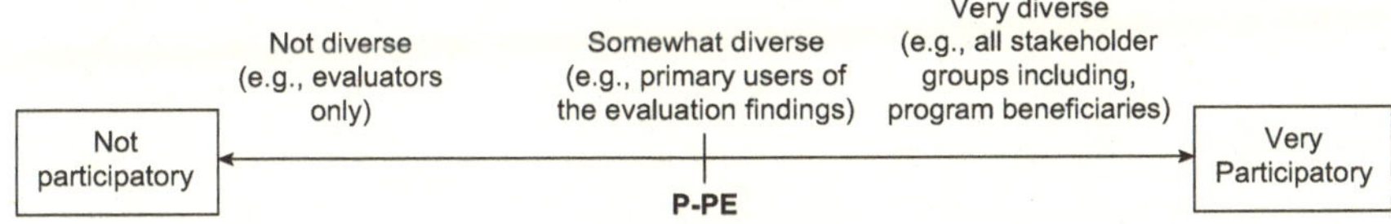

3. Depth of Participation:
To what extent are stakeholders involved in the different stages of the P-PE of the EL?

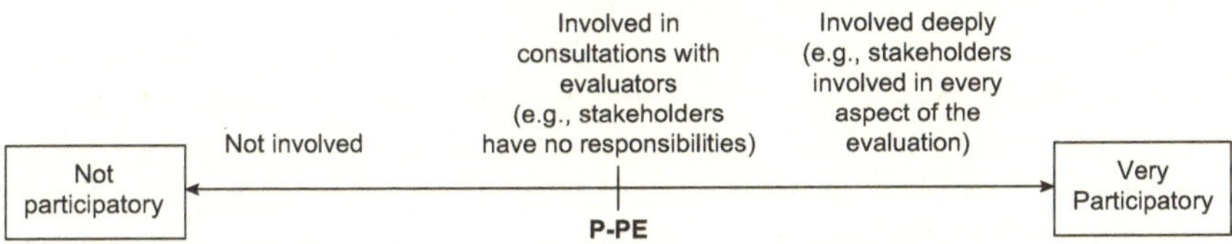

to the individuals among the EL community who are involved in carrying out the evaluation. For P-PE of EL, this involvement would include representatives from each of the primary stakeholder groups. Lastly, the third dimension, depth of participation, describes the extent to which stakeholders are involved in the different stages of the evaluation, including the design, data collection, processing and analysis, and reporting and dissemination phases. Involvement can range from consultation, where stakeholders have no direct responsibilities, to deep participation, where stakeholders are involved in every aspect of the evaluation (Cousins & Whitmore, 1998). Regarding the P-PE of EL, it would make most sense to involve representatives from each of the primary stakeholder groups in every aspect of the evaluation to share the evaluation responsibilities. Such involvement will not only ensure that the evaluation findings are useful and used but also build the stakeholders' knowledge, skills, and capacity to do future evaluations of the EL. Figure 6.1 summarizes what a P-PE of EL would look like in terms of the above-mentioned dimensions.

Challenges of Involving Primary Stakeholders in the Design, Teaching, Assessment, and Evaluation of Experiential Learning

It is important to recognize some challenges of involving primary stakeholders in the design, teaching, assessment, and evaluation of EL. In most cases, it is not feasible to involve all relevant primary stakeholders, and thus, those leading the EL need to identify and select representatives from various primary stakeholder groups who might be interested in actively participating in these various aspects. This selection of stakeholders or interested parties can be difficult as there are no definitive procedures for choosing stakeholders as well as a lack of research on stakeholder selection (Daigneault & Jacob, 2009). Next, despite the advantages of having a highly diverse group of stakeholders involved in EL, there is a risk that conflict among stakeholders can arise because of power differentials and differences in viewpoints or values (Cullen et al., 2011; Weaver & Cousins, 2004). Evidently, these conflicts and inclusion of multiple primary stakeholder representatives can result in the need for increased time and resources to mediate differences, solve logistical problems, and complete the design, teaching, assessment, and evaluation of EL. Nevertheless, while this diversity can add complexity to EL, it is often manageable if those leading the EL are skilled at group facilitation and are able to balance power differentials and foster trusting, respectful relationships among the various stakeholders (King, 1998).

Best Practices for Involving Stakeholders in Experiential Learning

The adoption of the following best practices can help to mitigate some of the above-mentioned challenges:

- Establish partnerships early and meaningfully involve partners in the design of the EL experience (e.g., developing the curriculum, learning outcomes, assessment strategies) (Greenhouse et al., 2022; Yardley et al., 2012).
- Take the time required to build trust with and among primary stakeholders and interested parties before embarking on EL (Choy & Delahaye, 2011; Mansoor & Cotton, 2006; Oldfield, 2008).
- Clearly communicate and negotiate the roles and expectations of the EL partnership, specifically key responsibilities of each stakeholder, each partner's individual contexts and needs, and who owns any knowledge that is created (i.e., intellectual property) (Bilous et al., 2018; Choy & Delahaye, 2011; Oldfield, 2008).

- Ensure that stakeholder involvement is authentic, rather than tokenistic. Authentic involvement may include, for example, stakeholders engaged in capacity building activities, involved on curriculum committees or as investigators on research projects, and being compensated for their contributions, where appropriate. Authentic, rather than tokenistic, involvement is an especially important consideration when involving stakeholders and interested parties from typically underrepresented groups (Epprecht, 2004; Inguva et al., 2018; Oldfield, 2008).
- Ensure the ethical treatment of all stakeholders and interested parties, with special consideration to unintended consequences or potential harms to the larger community resulting from EL activities (Epprecht, 2004; Grace et al., 2017; Logar et al., 2015; Meisel, 2008; Oldfield, 2008).

Concluding Thoughts

In this chapter, we have critically discussed how primary stakeholders and interested parties can be involved in designing, teaching, assessing, and evaluating EL activities. The EL activities discussed in the chapter typically occur off campus and in the community. Thus, this chapter focuses on EL in "town" and in local (and global) communities. We have also provided practical examples and best practices from the literature illustrating how this involvement may be done. Beyond the in-person examples provided in this chapter, an emerging trend in the literature appears to be the adoption of remote EL activities. Such practices have the potential to expand EL to students who may otherwise not be able to participate due to their financial, geographical, or physical circumstances. Additional research on the design, delivery, and evaluation of remote EL and its implications for town-gown connections is recommended. While not specific to remote EL necessarily, refer to Chapter 8 of this volume to learn more about the need to attend to equity in EL.

Experiential learning offers promises and pitfalls for equity, diversity, and inclusion efforts. As noted in the introduction of this chapter, if implemented incorrectly, EL has the potential to perpetuate existing inequities and problematic power dynamics. Even the term "stakeholder" has become somewhat contentious in recent years since it may be perceived as disempowering. Additionally, it cannot be applied to Indigenous Peoples, who are rights and treaties holders. Instead, discussions have begun to reference "interested parties" in an attempt to be more inclusive. Regardless of the terminology used, involving those who have vested interests in EL – and more critically, those whom it is likely to impact – in the design, delivery, and evaluation of these learning experiences may help to mitigate potential challenges and tensions with it. Ultimately, this active involvement of those EL activities are likely to impact can contribute to the development of learning experiences that are meaningful for students, respectful of communities, and address community or societal needs (Bilous et al., 2018; Greenhouse et al., 2022). Chapters 7 and 8 provide an excellent discussion of the equity implications associated with EL.

Finally, while much of this volume focuses on town-gown connections at the institutional level, it is important to consider the learner and their needs, goals, and objectives. Beyond integrating theory and practice – and teaching marketable skills – EL has the potential to help students become global citizens. If designed well, EL may present students with opportunities to learn about themselves, their local and global communities, and how to critically engage with knowledge in practice. For this to happen, involving learners in the design, delivery, and evaluation of EL is essential.

REFERENCES

Alkin, M., & Vo, A. (2017). *Evaluation essentials: From A to Z.* Guilford Press.

Aničić, K., & Divjak, B. (2022). Work integrated learning in higher education: Student, teacher and employer motivations and expectations. *International Journal of Work-Integrated Learning, 23*(1), 49–64.

Barsukov, D., Kuzmina, S., Morozova, N., & Pimenova, A. (2018). Professional education for digital economy: Trends and prospects. *MATEC Web of Conferences,* 170, 1–6.

Bilous, R., Hammersley, L., Lloyd, K., Rawlings-Sanaei, F., Downey, G., Amigo, M., Gilchrest, S., & Baker, M. (2018). "All of us together in a blurred space": Principles for co-creating curriculum with international partners. *International Journal for Academic Development, 23*(3), 165–78.

Brodie, P., & Irving, K. (2007). Assessment in work-based learning: investigating a pedagogical approach to enhance student learning. *Assessment & Evaluation in Higher Education, 32*(1), 11–19. https://doi.org/10.1080/02602930600848218

Broström, A., Feldmann, A., & Kaulio, M. (2019). Structured relations between higher education institutions and external organisations: Opportunity or bureaucratisation? *Higher Education,* 78, 575–91.

Buchmeyer, K. (2017). *Voluntourism discourse: A case study of Me to We* [Masters Thesis, University of Ottawa].

Buzzelli, M., & Asafo-Adjei, E. (2022). Experiential learning and the university's host community: Rapid growth, contested mission and policy challenge. *Higher Education,* 1–18. https://doi.org/10.1007/s10734-022-00849-1

Chan, C. (2022). *Assessment for experiential learning.* Routledge. https://doi.org/https://doi.org/10.4324/9781003018391

Chan, S. (2010). Applications of andragogy in multi disciplined teaching and learning. *Journal of Adult Education, 39*(2), 25–35.

Choy, S., & Delahaye, B. (2011). Partnerships between universities and workplaces: Some challenges for work-integrated learning. *Studies in Continuing Education, 33*(2), 157–72.

Costley, C. (2007). Work-based learning: assessment and evaluation in higher education. *Assessment & Evaluation in Higher Education, 32*(1), 1–9. https://doi.org/10.1080/02602930600848184

Cousins, J. B. (2005). Will the real empowerment evaluation please stand up? A critical friend perspective. In D. M. Fetterman, & A. Wandersman (Eds.), *Empowerment evaluation principles in practice* (pp. 183–208). Sage.

Cousins, J. B., & Chouinard, J. A. (2012). *Participatory evaluation up close: A review and integration of research-based knowledge.* Information Age Press.

Cousins, J. B., & Earl, L. M. (1995). *Participatory evaluation in education: Studies of evaluation use and organizational learning.* Falmer.

Cousins, J. B., & Shulha, L. M. (2008). Complexities in setting program standards in collaborative evaluation. In N. Smith, & P. Brandon (Eds.), *Fundamental issues in evaluation* (pp. 135–58). Guilford.

Cousins, J. B., & Whitmore, E. (1998). Framing participatory evaluation. In E. Whitmore (Ed.), *New directions for evaluation: Understanding and practicing participatory evaluation* (pp. 5–23). Jossey-Bass Inc.

Cullen, A. E., Coryn, C., & Rugh, J. (2011). The politics and consequences of including stakeholders in international development evaluation. *American Journal of Evaluation, 32,* 345–61.

Daigneault, P. M., & Jacob, S. (2009). Toward accurate measurement of participation: Rethinking the conceptualization and operationalization of participatory evaluation. *American Journal of Evaluation, 30*(3), 330–48.

Epprecht, M. (2004). Work-study abroad courses in international development studies: Some ethical and pedagogical issues. *Canadian Journal of Development Studies, 25*(4), 687–706.

Gosenpud, J. (1990). Evaluation of experiential learning. In J. W. Gentry (Ed.), *Guide to business gaming and experiential learning* (pp. 301–29). Nichols/GP Publishing.

Government of Canada. (2020). *Canada student service grant.* https://pm.gc.ca/en/news/backgrounders/2020/06/25/canada-student-service-grant

Grace, S., Innes, E., & Stockhausen, L. (2017). Ethical experiential learning in medical, nursing, and allied health education: A narrative review. *Nurse Education Today,* 51, 23–33.

Greenhouse, A., Goldstein, R., Bradley, C., Spell, N., Spicer, J., & George, M. (2022). Student-faculty co-creation of experiential learning in health systems science. *Medical Teacher, 44*(3), 328–33.

Henrich, J. (2016). Competency-based education: The employers' perspective of higher education. *The Journal of Competency-Based Education, 1*(3), 122–9. https://doi.org/10.1002/cbe2.1023

Herzog, L. (2017). The need for narrative reflection and experiential learning in medical education: A lesson learned through an urban Indigenous health elective. *Medical Teacher, 39*(9), 995–6.

Horton, R. (2010). A new epoch for health professionals' education. *The Lancet, 376*(9756), 1875–7. https://doi.org/10.1016/s0140-6736(10)62008-9

Hunt, J. B., Bonham, C., & Jones, L. (2011). Understanding the goals of service learning and community-based medical education: A systematic review. *Academic Medicine, 86*(2), 246–51. https://doi.org/10.1097/ACM.0b013e3182046481

Inguva, P., Lee-Lane, D., Teck, A., Anabaraonye, A., Chen, W., Shah, U., & Brechtelsbauer, C. (2018). Advancing experiential learning through participatory design. *Education for Chemical Engineers*, 25, 16–21.

Keehn, M. (2016). *Unsettling good intentions: The dismantling of benevolence as discursive practice within global citizenship education* [Masters Thesis, The University of New Brunswick].

King, J. A. (1998). Making sense of participatory evaluation practice. In E. Whitmore (Ed.), *New directions for evaluation: Understanding and practicing participatory evaluation* (pp. 57–67). Jossey-Bass.

Kline, C., Asadian, W., Godolphin, W., Graham, S., Hewitt, C., & Towle, A. (2018). From "Academic Projectitis" to partnership: Community perspectives for authentic community engagement in health professional education. *Engaged Scholar Journal: Community-Engaged Research, Teaching, and Learning, 4*(1), 79–96. https://doi.org/10.15402/esj.v4i1.310

Lester, S., & Costley, C. (2010). Work-based learning at higher education level: value, practice and critique. *Studies in Higher Education, 35*(5), 561–75. https://doi.org/10.1080/03075070903216635

Logar, T., Le, P., Harrison, J., & Glass, M. (2015). Teaching corner: "First, do no harm": Teaching global health ethics to medical trainees through experiential learning. *Bioethical Inquiry*, 12, 69–78.

Mansoor, A., & Cotton, A. (2006). Working with partners: Government ministries. In V. Desai & R. Potter (Eds.), *Doing development research* (pp. 87–93). Sage.

Marshall, S. J. (2018). Internal and external stakeholders in higher education. In S. J. Marshall (Ed.), *Shaping the university of the future* (pp. 77–102). Springer.

McCale, C. (2008). It's hard work learning soft skills: Can client based projects teach the soft skills students need and employers want? *The Journal of Effective Teaching, 8*(2), 50–60.

Meisel, J. (2008). The ethics of observing: Confronting the harm of experiential learning. *Teaching Sociology*, 36, 196–210.

Moreau, K. A. (2017). Twelve tips for planning and conducting a participatory evaluation. *Medical Teacher, 39*(4), 334–40.

Moreau, K. A., & Eady, K. (2015). Connecting medical education to patient outcomes: The promise of contribution analysis. *Medical Teacher, 37*(11), 1060–82.

Nghia, T. L. H. (2017). External stakeholders' roles and factors influencing their participation in developing generic skills for students in Vietnamese universities. *Journal of Education and Work, 31*(1), 72–86. https://doi.org/10.1080/13639080.2017.1386774

Oldfield, S. (2008). Who's serving whom? Partners, process, and products in service-learning projects in South African urban geography. *Journal of Geography in Higher Education, 32*(2), 269–85.

Prose, N., Diab, P., & Matthews, M. (2013). Experiential learning outside the comfort zone: Taking medical students to downtown Durban. *African Journal of Health Professions Education, 5*(2), 98–9.

Rowland, P., & Kumagai, A. K. (2018). Dilemmas of representation: Patient engagement in health professions education. *Academic Medicine, 93*(6), 869–73.

Steghöfer, J.-P., Burden, H., Hebig, R., Calikli, G., Feldt, R., Hammouda, I., Horkoff, J., Knauss, E., & Liebel, G. (2018). Involving External Stakeholders in Project Courses. *ACM Transactions on Computing Education, 18*(2), 1–32. https://doi.org/10.1145/3152098

Tiessen, R., & Kumar, P. (2013). Ethical challenges encountered on learning/volunteer abroad programmes for students in international development studies in Canada: Youth perspectives and educator insights. *Canadian Journal of Development Studies, 34*(3), 416–30.

Towle, A., Brown, H., Hofley, C., Kerston, R. P., Lyons, H., & Walsh, C. . (2014). The expert patient as teacher: An interprofessional health mentors programme. *The Clinical Teacher, 11*(4), 301–6.

Towle, A., Farrell, C., Gaines, M. E., Godolphin, W., John, G., Kline, C., Lown, B., Morris, P., Symons, J., & Thistlethwaite, J. (2016). The patient's voice in health and social care professional education. *International Journal of Health Governance, 21*(1), 18–25. https://doi.org/10.1108/ijhg-01-2016-0003

Towle, A., & Godolphin, W. (2011). A meeting of experts: The emerging roles of non-professionals in the education of health professionals. *Teaching in Higher Education, 16*(5), 495–504.

University of Toronto MD Program. (2018). *Pre-clerkship foundations curriculum: Indigenous health.* https://md.utoronto.ca/sites/default/files/2018-10-18%20Preclerkship%20Curriculum%20in%20Indigenous%20Health.pdf

Waldner, L., & McGorry, S. (2012). E-service learning: The evolution of service-learning to engage a growing online student population. *Journal of Higher Education Outreach and Engagement*, 16, 123–50.

Weaver, L., & Cousins, J. B. (2004). Unpacking the participatory process. *Journal of Management and Digital Business*, 1, 19–40.
Yardley, S., Teunissen, P., & Dornan, T. (2012). Experiential learning: AMEE guide no. 63. *Medical Teacher, 34*(2), e102–e115.

7 Dismantling Colonialism Through Indigenous Storytelling, Experiential Learning, and Town-Gown Collaboration

CAROLYN BJARTVEIT, ROY BEAR CHIEF, AND HANNELE GORDON

Mount Royal University, Canada

Introduction[1]

Experiential learning and partnerships between academic institutions and community organizations are being reimagined in ways that demonstrate positive teaching, learning and economic outcomes, particularly with Indigenous communities. As part of an ongoing research study,[2] this chapter is rooted in critical pedagogy where experiential learning (EL) includes "participation, voice and social action within the classroom" (Darder et al., 2003), and, moreover, the community is crucial and recognizes that on-campus and field work can widen students' perspectives and scope of practice. Relationships are at the heart of community work and commitment to the well-being of students and those with whom they interact (McNamara & Naepi, 2018); yet, the resources and support offered by universities are often constrained by time, budget, and staffing limits. Post-secondary institutions' commitment to students working in the field and their investment in nurturing relationships for university-community collaboration is central to our inquiry and work related to decolonization and reconciliation.

Gaudry and Lorenz (2018) have explained that on-the-land and community-based research and learning are essential and that universities are not necessarily the main sites of "decolonial indigenization … [but] may be best directed from outside of their own tradition" (p. 225). Although educators have focused on teaching Indigenous knowledges to post-secondary students through in-class and community-based learning experiences (Bang & Marin, 2015; Fiola & MacKinnon, 2020; Kinzel, 2020; McNamara & Naepi, 2018), their intent of increasing students' understanding of decolonization through community-based learning is not as evident. In response to Canada's Truth and Reconciliation Commission's (TRC) Calls to Action,[3] this chapter will explore how university-community or so-called town-gown collaboration and relationship building can dismantle or "tear down" (Online Etymology Dictionary, n.d.) colonial ideals and practices in academic and community settings. Gaudry and Lorenz (2018) have prompted an exploration of town-gown partnerships in post-secondary education contexts, and our own research ask the questions: What is the role of the university in effectively supporting students and town-gown collaborations? What can students and community partners learn about decolonization through EL both in the university classroom and in the local community with Indigenous organizations? What is the relevance of Indigenous stories and storytelling in decolonizing academic and professional practices?

Contextual and relational definitions of decolonization will be considered in the context of an exemplar community-based project named the alliedFutures Project,[4] described later in the chapter. The goal of this Calgary-based project was to partner with students and support their achievement in understanding and enacting decolonization in professional pedagogy and practice, learn about and value sociocultural worldviews and perspectives on the care and education of children and youth, and build relationships and collaborate with members of Indigenous community organizations. Through sharing the students' learning experiences, and excerpts from their written journals, we hope to emphasize the relevance of Indigenous teachings and stories in decolonizing pedagogical and professional practices. We will explain how the application of students' personal narratives to an Indigenous creation story – the layering of stories within a story – can widely support higher education teaching EL and town-gown collaboration in multiple fields and disciplines.

The Social Location of the Authors

It is important to share our personal connections to the land and social locations, recognizing that our sense of place, histories, and cultures have shaped who we are, our worldviews and interpretations of lived experiences, relationships, and project work.

Carolyn Bjartveit was born in Northern British Columbia which is in Treaty 8 territory and the ancestral land of the Sikanni and Beaver Peoples. She identifies as a white settler of northern European ancestry with strong family connections to Calgary, Alberta where she has lived for more than thirty years. She is an Associate Professor and currently teaches in the Bachelor of Child Studies (BCST) degree program at Mount Royal University (MRU) in Calgary, Alberta.

Roy Bear Chief was born and raised in the Treaty 7 territory as a member of the Siksika Nation which is part of the Blackfoot Confederacy. Siksika is about 90 km east of the City of Calgary. His ancestors have left their footprints and inhabited this territory since time immemorial. The animals have also left their claw and hoof prints including the birds as well as the plants that have their roots firmly planted onto Mother Earth. He has lived in the City of Calgary since 1980 and has worked as an Espoom Taah (Helper) for the Health, Community, and Education faculty at MRU since 2018.

Hannele Gordon grew up in Robinson-Huron Treaty territory, in an area traditionally known as Bawating, which means place of the rapids. Her childhood was spent exploring what is now known in Canada as the Great Lakes. She identifies as a settler as her maternal ancestors are from Finland and paternal ancestors are from Scotland and England. She has been a visitor on Treaty 7 territory since 2014 and worked as a Culture and Inclusion Strategist at WilderFutures Institute[5] and community partner with Mount Royal University students and faculty.

Decolonizing Education: Experiential, Relational, and Land-Based

In Canada, decolonization is often understood and discussed in the context of "Indigenous resurgence" (Attas, n.d.) which includes the reclamation of culture, land, language, relationships, and health. Academic journals spanning six years after the publication of the TRC's *Calls to Action* (2015a) provide definitions of decolonization and evidence of the benefits of student-community partnerships relative to decolonization work and learning (Bang & Marin, 2015; Fiola & MacKinnon, 2020; McNamara & Naepi, 2018). The definition of decolonization is not universal but rather contextual, sometimes disputed, and holds multiple meanings (Andreotti et al., 2015; Battiste, 2013; Smith, 2012), and post-secondary students will interpret the term differently according to their social locations and lived experiences. Tuck and Yang (2012) have emphasized that developing a contextual understanding of decolonization avoids "the risk of reducing it to a metaphor."

Decolonization involves the deconstruction of colonial influences and raises questions about existing social structures and the need for major systemic change within political, economic, and social institutions. Fiola and MacKinnon (2020) note that decolonization identifies the impacts of colonization, power differentials, promotes Indigenous self-determination and the "repatriation of Indigenous land and life" (Tuck & Yang, 2012, p. 1). In the context of education, McNamara and Naepi (2018) emphasize that working toward decolonization involves "adopting indigenization approaches, building bridges that better address the needs of Indigenous communities … and supporting Indigenous learners who attend classes" (p. 347).

Throughout the course of the alliedFutures Project, journal entries of post-secondary students demonstrate a change in understanding from a dictionary definition of decolonization, focused on Indigenous reclamation and resurgence, to a contextual meaning related to their project work. Themes in the students' journals included creating ethical spaces for cross-cultural dialogue, building relationships, inclusion, cooperation, and transformational change within community organizations. Evidence of students' understanding of decolonization as an ongoing process of reciprocal and relational exchange between Indigenous people and Settlers is reflected in the following student's journal post:

> My understanding of decolonization has shifted considerably since the beginning of the year. Decolonization is an ongoing process dedicated to relationship building. Decolonization intends to establish connections between people to their land, to their community, and to their environments. Decolonization recognizes that Truth and Reconciliation is not an end goal, rather, a state of living; of accepting truth, and building a positive, reciprocal, respectful relationships between Indigenous people and Settlers. This is what decolonization means to me. (Personal communication, March 26, 2022)

In response to the TRC's Calls to Action (2015a), it is important for post-secondary institutions, faculty, and students to understand the meaning of decolonization and how it can be enacted within community and education settings. By sharing historical and theoretical perspectives (Indigenous and settler) on EL layered with research findings from the alliedFutures Project, we aim to show how undergraduate students' collaboration with Indigenous youth organizations elevated and enriched their knowledge of decolonization and discipline-specific decolonizing practices.

Historical Residential Schools: The Dark Side of EL and Canada's Colonial Legacy

The Truth and Reconciliation process is rooted in Indigenous experiences including the establishment and impacts of the residential school system in Canada. The residential school system was implemented to eradicate Indigenous knowledge, cultures and languages (Battiste, 2013). In Canada, 150,000 children attended residential schools over a span of 150 years. During this time, over six thousand children died while in the care of these church and government-operated schools. Children were taken from their homes to force "aggressive assimilation," and detach them from their customs, traditions, and ancestors (Loyie et al., 2014). The last school closed in 1996. Prior to 1960, Indigenous People were not considered as persons and subsequently did not have a legal right to dispute the government and the residential school system (Frideres, 2019). Self-confidence, self-worth, and the concept of healthy relationships were shattered through the mental, emotional, physical and sexual abuse of Indigenous children while in the residential school system (Battiste, 2013; Vowel, 2016). Indigenous scholar Marie Battiste's (2020) explanation of EL as independent learning, agency, and freedom to engage in cultural practices is far removed from the experiences of children who attended residential schools. Their daily experiences, hidden under a façade of learning, included rote drills, memorization, and forced labour as described in the final report of the TRC (2015b):

> Students were expected to raise or grow and prepare most of the food they ate, to make and repair much of their clothing, and to maintain the schools. As a result, most of the residential schools operated on what was referred to as the "half day system" … which amounted to institutionalized child labour … and served to maintain the school operations. (pp. 77–8)

In recent years, the BCST faculty and students at MRU have worked with Elder Roy Bear Chief who, through sharing his Blackfoot culture, history, and personal experiences as a residential school survivor, has helped students and faculty learn and discover ways to decolonize course curriculum and work toward reconciliation. Bear Chief explained his perspective on decolonization work in relation to Blackfoot history and the raising up and taking down of tipis:

> The Blackfoot people moved their entire camp for a variety of reasons such as moving to a winter camp, for picking their medicines or for berry picking or for hunting game. Tipis served that purpose because they are quickly taken down and raised again in a different environment. A program or project is much like raising and dismantling a tipi. A tipi represents a project and is developed to serve participants and once it's done can be taken down and moved to a different location or environment. An evaluation of the project will help to dismantle what is working and what isn't working. (Personal correspondence, February 23, 2023)

Relationality, reciprocity, and creating an environment of trust in the classroom, or as Elder Bear Chief emphasizes "kimma pi pitsin" in the Blackfoot language (translated as "kindness and compassion"), are at the centre of his work with students. His poignant recollection of dark experiences at Old Sun[6] Residential School are a reminder that the journey from truth to reconciliation begins with hearing the stories, acknowledging history, and attempting to fix what is broken (Rogers et al., 2012). Memories of Residential School (text box) helps to further situate the experience and importance of understanding the need to develop meaningful and reciprocal EL.

Memories of Residential School

Prior to 1955, I was at home being raised and nurtured by my parents and then at the age of seven my world was turned upside down in a matter of 24 hours when my mother gave me up to the residential school system. I cannot recall any preparation or conversation around being placed into the residential school from my parents. It seems to me that one day you're at home and the next day you're at the residential school that would be your home away from home. I did not speak a word of English as Blackfoot was the only language that I knew and only knew my English name was Roy Bear Chief when I went into the school. I can recall my first day of school and holding onto my older brother's hand and looking up at this great, big red brick building and talking in Blackfoot asking him what is this place? He whispered in my ear not to talk. Little did I know that I was not supposed to speak my language and I quickly learned that you will be punished if you got caught speaking your language.

That was really my first taste of EL in a different and harsh environment, and it deviated sharply from the comfort of home. In the Blackfoot culture, the old people or Elders would often say to look, listen and learn from the interaction with the environment as well as other people. The Elders are really talking about EL through looking, listening and learning. We look, listen, and learn on a daily basis and it is done within the context of EL.

I come from a family of 12 and 10 of us went through the residential school system and each one of us had our first day experience entrenched in our memories. As my brother, Arthur, stated, "I was seven years old when I entered Old Sun in September of 1949. I did not speak English, nor did I understand it. I was scared out of my wits (Bear Chief, 2016. p. 24)." The daily learning experience became a reality when we went to bed and the lights went out and suddenly you realize that both parents are not there to comfort you, and this is echoed by my brother: "We crawled into bed. Once the lights were out. I got scared and started to cry for my mother" (Bear Chief, 2016 p. 24). I remember those lonely nights with those empty and haunting white walls that if given a chance, they could relate stories of what happened to children that went there. The walls could say I remember the time when Roy got caught wetting his bed and he was forced to strip his bed and wear the sheet soaked in piss over his head while sitting at the edge of the bed. I remember the sheet was sticking to my face while I tried to breathe through it. The sheet was firmly stuck to my face, and I didn't take it off until I was given permission. Even after taking the sheet off my head, I was not allowed to wash my hands or my face or my hair and I must have smelled like piss walking around all day.

What did I learn from this experience other than humiliation even as a young 7–8-year-old boy? The 10 years that I spent at the residential school did not provide me with any positive experiences to learn from, instead, it brought guilt and helplessness because I couldn't help others that were younger than me when they got punished. EL at home during my formative years is something that I will never get to do over again or get my childhood back because I spent them in a different environment. I could not speak my language nor practice my culture because once you take that away then you are forced to speak another foreign language. My brother summed it up this way, "I would give anything to take this life back and to be able to enjoy it and feel what it's really like to be a child. It was so unfair on the government's part because of their policies regarding Indians living on reserves. I lost so much as a child. How can anyone put a price to it and simply say, 'Sorry, we were wrong. It should not have happened?'" (Bear Chief, 2016. p. 23).

Indigenous scholar Thomas King (2003) wrote that "the truth about stories is that's all we are" (p. 2), and points to the role of stories and lived experiences in shaping the self of individuals and professionals. Through sharing his personal story, Roy uncovered the dark truth about the experiences of Indigenous children in Canadian residential schools and the students came to recognize the powerful impact of life stories on their understanding of colonization and relevance to the alliedFutures Project. The feminist writer Rebecca Solnit (2005) said to "leave the door open for the unknown, the door into the dark. That's where the most important things come from" (p. 4). Sitting in truth and engaging in dialogue created opportunities for students to build relationships and moved them out of the darkness toward the light of new Indigenous cultural understandings.

EL: Settler Colonial and Indigenous Perspectives

Education theorist David Kolb (1984) explained the role of experience in the learning process and drew ideas from earlier education theorist John Dewey (1938). Kolb (1984) described EL theory as a "holistic, integrative perspective on learning that combines experience, perception, cognition, and behavior" (pp. 20–1). According to Kolb, learners gain deep understanding of concepts if they proceed through the four steps of the learning cycle – reflective observation, abstract conceptualization, active experimentation, concrete experience – and co-construct meaning from their lived experiences through dialogue. John Dewey's EL theory emphasized development and how interactions with the environment and learning can transform feelings and desires for concrete experience into purposeful action (Kolb, 1984, p. 22).

It is important to repeat this broad outline of Kolb's and Dewey's models in the context of this edited volume because EL is understood differently in the context of Indigenous worldviews and pedagogies (Smith & McGee, 2005). Our own understanding of EL aligns with First Nations pedagogy – a four-step EL cycle that includes experiencing, reflecting, meaning making, and acting. Learners do not always follow the steps in a logical order – all steps might occur at once for multitaskers or out of sequence according to context and unique learning styles. Battiste (2002) has emphasized the importance of EL for Indigenous learners and how it includes reflexivity, meditation, prayer, and anonymity (p. 16):

> The first principle of Aboriginal learning is a preference for experiential knowledge. Indigenous pedagogy values a person's ability to learn independently by observing, listening, and participating with a minimum of intervention or instruction. This pattern of direct learning by seeing and doing, without asking questions, makes Aboriginal children diverse learners. (p. 15)

Knudson (2015) has noted that "in contrast to positivism and western worldviews, Indigenous knowledge systems are highly contextualized and emphasize story, local knowledge, and the experiential" (González y González & Lincoln, 2006; Romm, 2015). EL relates to the agency and interests of individual learners living and working within their own Indigenous communities where they can participate in the planning, implementation, and evaluation of their learning (Kaminski, 2011). In a later section of the chapter, we will explain how the application of the four-step Indigenous EL cycle increased the students' understanding of decolonization, strengthened collaboration between the university and community organization and Indigenous-settler relations, and decolonized professional practices and academic teaching and learning.

The Relevance of Indigenous Storytelling in Decolonizing Academic and Professional Practice

Opaskwayak Cree researcher Shawn Tafoya (1995) noted the complexity of stories and the importance of listening closely to understand and apply cultural narratives to one's lived experiences.

> Stories go in circles. They don't go in straight lines. It helps if you listen in circles because there are stories inside and between stories and finding your way through them is as easy and as hard as finding your way home. Part of finding is getting lost, and when you are lost you start to open up and listen. (Tafoya, 1995, p. 12)

To further increase students' understanding of Indigenous worldviews and culture, Roy Bear Chief told them a creation story, *Ani to pisi,* provided below. It was first told by his older brother, Elder Clement Bear Chief. Attempting to layer lived experiences and a Blackfoot creation story within the course curriculum required critical thinking to determine effective pedagogical strategies to create relevant and authentic learning opportunities for students working within the university and in the wider community.

Ani to pisi: A Blackfoot Creation Story

My brother, the late Clement Bear Chief, was a kipi tai po'ka or someone raised by grandparents and in this case, he was raised by paternal grandparents. They are the fortunate ones as they are raised deeply embedded in the language and culture. One of the creation stories related by my brother, Clement, was *Ani to pisi*:

> He* [Creator] instructed Ani to pisi to wrap the world, with the people in it, in his web and let them down to the lower world. Ani to pisi did as he was told and let them down from the upper world through a hole. After the people were lowered from the upper world (spoomootsi) to here below, Ani to pisi explained to them that the web would remain with them so that the Creator would know when to help them. Whenever there is trouble or an emergency, one string of the web would vibrate and this would signal the Creator who would

come to help. Man was told to pattern his life after the web so that they can stay close together and help each other whenever there is a problem, anywhere on the web. When there is no trouble, the web would remain calm; otherwise it would vibrate and everyone on the web would know and come to help with whatever the problem may be (as told by Clement Bear Chief).

Creation stories are handed down from generation to generation and *Ani to pisi* was one that was handed down to my brother and he allowed me to use the story. The importance of this story is that when there's a problem anywhere on the web would vibrate and respond to it by assisting. We can also look at vibrations as another way of reframing situations and not always look at vibrations as negative but also as good vibrations too and to celebrate them. When students begin to understand and use the story of *Ani to pisi* it validates the notion that creation stories have relevance in the institutional landscape of learning.

Student participants in the alliedFutures Project embodied the *Ani to pisi* story and evidence of how the narrative and Blackfoot teachings impacted them personally and professionally was reflected in their practices, journal writing, and ways they supported each other. A student created a visual representation of *Ani to pisi* (spiderwebs) to track the development of her leadership competencies and project work and explained:

> The outcome of this project was beyond anything that we could have dreamt of. However, this success did not come without challenges. Elder Roy Bear Chief guided our project and he taught us to envision our challenges and successes as vibrations on a spider web … as described in a Blackfoot Creation story. (cited in Bjartveit et al., 2022, p. 41)

Applying King's (2003) and Tafoya's (1995) ideas about the importance of stories with the students' understanding of *Ani to pisi* has created different narratives centred on relationship, curriculum, and practice in the BCST program. Through partnering with community organizations and students, we have come to recognize the relevance of Indigenous storytelling in decolonizing academic practice and how the self of students and educators are continuously changing and evolving based on history, culture and lived experiences – the stories of our lives. The following section explains how applying the four-step Indigenous EL cycle (experiencing, reflecting, meaning making, and acting), layered with the *Anti to pisi* story and collaborations with community organizations, increased the students' understanding of decolonization.

The Four-Step Indigenous EL Cycle

Step 1: Experiencing the alliedFutures Project: A Journey from Truth to Reconciliation

During the 2021/22 academic year, the students' collaboration on a joint community project with WilderFutures Institute[7] (WFI) and an Indigenous-led organization, Urban Society for Aboriginal Youth[8] (USAY), involved developing education workshops and a toolkit for local Calgary businesses related to decolonizing professional practice, increasing knowledge of Indigenous worldviews and steps toward reconciliation. The student project team was composed of both Child and Youth Care Counsellor (CYCC) and Early Learning and Child Care (ELCC) majors. The participants, who identified as Indigenous and settlers, were enrolled in the final year of a BCST program. Through their ongoing discussions, EL and collaboration with Indigenous Elders, Knowledge Holders, and community organizations over a nine-month period (2021–2), the students designed and implemented a fundraising initiative to support an Indigenous youth organization in Calgary. A long-term goal of the alliedFutures Project was to raise public awareness about post-secondary community-based initiatives and student partnerships with Indigenous organizations and to increase knowledge and provoke dialogue about decolonization and anti-biased pedagogy and practice. Town-gown collaboration and project work involving USAY and MRU increased post secondary students' understanding of decolonization relative to their academic and professional practices.

The theoretical framework for the alliedFutures Project included Indigenous scholar Willie Ermine's (2007) concept of "ethical space," which focuses on cultural hybridity and creating opportunities for Indigenous and non-Indigenous dialogic engagement. An ethical space is formed when two societies with different worldviews engage each other, and the space in between them contributes to the development of a framework for dialogue (Ermine, 2007). The work of decolonization includes creating ethical spaces and remaining open and listening to diverse perspectives. In-class discussions about ethical space fueled dialogue among the students about human rights and social justice and became an important topic of reference as the project unfolded. Through discussing social justice and engaging in EL, the project team challenged colonial ideologies and false assumptions about Indigenous history and contemporary on-reserve realities.

The students participated in a weekly three-hour seminar and their EL opportunities within the university involved leading class discussions based on Sensoy and DiAngelo's (2017) social justice text, project planning, conducting a literature review, and writing evaluation reports. The students also conducted a literature review to understand the impacts of colonization on academic and professional practice.

Decolonizing course curriculum across the faculties at MRU closely aligns with our pedagogy and research interests in human rights and social justice. Equity, Diversity, and Inclusion (EDI) are at the centre of classroom and fieldwork in the BCST program. In the first weeks of the academic semester, the students read about and discussed Canada's colonial past and the impacts of colonization on Indigenous Peoples. Sitting in the truth about cultural genocide, lost lives, lost languages, and intergenerational trauma linked to the Indigenous residential schools brought the dark side of EL into sharp focus. Reading the lived experiences of residential school survivors in government reports (Truth & Reconciliation Commission of Canada, 2015a, 2015b, 2015c), academic texts (Rogers et al., 2012), and media reports about the discovery of unmarked graves on residential school sites in Canada uncovered the truth about the fate of children who attended the schools from the 1880s to the end of the 20th century (Heidenreich, 2021; Meissner, 2021).

Each week the students' learning experiences in the community included eight hours of project work with Indigenous community partners to develop the *alliedFutures* toolkit to increase knowledge about decolonization, Indigenization, and the steps from truth to reconciliation, as outlined in Canada's Truth and Reconciliation Commission's (TRC) 94 Calls to Action (2015a). The project team researched and wrote sections of the toolkit together which included: Sitting in Truth, Allyship, Accomplice, Decolonization, and Reconciliation. They also developed and facilitated five public education webinars related to the toolkit topics. More than one hundred businesses in Calgary purchased the toolkit and the funds raised were directed to USAY. The students promoted the toolkit on social media and together with their professor and community partner disseminated the project work at an international academic conference and co-authored an academic journal article (Bjartveit et al., 2022).

The students' understanding of decolonization, their project experiences including their successes and challenges while working on the project were recorded in electronic journals at the beginning, mid-point and end of the academic year. Some students opted to write journals while others created video recordings or visual representations of their reflections. The journal postings were collected as research data and analyzed after the course work ended.

Steps 2 and 3: Reflecting and Meaning Making – Capstone Project Outcomes

> Arising out of Aboriginal philosophy of constant motion or flux is the value of wholeness or totality. The value of wholeness speaks to the totality of creation, the group as opposed to the individual, the forest as opposed to the individual trees ... The circle of kinship can be made up of one circle or a number of concentric circles. These kinship circles can be interconnected by other circles such as religious and social communities. This approach to Aboriginal organization can be viewed as "spider web" of relations.[9] (Little Bear, 2000, p. 79)

Leroy Little Bear's (2000) words point to the importance of interconnection and his reference to a "spider web of relations" aligns closely with the *Ani to pisi* story. Through reading the students' journals and reflecting on our leadership roles and project experiences, we came to recognize how town-gown work on the alliedFutures project was rooted in cross-cultural relationships and collaboration between the university and wider community. The research findings and themes in the journals reflect the positive impacts of town-gown collaboration on building and strengthening relationships, and decolonizing academic teaching, learning, and professional practice.

Town-Gown Project Work Created a "Spider Web of Relations"

Elder Bear Chief explained that Blackfoot creation stories evolve from the sky or the cosmic world, from the animal world, from the underground world, or from nature. These stories are passed down through generations. The story, *Ani to pisi* or the spider web, is about vibrations that require help and about celebrating good vibrations when they are felt. It gives people an opportunity to look at situations through a creation story as students carry *Ani to pisi* into their fieldwork and community agencies. *Ani to pisi* is universal and touches every aspect of life because of the vibrations.

Ani to pisi story was applied to practice in the community as students interacted with partner organizations and developed a spider web of professional relationships. The creation story reminded the project participants that building relationships and exercising "kimma pi pitsin" (Blackfoot to English translation: kindness and compassion) are crucial in decolonization. The creation story is about connection and action and when one person struggles, all members of the community feel the vibrations and should feel drawn to assist them. When the students experienced challenges while engaged in project work, they remembered the cultural teachings and supported each other. The project participants' enactment of *Ani to pisi* would not have happened without town-gown partnerships as reflected in a student's journal entry:

> Although we faced much uncertainty and strained relationships, this was profound for my professional practice. Having these unpleasant experiences while having the support of other students and my professor allowed me to navigate the situations much more effectively and appropriately … I'm grateful for these experiences. I now have better communication skills, more experience voicing my displeasure/compromising with others, and I ultimately can navigate my professional relationships better. (Personal communication/journal, March 2022)

The alliedFutures Project was formed from a series of reciprocal relationships between the students, partner organizations, Elders and Knowledge Holders. Project work on campus and in the community widened students' perspectives and scope of professional practice. All parties came together to share and exchange information, knowledge, and skills to advance the project. Through enacting reciprocity, the students learned to value relationships as the fundamental component of decolonization in professional settings. Based on the journal entries and research findings, the students' understanding of decolonization increased as they engaged in reciprocal relationships with their Indigenous community partners.

Town-Gown Project Work Decolonized Professional Practices

Community organizations profit from town-gown partnerships by recruiting students for hands-on project work and in turn students benefit through gaining work experience and skills. The WFI staff's goal in partnering with MRU was to develop and implement a public fundraiser and provide students with professional experience. The importance of ethical space, relationships, and reciprocity was recognized by the project participants as they interacted with each other and Indigenous community organizations.

An unexpected project outcome became evident when feedback from the students and Indigenous leaders influenced WFI to dismantle their colonial practices. During an early stage of the project, a power differential was felt between the students and WFI staff. The first change to colonial practice emerged out of a need to eliminate hierarchy and create an ethical space where the project team members could engage in honest and open dialogue about their ideas and roles in the project work. It took time and practice to recognize when power dynamics arose in the student-community partner relationships and how they negatively affected the group's work and relationships. After the project partners recognized and dismantled the power differential, meaningful connections and authentic collaboration on the project ensued. The students' roles and ideas were valued equally, which improved group dynamics and the project partners began to build trust and lean on each other's strengths and support.

Another change in colonial practice became necessary when the project team asked an Indigenous organization for assistance and were firmly reminded by a leader within the organization that establishing a reciprocal relationship is necessary before making requests. The vibrations created by this unexpected response caused the team to step back and reflect on what they had asked for and their approach. The project team had assumed that the Indigenous organization would agree to assist them on their terms and within their timeframe and they were surprised when this was denied. Their embedded neoliberal and colonial practices based on efficiency and productivity were uncovered. This pivot point in the project resulted in a realignment of the project goals and schedule to allow time for relationship building, to establish trust and to understand how reciprocity – equal give and take for all parties – would be honoured. A final change to colonial practice was discovered through reflection after the project had ended. Project deliverables such as written reports and tangible outcomes were a course requirement and rewarded in both on-campus and community work environments. Relationships, on the other hand, could neither be measured nor quantified. While reflecting on their collaborative experiences during the academic year, the project team came to understand that relationships are central to decolonial, human rights, and social justice work.

Town-Gown Project Work Decolonized Academic Teaching and Learning

Recognizing their social locations as white settlers of European ancestry and living on Treaty 7 land caused some students and project leaders to feel vulnerable while teaching and learning course content focused on decolonization. Rather than backing away from the challenges due to fear and vulnerability, they embraced the risks and partnered in learning with Elders, and community partners. Creating brave and ethical spaces to discuss personal and professional challenges and successes, drawing on resources and support from Indigenous leaders on campus and in the community, and viewing curriculum topics through multiple critical lenses (history, culture, theory, practice) strengthened relationships in the classroom and community, deepened their learning together, and created an environment of trust.

Blackfoot language, tipi pole teachings, the Medicine Wheel and Creation stories were woven into curriculum content and course resources. Students engaged in sharing circles and cultural ceremonies led by Indigenous leaders in the classroom and community. In alignment with Indigenous cultural traditions, the students wanted to present their project and course work through visual representations and oral presentations rather than written reports. Decolonizing teaching and learning interrupted colonial pedagogical strategies, requiring changes to course syllabi, assignments, and assessments. These curriculum adjustments required the professor to be flexible and address the vibrations that she herself experienced when asked to change what she believed were reliable, valid, and measurable assessment tools and strategies. The discovery of these deeply embedded colonial ideologies was uncovered and prompted reflexive and critical thinking about hidden biases, presuppositions, and what counts as "good" pedagogy. The alliedFutures project catalyzed transformative change and uncovered truth about the self of faculty, community leaders, and students and their embedded colonial discourses and beliefs.

Step 4: Acting – Finding a Pathway Forward

Viewing EL through an Indigenous lens assisted the project team in creating an ethical space for dialogue within the university and community and increased their understanding of decolonization. It took time to establish a culture of trust between the students and community partners which began with the creation of a brave space where honest ideas could be shared prior to ethical understanding, learning, and changemaking. The project team discovered that creating an ethical space is a process and requires the development of relationships and an openness on the part of dialogic partners to look, listen, learn, and consider the ideas of others, even to the point of changing dominant cultural ideas, beliefs, and practices. The process required reflexivity, raising self-awareness about deeply embedded biases, prejudices and presuppositions, and honest dialogue.

Learning Decolonization in Collaboration With Indigenous Organizations

Town-gown work within the university and community had a transformative impact on the students' and community partners' engagement and learning. When given EL opportunities, the students were able to "think outside the box of the institutions … and help as agents of social justice"

(Bear Chief as cited in Bjartveit et al., 2022, p. 52). The students demonstrated respect for the Elders who mentored and guided their work during each phase of the project as Bear Chief noted: "The transformation I see amongst the young is comforting because I see them as future leaders ready to take on what they are inheriting in the future" (Bjartveit et al., 2022, p. 53). This transformative change in students' learning and their understanding of decolonization is echoed in the following journal entry which a student posted in the final week of the course:

> I now understand that decolonization is so much more than I had thought. Coming into this year I viewed decolonization so simply, as the process of undoing the effects of colonization. What I learned was that it could not be a more complex, challenging, intricate, systemic, and a lifelong process. I've learned that it is not something solely conducted by society and its institutions, but is also a very individual process that everyone should participate in. It is about unlearning and relearning. It is about sitting in our own truth, recognizing our privilege and how we can use it to become an accomplice for those who are marginalized and experience systemic barriers. It is about first decolonizing ourselves and then acting to decolonize societal systems. It is about giving a voice to those who have been silenced and to stand with, and in front of them, in the process of advocacy and changemaking. It is about building bridges between two worlds so we can live in harmony as equals. It is about reconciling past mistakes and making a promise and a commitment to doing better moving forward. It is about breaking down our current society and its oppressive functioning and rebuilding a better world where everyone is celebrated. It is a long and arduous process, and we most likely will not see the outcome that we would like to in this lifetime, but we can sure as hell work as hard as we can to build a better and stronger foundation for future generations to build upon so that one day our world will be a better place where everyone can flourish. (Personal correspondence, March 27, 2022)

What Is the Role of the University in Effectively Supporting Students and Town-Gown Collaborations?

The university's commitment and role in supporting the students' fieldwork and building solid community partnerships is crucial and requires critical consideration of time, labour (faculty support), and funding. We appreciate the emphasis that Chapter 8 places on equity, inclusion, dismantling power dynamics and broadening the definition of EL through town-gown partnerships. The alliedFutures Project exemplifies the importance of reciprocity and equity through building inclusion and developing local town-gown relationships and EL collaborations with Indigenous community partners. In post-secondary education institutions, built on colonized systems, policies, and practices, EL offers opportunities to dismantle power imbalances and raises cultural awareness through transcultural teaching and learning practices both within universities and local communities. The prefix "trans" in "transcultural," in the context of the alliedFutures Project refers to the transformative potential for creating "ethical spaces" (Ermine, 2007) and a culture of engagement to support reciprocal teaching and learning in EL activities. Partnering with community partners on EL initiatives also aligns with the university's core mission for teaching and learning and is the first goal in MRU's 2023–2030 Strategic Plan: "Through the delivery of a broad liberal education, students will have numerous opportunities to develop transversal skills by participating in various forms of experiential learning such as work-integrated learning, community service learning, labs, working with professors on research and scholarship projects, and co-curricular activities." (p. 9)

The investment and far-reaching impact of effective town-gown collaboration is demonstrated through the alliedFutures Project – specifically its response to the TRC's *Calls to Action* (2015a). The university was able to extend its decolonization and reconciliation work in the areas of teaching, service, and scholarship beyond the institution into the wider community. Town-gown collaboration increased the project participants' understanding of ways to include Indigenous knowledge, methods and stories into classrooms and child and youth care programs (TRC, 2015a, Call 63). Management and staff of Calgary businesses that purchased the toolkit learned about "the history and legacy of residential schools, the United Nations Declaration on the Rights of Indigenous Peoples, Treaties and Aboriginal rights … training in intercultural competency, conflict resolution, human rights, and antiracism" (TRC, 2015a, Call 92). The positive learning outcomes and strengthened relationships between the university and community organizations are evidence that land-based and community-based research and learning are essential and that decolonial indigenization might be best facilitated outside of post-secondary institutions (Gaudry & Lorenz, 2018).

EL is by and of itself a decolonial practice. Before settlers arrived in Canada, Indigenous knowledge was passed through experiencing, reflecting, meaning making, and acting – relevant to oral traditions, stories, and storytelling. The alliedFutures Project and our partnerships with Indigenous organizations in Calgary have motivated us to continue decolonization efforts, knowing it is firmly rooted in EL and relationships, within the university and wider community, as we advocate for human rights and social justice in the fields of Early Learning and Child and Youth Care and work toward reconciliation.

NOTES

1 We dedicate this chapter to Elder Clement Bear Chief (November 1938–February 2022), who told the Blackfoot Creation story, *Ani to pisi.* His legacy and the story live on in our hearts, minds and souls as we continue the work of decolonization, reconciliation and healing within the university and in our work with children, youth and families in community care settings.

2 This chapter describes post-secondary project work that is part of a continuing research study entitled – Untangling Post-Secondary Students' Understanding of Decolonization through Community-based Projects with Indigenous Partner Organization. The study has received ethics approval from the Human Research Ethics Board at Mount Royal University (Application Number #102977). Excerpts from this article were presented at the Reconceptualizing Early Childhood Education (RECE) conference, Being together in/with place: Reimagining Pedagogies in Transformational Times (Vancouver, British Columbia, June 2022).

3 In 2008, the Canadian Government formed the Truth and Reconciliation Commission to investigate the harm caused to Indigenous peoples by church-run residential schools across Canada, and to recommend solutions so that future abuses would never again be inflicted on Indigenous people and communities in the future. The Commission's 94 Calls to Action are policy recommendations meant to aid people in the healing process by acknowledging the truth of historical events and creating systems to break the cycle of abuse (Reconciliation Education, First Nations University of Canada).

4 The alliedFutures Project was published online in March 2022. It is an interactive digital toolkit that guides readers through a five-step journey with multiple resources and reflexive activities.

5 https://www.wilderfutures.com/.

6 Old Sun Residential School opened in 1886 and was operated by the Anglican church and the Canadian federal government. "Leaders of the Siksika Nation in the 1970s took control of the Old Sun Residential School building and transformed it into the Old Sun Community College for Niitsitapi (Blackfoot) students." See https://www.mtroyal.ca/AboutMountRoyal/MediaRoom/Stories/2021/09/from-darkness-to-light-old-sun-community-college-marks-50th-anniversary.htm.

7 WilderFutures Institute is a non-profit organization based in Treaty 7 territory, aimed at addressing intersecting social issues by empowering organizations, families, educators, and the next generation of leaders with the tools and resources they need to make meaningful change in our communities.

8 The Urban Society for Aboriginal Youth (USAY) has been an influential not-for-profit organization in Calgary since 2001. USAY strives to provide

essential programming and services to Indigenous youth between the ages of twelve and twenty-nine living in Calgary.

9 Reprinted with permission of the Publisher from *Reclaiming Indigenous Voice and Vision* by Marie Battiste © University of British Columbia Press 2000. All rights reserved by the Publisher.

REFERENCES

Andreotti, V., Stein, S., Ahenakew, C., & Hunt, D. (2015). Mapping interpretations of decolonization in the context of higher education. *Decolonization: Indigeneity Education & Society*, 4, 21–40.

Attas, (n.d.). *What is decolonization? What is Indigenization?* Centre for Teaching and Learning, Queen's University. https://www.queensu.ca/ctl/resources/decolonizing-and-indigenizing/what-decolonization-what-indigenization

Bang, M., & Marin, A. (2015). Nature-culture constructs in science learning: Human/non-human agency and intentionality. *Journal of Research in Science Teaching, 52*(4), 530–44.

Battiste, M. (2002). *Indigenous knowledge and pedagogy in First Nations education: A literature review with recommendations.* National Working Group on Education.

– (2013). *Decolonizing education: Nourishing the learning spirit.* UBC Press.

– (2022, May 2) *Indigenous and Trans-Systemic Approaches Toward Decolonizing the Academy* [Conference presentation] Postsecondary Learning and Teaching, University of Calgary, Calgary, AB. http://hdl.handle.net/1880/114891

Bear Chief, A. (2016). *My decade at Old Sun: My lifetime of hell.* AU Press.

Bjartveit, C., Gordon, H., Manywounds, E., Larden, A., Oschipok, K., & Arnfinson, K. (2022). Ethical space as a relational place: Increasing postsecondary students' understanding of decolonization through the alliedFutures Project. *Relational Child and Youth Care Practice, 35*(2), 32–56.

Darder, A., Baltodano, M., & Torres, R. D. (Eds.). (2003). *The critical pedagogy reader.* Routledge-Falmer.

Dewey, J. (1938). *Experience and education.* Colliers Book.

Ermine, W. (2007). The ethical space of engagement. *Indigenous Law Journal*, 6, 193–293.

Fiola, C. & MacKinnon, S. (2020). Urban and inner-city studies: Decolonizing ourselves and the University of Winnipeg. In S. Cote-Meek & T. Moeke-Pickering's (Eds.), *Decolonizing and Indigenizing Education in Canada* (pp. 155–173). Canadian Scholar.

Frideres, J. (2019). *Arrows in a quiver: Indigenous-Canadian relations from contact to the courts.* University of Regina Press.

Gaudry, A., & Lorenz, D. (2018). Indigenization as inclusion, reconciliation, and decolonization: Navigating the different visions for indigenizing the Canadian Academy. *AlterNative: An International Journal of Indigenous Peoples, 14(*3), 218–27. https://doi.org/10.1177/1177180118785382

González y González, E. M., & Lincoln, Y. S. (2006). Decolonizing qualitative research: Non-traditional reporting forms in the academy. *Forum Qualitative Sozialforschung/Forum: Qualitative Social Research,* 7(4).

Heidenreich, P. (2021, December 31). "The story was hidden": How residential school graves shocked and shaped Canada in 202. *Global News.* https://globalnews.ca/news/8458351/canada-residential-schools-unmarked-graves-indigenous-impact/

Kaminski, J. (2011). Experiential Learning. *First Nations Pedagogy.* https://firstnationspedagogy.com/experiential.html

King, T. (2004). *The truth about stories: A native narrative.* Anansi.

Kinzel, C. (2020). Indigenous knowledge in early childhood education: Building a nest for reconciliation. *Journal of Childhood Studies, 45*(1), 19–32.

Knudson, S. (2015). Integrating the self and the spirit: Strategies for aligning qualitative research teaching with Indigenous methods, methodologies, and epistemologies. *Forum Qualitative Sozialforschung/Forum: Qualitative Social Research, 16*(3), Art. 4. https://www.qualitative-research.net/index.php/fqs/article/view/162

Kolb, D. (1984). *Experiential learning: Experience as the source of learning and development.* Prentice Hall.

Little Bear, L. (2000). Jagged worldviews colliding. In M. Battiste (Ed.), *Reclaiming Indigenous voice and vision* (pp. 77–85). UBC Press.

Loyie, L., Spear, W., & Brissenden, C. (2014). *Residential schools: With the words and images of survivors.* Indigenous Education Press and Shingwauk Residential Schools Centre.

McNamara, R., & Naepi, S. (2018). Decolonizing community psychology by supporting indigenous knowledge, projects, and students: Lessons from Aotearoa New Zealand and Canada. *American Journal of Community Psychology, 62*(3–4), 340–9. https://doi.org/10.1002/ajcp.12296

Meissner, D. (2021, December 16). Canadian Press names Kamloops unmarked graves discovery Canada's news story of the year. *CBC News.* https://www.cbc.ca/news/canada/british-columbia/canadian-press-story-of-the-year-unmarked-grave-discovery-1.6288978

Online Etymology Dictionary (n.d). Dismantle. In *www.etymonline.com.* Retrieved December 11, 2024, from https://www.etymonline.com/search?q=dismantle

Rogers, S., DeGagné, M., Dewar, J., & Lowry, G. (2012). *Speaking my truth. Reflections on reconciliation & residential school.* Aboriginal Healing Foundation.

Romm, N. (2015). Conducting focus groups in terms of an appreciation of indigenous ways of knowing: Some examples from South Africa. *Forum Qualitative Sozialforschung/Forum: Qualitative Social Research, 16*(1), Art. 2.

Sensoy, O., & DiAngelo. (2017). *Is everyone really equal?* (2nd ed.). Teacher's College Press.

Smith, L. T. (2012). *Decolonizing methodologies: Research and Indigenous peoples* (2nd ed.). Zed Books.

Smith, R., & McGee, M. (2005). Experiential Learning Models. *First Nations Pedagogy*. https://firstnationspedagogy.com/experiential.html

Solnit, R. (2005). *A field guide to getting lost.* Penguin.

Tafoya, T. (1995). Finding Harmony: Balancing Traditional Values with Western Science in Therapy. *Canadian Journal of Native Education, 21*(supplement), 7–27.

Truth and Reconciliation Commission of Canada (2015a) *Calls to Action.* https://www2.gov.bc.ca/assets/gov/british-columbians-our-governments/indigenous-people/aboriginal-peoples-documents/calls_to_action_english2.pdf

– (2015b). *Final report of the Truth and Reconciliation Commission of Canada Volume One: Summary.* Lorimer

– (2015c). *The survivors speak.*

Tuck, E., & Yang, K. W. (2012). Decolonization is not a metaphor. *Decolonization: Indigeneity, Education & Society, 1*(1), 1–40.

Vowel, C. (2016). *Indigenous writes: A guide to First Nations, Métis & Inuit issues in Canada.* Highwater Press.

8 Experiential Learning as Community Engagement and the Need to Attend to Equity

REBECCA COLLINS-NELSEN, HANNAH EGERT, JOHN MACLACHAN, AND SANDEEP RAHA

McMaster University, Canada

Introduction

The popularity of experiential learning (EL) as a philosophy of education (Dewey, 1971) continues to grow. Bates (2014) defines EL as the opportunity to learn through doing and then reflect to apply theoretical and practical knowledge in and out of the classroom. With that relatively broad definition, instructors have applied it to a variety of experiences and disciplines recognizing the value of including a hands-on approach to teaching at the post-secondary level. As EL has become more prevalent, the associated definition, practices, and values have expanded and evolved (Lewis & Williams, 1994; Kolb et al., 2014). For instance, the ways in which learners apply information in an experiential-based approach has taken the form of seminars, laboratory settings, clinical experiences, and even experiential pedagogies within virtual environments (Vo & Morris, 2006; Abdulwashed & Nagy, 2009; Carroll et al., 2021). In conjunction with an increased interest in EL, there has also been a greater call for community engaged learning (CEL) and responsible community engagement from post-secondary institutions (Berard & Ravelli, 2021; Soyer et al., 2022). The European Union has called for a renewed agenda in higher education to include community engagement (Farnell et al., 2020). If you have not already done so, consider reading Chapter 7 for more discussion on community engagement. Community engaged learning (also commonly referred to as Service Learning) can be broadly defined as the combination of service and academic activities that are intended to benefit both the recipient and the provider (Hou, 2014). This focus on reciprocity means that all CEL initiatives should be able to clearly identify the benefit for both the students and community partners (Meurer et al., 2011; Comeau et al., 2019; Goggins & Hajdukiewicz, 2022). Community partners can range from larger units such as community organizations to smaller units, such as individual members of the community, depending on the particular focus of the project. The focus of this chapter, Community Engaged Experiential Learning (CEEL), is a combination of EL and community engaged learning whereby the experiential component of the course involves engaging with the broader community, most commonly in an off-campus setting.

Related to the greater emphasis on EL, CEL, and CEEL is an amplified demand for universities to pay attention to issues of equity, diversity, and inclusion (EDI). Some have even stated that beyond research and teaching, there is a "third mission" for universities to "contribute to society" (Compagnucci & Spigarelli, 2020). This concept works exceedingly well with the impacts of CEEL benefiting the community and the learners (Goggins & Hajdukiewicz, 2022). While some would argue that the teaching and research emerging out of post-secondary institutions has been contributing to society for years, others would note that much of this work stays in the realm of intellectual debates among small populations of like-minded individuals with little practical application to many citizens' day-to-day lives (Kalles & Thomas, 2015). There can be a significant gap between what happens at the university and the broader community, which creates barriers for CEEL. Better university and community relations are important, as the university is both part of the community and often relies on the community for funding and research opportunities. Conversely, it makes sense for the community to benefit from a nearby institute of research and higher learning. Complicated histories and power dynamics have long existed between universities and the broader communities they are situated within (Wallerstein et al., 2019, Parker et al., 2020). For instance, universities are often considered to be elitist institutions that have created physical and moral barriers between themselves and the broader community, particularly high priority neighbourhoods. Additionally, with this elitism, universities often carry on colonial legacies, which has led to exploitative relationships with communities. The greater power that post-secondary institutions historically and presently hold, has created barriers to bridging the "town and gown" divide which means that responsible community engagement, and the associated CEEL, is easier said than done.

With this context in mind we ask, how can the university encourage and support CEEL without continuing to reproduce problematic power dynamics and exclusion? More specifically, we consider what efforts can be made to engage populations outside of the academic community who choose to disassociate from the university, further expanding the town and gown divide. While it can be difficult to identify who is disassociated by the sheer fact that they are not around, it is safe to say that we are less likely to see communities engaging who do not have any connection to the university. There are many considerations when implementing CEEL, including, what policies does the university need to have in place, what process is needed to make this happen, how to build relationships within the community, how do these experiences fit within pedagogical and curriculum goals, and so on. What is perhaps considered less in the design process is how to ensure that CEEL is not reproducing exclusionary practices by continuing to ignore certain sectors of our communities. Dismantling power dynamics is a huge feat that requires continued and coordinated efforts from the academy and beyond. Offering solutions to eliminate long-standing power dynamics is beyond the scope of this chapter. Rather, this chapter argues that in order to implement responsible CEEL, it is necessary to use a lens of equity in conjunction with a pedagogy of listening (Rinaldi, 2012) in order to attend to populations in the community that have traditionally been excluded. It is particularly important to facilitate engagement with those who distrust the university and/or see it as irrelevant. We draw on an empirical example of twenty interviews with parents whose children participate in a children's university (CU) in Hamilton, Ontario, Canada. These interviews show that positive experiences and attitudes associated with learning and post-secondary institutions significantly influence people's decisions to engage. Lastly, we elaborate on the "pedagogy of listening" as a strategy to improve community relations with equity deserving groups and get the most out of CEEL.

Literature Context

There is a history of disconnect, and in some cases tensions, between the university and the wider communities where they reside. It is common to have spatial, economic, and social differences between universities and their broader communities (Massey et al., 2014). However, Massey, Field and Chan (2014) note that more recently there have been efforts at improving these town-gown relations, with communities standing to gain economic benefits and universities recognizing that "partnerships with the local community are politically important" (p.154). The facility by which these relations can be bridged is, of course, in part based on the context of the university/community dynamic. For example, Hamilton, Ontario, Canada is a traditionally working-class town that houses a top-ranking research institution, McMaster University (Johnston, 2015). The City of Hamilton was built on the steel industry as an economic driver and therefore has a foundation of being a blue-collar city (Dear et al., 1987; Eyles & Peace, 1990). Thus, the white-collar environment of the university brings a contrasting identity that does not organically lead to a natural partnership. Beyond the class divide, there is also a physical divide created by the 110-metre high Niagara Escarpment splitting Hamilton into, what locals refer to as, the Lower and Upper City (Maclachlan & Eyles, 2011; Gage et al., 2022). Additionally, the effects of socioeconomic variability (Williams et al., 2010), arguably associated with the blue- and white-collar gap, have been shown to have an effect when it comes to inequality around air pollution (Buzzelli et al., 2003; Jerrett et al., 2004; Maclachlan et al., 2007), access to and quality of health care (DeLuca et al., 2012), and access to basic needs (Latham & Moffat, 2007; Dosen et al., 2017). As is the case in this example, certain contexts provide an even greater challenge in bridging the divide between the university and the city.

One of the outcomes of this kind of dynamic is that there are populations within the broader community that tend to be disconnected from the university (Maurrasse, 2002; Sandy & Holland, 2006). Many of these people can be grouped into two prominent camps, those that distrust the university and those who see the university as irrelevant, with inevitable overlap between these two categories. There are many reasons as to why people may feel this way. For example, people may have had little interaction with the university if no one they know has attended, they may see it as an exclusive and intimidating space, or they may have had bad experiences with education and/or institutions and research. As such, in many of these cases, avoiding the university becomes a response to social inequality (Strier, 2011). These attitudes are, of course, more or less prominent depending on the context of the community where the university resides. For instance, given the history and power dynamics in the example cited above, Hamilton, Ontario, Canada, has sectors of the population who do not trust the university and/or see it as peripheral to their lives.

While those who distrust the university or see it as irrelevant are not exclusively associated with social categories, we do know that intersections of race, class, gender, sexuality, ability, and age (Crenshaw, 1991) contribute to broader patterns of relationships with education and post-secondary education in particular. For example, people who are poor and people of colour have often, and continue to be, regularly left out of research studies often conducted through post-secondary institutions (Cote-Meek, 2020). Moreover, when they have been included, there are many examples of exploitation. In fact, several standards for research ethics have been put into place as a direct response to these circumstances (Ross et al., 2010; Anderson et al., 2012). Additionally, universities make efforts to attract first generation students, recognizing that there is a large sector of the population who do not see university as a viable path for them. If one has limited engagement with the university, it is not surprising that they may distrust or be indifferent towards it.

Scholars note that recent attempts to bridge university activities with the broader community has served to further strain rather than improve relationships. For example, Dean's (2007) analysis of a "service-learning" model that she employed in her class affirms that, in many cases, efforts to benefit students' and professors' curriculum and learning needs ultimately created more work for community organizations with little benefit in return. This and similar examples have increased skepticism about the possibility of a reciprocal relationship between the university and broader community.

Responsible community engagement requires continuity and respect for the time of community partners and members. Both have proven challenging when incorporating CEEL into university classrooms, particularly because universities tend to run on a semester system, which is rarely consistent with other societal institutions and schedules. Even if schedules align so that a CEEL opportunity begins at the start of a semester, it is difficult to build relationships and execute projects under such a tight timeframe (Radonic et al., 2021). This can result in a superficial relationship with the community (Wellman, 1987; Mtawa et al., 2017), as well as incomplete engagement and/or follow-through (Beckman et al., 2011).

Universities are dogmatic institutions where institutional change comes slowly, if at all. They are also institutions that have been given prestige and status, making change difficult. Thus, logistics and tradition present barriers to inclusive and meaningful CEEL. Similar trends can be seen with the rate at which research is now expected at the university. Professors cannot spend a lot of time building and sustaining trusting relationships in the community, when data is expected to be collected quickly in order to meet institutional and granting timelines. Despite some universities prioritizing community connections, there are very few institutional incentives for this kind of work. Thus, devoting time to responsible community engagement rarely comes with professional or promotional payoffs.

For CEEL to work, it must be reciprocally beneficial for the communities, students, and faculty, as well as equitable and inclusive. There are many ways the community can benefit from CEEL, such as contributing relevant research or hours worked, but most importantly, the specifics need to be developed with the community partners themselves. This involves approaching these initiatives with a lens of equity and using a great deal of listening and reflection. Without careful design of CEEL, there is a likely chance of reproducing problematic circumstances, including the exclusion of populations who have negative views and/or are indifferent towards the university. The following case study shows that people who have had positive experiences with education and post-secondary institutions are far more likely to feel a connection to the post-secondary community and willingly engage with university-led initiatives.

The Case of McMaster Children and Youth University

Children and youth universities exist around the world (e.g., McMaster Children and Youth University (MCYU), Canada; European Children's University Network, Vienna; Manchester, U.K.; Nã Pua No èau, U.S.A.). Their general mandate is to inspire an interest in learning by sharing university research and ideas with children in the local community. Many started by focusing on topics related to science, technology, engineering and math (STEM) in order to increase interest in those areas. Since then, many have added Arts (making the acronym STEAM) in order to offer a comprehensive array of subjects. In addition to being a space for learning, some children's universities are also trying to centre the voices of young people and advocate for their rights as active citizens. Currently, dominant narratives of childhood position young people as recipients of knowledge as though they exist only in a forward focused state of becoming, rather than promoting young people as already capable of contributing to society in important ways (Cassidy & Mohr Lone, 2020; Uprichard, 2008). The example below focuses specifically on a children's university in Hamilton, Ontario, Canada.

The case of MCYU serves to highlight some of the ways that community members make decisions about whether to engage with the university. MCYU is a free program that invites children and their families to McMaster University to attend a lecture given by a university instructor. One purpose of this initiative is to bridge what is happening at the university with the broader community, as well as to encourage children to feel comfortable in university settings so that they can see themselves fitting in if they choose to attend in the future. To establish what motivates parents to bring their families to these lectures, we conducted interviews with twenty parents of families who attend MCYU lectures.

This case shows that positive educational experiences influence parents' decisions to engage with MCYU. Positive educational experiences refer to any experience that instills a positive value of education and learning within participants. The results posit two primary positive values, extrinsic and intrinsic. Extrinsic motivation refers to motivation to do something to achieve a goal, whereas intrinsic motivation stems from the enjoyment or interest of the task itself (Hennessey et al., 2015; Serin, 2018). The experiences were categorized into three core environments: home, school, and community.

Positive experiences in the home, which include learning through parents or family members, shaped both extrinsic and intrinsic values of education for parents. For many participants, their families instilled extrinsic values of education by sharing the positive implications of pursuing post-secondary, such as upward social mobility or career success.

> My father always reminded me that if I were to get an education that no one can take that away from me. And it's a way out of poverty.
>
> My parents kind of ingrained in my head that education is important and without an education you're going to end up with kind of, you know, those jobs that look not so desirable … and with a great education you can do anything.

For others, their at-home experiences instilled intrinsic values of education. This included activities where an organic curiosity was enjoyable or where participants were told that pursuing an education will help them become a well-rounded person.

> So, I just think they always raised us that it wasn't really optional, that that's what you did after high school, and so it wasn't really a questioning about it. So, I guess that shaped my views as well … I've always told my children that your university or college years are your time to explore and to learn about yourself, but it's fine if that's not career driven, it's more just to become a better, rounded person.

These examples highlight that an appreciation and positive regard for learning and post-secondary education, in particular, is often passed down intergenerationally within the home.

The school was identified as another key place for shaping positive attitudes of education. Many participants formed positive values of education through their own postsecondary experiences where they enjoyed learning. They view attending post-secondary school as a positive experience because it leads to extrinsic values such as gaining marketable skills or a desirable occupation.

> For most occupations, high school education is just basic, and if you want to pursue any kind of profession or a trade or anything of that nature, you have to continue with your education beyond the basics.

Additionally, many participants had intrinsic motivations to pursue post-secondary school, such as learning to critically evaluate oneself or providing a space to explore and be creative.

> Beyond just the educational component, I think it is an invaluable opportunity for people to explore and be creative and come up with new ideas and I think it really does help form who we are as people.

The school environment for participants is critical in shaping their own positive values of education. The examples demonstrate how attending postsecondary instills a personal value of the university for parents, as they experience first-hand the benefits that come from attending. Conversely, those who have not had experience with post-secondary schooling cannot pass this down to their children.

The final environment we identified was the community, referring to educational experiences taking place in the participant's physical and social environment. This environment may extend to the global and local community, as some participants are immigrants to Canada or have travelled around the world. For many parents, there is a shared value of education that has been shaped by their community, particularly by experiencing barriers to educational opportunities. Within this environment, the connection to specific intrinsic and extrinsic values appears to be equally linked. For instance, in the following examples, the community environment could have shaped either intrinsic or extrinsic values, as "[starting] a better life" or being encouraged to pursue education "no matter what" may hold multiple meanings.

> I've worked in lots of different environments, and you see people that are oppressed and you see people that have grown up with different opportunities. I mean, the environment that I live in here, right now, I've got a lot of people from all over the world … they've been extremely lucky because they've been able to get out [of their native countries] because they've had an education to be able to come to Canada and start a better life here.
>
> I'm actually from South America, and I grew up in a tiny village where educational opportunities were very few. And my father always encouraged us to pursue education, no matter what, at all means.

Both extrinsic and intrinsic values of learning instilled through the home, school, and community led parents to engage with MCYU lectures. Parents sought out MCYU to provide positive experiences for their own children and to engage in learning themselves. With this in mind, we can postulate that those who are not attending MCYU lectures are those who have *not* developed extrinsic and intrinsic values for post-secondary education. Therefore, we need to consider who in our society is less likely to get opportunities through home, school, and community to cultivate these values and ensure that we do a better job of engaging them. The participants in this study recognize the university as useful and impactful, thus, choosing to engage in MCYU. Below we explore the value of listening with a lens of equity as a way to create community and belonging for those who do not yet share this value.

Meaningful and Equitable CEEL

In considering the above in relation to our initial question, how universities can support CEEL by tempering problematic power dynamics and exclusion in order to engage populations within the broader community, it is clear that early intervention is helpful. As discussed above, one's experiences with learning as it relates to the home, school, and community, shape attitudes and play a role in determining whether people seek out opportunities to be involved with the university in the future. Many of the participants mentioned that they grew up in families, schools, and communities that encouraged learning and post-secondary aspirations. Thus, the most effective way to engage all community members requires active intervention from an early age before people regard the university to be either irrelevant or suspicious. Interestingly, this is something that children's universities may help with as they look to offer positive, inclusive, and welcoming university experiences to children from all backgrounds. While this may be an effective approach to the problem, it will require intergenerational time in order to take effect. It also requires parents to dare to participate and attend, which is where universities must consider how to encourage equitable CEEL within children's university programs.

In the interim, creating positive relations with community necessitates a responsible approach to engagement when working with any community group and/or member. McMaster University has outlined six principles of responsible community engagement: respectful relationships, reciprocity, equity, continuity, openness to learning, and commitment to act (McMaster Office of Community Engagement, 2023). These principles require ongoing work and reflection to achieve. Put simply, responsible community engagement takes a lot of time, effort, and is never finished.

The emphasis on reflection that is required for responsible community engagement fits helpfully with EL. Many would argue that EL cannot happen without reflection. As such, reflection is firmly built into

Kolb's (1984) cycle of EL which involves concrete experience, followed by *reflective observation,* to abstract conceptualization, and finally active experimentation. Therefore, students need to learn how to effectively reflect to establish a foundation for both community engagement and EL. While reflection may come naturally to some people, it is also a skill that instructors need to commit to thoughtfully teaching and dedicating time to practice in CEEL-incorporated courses. A genuine emphasis on reflection will make positive contributions to both EL and community engagement.

Another key to inclusive and responsible community engagement, embedded within numerous McMaster principles, is listening. There is a history of people in privileged positions assuming they know what is best and imposing their ideas on others. This is evident within Canada's colonial history with Indigenous Peoples. It is this kind of method that has spurred the mantra of "nothing about us, without us" (Charlton, 1998). In this spirit, it is crucial that we listen to those in the community who do not trust the university or see it as irrelevant.

It is here that Rinaldi's (2012) "pedagogy of listening" could go a long way in helping create conditions for inclusive and responsible CEEL. While Rinaldi applies her theory to early childhood education, she also contends that it has a much broader application:

> The pedagogy of listening is not only a pedagogy for school, but also an attitude for life. It can be a tool but it can also be something more. It means taking responsibility for what we are sharing. If we need to be listened to, then listening is one of the most important attitudes for the identity of the human being, starting from the moment of birth. (p. 235)

Here, we can see that employing a wider lens of equity that reaches beyond children as an equity-deserving group allows this theory to connect with anyone with whom we wish to have mutual respect and meaningful dialogue. We cannot begin to repair relationships with the community or advocate that they engage with universities without a deep commitment to listening. As Rianaldi (2012) argues, "Through actions and reflection, learning takes shape in the mind of the subject and, through representation and exchange, becomes skill and knowledge" (p. 236). Historically, the university has often approached learning as a one-way relationship rather than seeing the opportunities for everyone to learn from each other. The pedagogy of listening pushes beyond the general bounds of "professing" to see possibilities of a requited relationship.

Similar to reflection, it is often thought that listening is a "natural" skill. It is true that we are almost always immersed in sound but that does not necessarily mean we are listening. Even to hear is different than to listen. As Rinaldi (2012) writes, "listening is not easy. It requires a deep awareness and a suspension of our judgements and prejudices. It requires openness to change" (p. 236). Like reflection, listening is a learned skill that must be deliberate and practiced.

The pedagogy of listening recognizes that in order for information to exist, it has to be listened to by others. This sharing moves us away from individualism and towards community, a necessary component of CEEL. Rinaldi (2012) also notes that listening should welcome difference, so that the messages and people being listened to are given value. Ultimately, this removes the individual from anonymity. It is this value that existing power dynamics often thwart and applying listening can bridge. Relationships build communities, and trust and respect are foundational to relationships. To listen in this way is to show trust and respect.

This is not to say that through listening, these relationships will change overnight. In fact, people must agree to conversations before we can even enact a pedagogy of listening which highlights the amount of work that lies ahead. It takes time and continued effort to build and maintain trust, but attending to issues of equity, reflecting, and listening are key ingredients toward this direction.

In sum, equitable and meaningful CEEL involves several steps that must be considered at the very start of the engagement and continue throughout. First, when thinking of an EL opportunity that involves community engagement, it is crucial to consider the communities you will engage, and those you will not. This can lead to further questions about why such boundaries have been created and whether or not they ought to be reconsidered. Next, one must apply the pedagogy of listening and reflection throughout the entire process. Doing so will help ensure that the following principles are present throughout the CEEL experience: respectful relationships, reciprocity, equity, continuity, openness to learning, and commitment to act.

Conclusion

The current interest in expanding the scope of learning from the university towards the community offers opportunity to reconfigure the relationship between the university and the broader community where it resides. That said, we cannot expect these relations to organically transpire or that equitable values will simply have a trickle-down effect in engagement with the community. Rather, we need to be deliberate about our approach and do the work to break down problematic power imbalances to create respectful and meaningful relationships with our communities. As highlighted in the case study, positive educational experiences can determine if a person will continue to engage throughout their life and/or try to engage their children. The university can have a significant role in providing positive experiences to the broader community that set the trajectory for how learning and post-secondary involvement will be perceived in the future. Effective and meaningful CEEL means that the university must find ways to connect with communities that have traditionally been excluded. This requires an awareness about these communities to prioritize equity, reflection, and listening when engaging with them. There is a great deal to be gained from emphasizing equity in CEEL, including a reciprocity between a greater emphasis on social justice in our communities and particularly meaningful learning opportunities for students and instructors. This is a process that is sure to take a great deal of time and effort, with success being difficult to measure (O'Brien et al., 2021), but will also result in reaching a fuller potential of CEEL while continuing to close the gap between "town and gown."

REFERENCES

Abdulwahed, M., & Nagy, Z. K. (2009). Applying Kolb's experiential learning cycle for laboratory education. *Journal of Engineering Education, 98*(3), 283–94.

Anderson, E. E., Solomon, S., Heitman, E., DuBois, J. M., Fisher, C. B., Kost, R. G., Lawless, M. E., Ramsey, C., Jones, B., Ammerman, A., & Ross, L. F. (2012). Research ethics education for community-engaged research: A review and research agenda. *Journal of Empirical Research on Human Research Ethics, 7*(2), 3–19.

Bates, A. (2014, December 1). Can you do experiential learning online? Assessing design models for experiential learning. *Online Learning and Distance Education Resources. Contact North.* https://www.tonybates.ca/2014/12/01/can-you-do-experiential-learning-online-assessing-design-models-for-experiential-learning/

Beckman, M., Penney, N., & Cockburn, B. (2011). Maximizing the impact of community-based research. *Journal of Higher Education Outreach and Engagement, 15*(2), 83–104.

Berard, A., & Ravelli, B. (2021). In their words: what undergraduate sociology students say about community-engaged learning. *Journal of Applied Social Science, 15*(2), 197–210.

Buzzelli, M., Jerrett, M., Burnett, R., & Finklestein, N. (2003). Spatiotemporal perspectives on air pollution and environmental justice in Hamilton, Canada, 1985–1996. *Annals of the Association of American Geographers, 93*(3), 557–73.

Carroll, M., Lindsey, S., Chaparro, M., & Winslow, B. (2021). An applied model of learner engagement and strategies for increasing learner engagement in the modern educational environment. *Interactive Learning Environments, 29*(5), 757–71.

Cassidy, C. & Mohr Lone, J. (2020). Thinking about childhood: Being and becoming in the world. *Analytic Teaching and Philosophical Practice, 40*(1): 16–26.

Charlton, James I. (1998). *Nothing About Us Without Us.* University of California Press.

Comeau, D. L., Palacios, N., Talley, C., Walker, E. R., Escoffery, C., Thompson, W. W., & Lang, D. L. (2019). Community-engaged learning in public health: An evaluation of utilization and value of student projects for community partners. *Pedagogy in Health Promotion, 5*(1), 3–13.

Compagnucci, L. & Spigarelli, F. (2020). The third mission of the university: A systematic literature review on potentials and constraints. *Technological Forecasting and Social Change,* 161, 1–30.

Cote-Meek, S. (2020). *Colonized classrooms: Racism, trauma and resistance in post-secondary education.* Fernwood Publishing.

Crenshaw. K. W. (1991). Mapping the margins: Intersectionality, identity politics, and violence against women of colour. *Stanford Law Review, 43*(6), 1241–99.

Dean, A. (2007). Teaching feminist activism: Reflections on an activism assignment in introductory women's studies. *The Review of Education, Pedagogy, and Cultural Studies,* 29, 351–69.

Dear, M. J., Drake, J. J., & Reeds, L. G. (Eds.). (1987). *Steel city: Hamilton and region.* University of Toronto Press.

DeLuca, P. F., Buist, S., & Johnston, N. (2012). The code red project: Engaging communities in health system change in Hamilton, Canada. *Social Indicators Research,* 108, 317–27.

Dewey, J. (1971). *Experience and education.* Collier Books. (Originally work published 1938)

Dosen, K. M., Karasiuk, A. A., Marcaccio, A. C., Miljak, S., Nair, M. H., & Radauskas, V. J. (2017). Code grey: Mapping healthcare service deserts in Hamilton, Ontario and the impact on senior populations. *Cartographica: The International Journal for Geographic Information and Geovisualization, 52*(2), 125–31.

Eyles, J., & Peace, W. (1990). Signs and symbols in Hamilton: An iconology of Steeltown. *Geografiska Annaler: Series B, Human Geography, 72*(2–3), 73–88.

Farnell, T., Veidemane, A., & Westerheijden, D. (2020). *Assessing the feasibility of developing a framework for community engagement in European higher education.* Zagreb: Institute for the Development of Education. https://iro.hr/wp-content/uploads/2022/10/TEFCE_Feasibility.pdf

Gage, H. J., Eyles, C. H., & Peace, A. L. (2022). Winter weathering of fractured sedimentary rocks in a temperate climate: observation of freeze–thaw and thermal processes on the Niagara Escarpment, Hamilton, Ontario. *Geological Magazine,* 1–22.

Goggins, J., & Hajdukiewicz, M. (2022). The role of community-engaged learning in engineering education for sustainable development. *Sustainability, 14*(13), 8208.

Hennessey, B., Moran, S., Altringer, B., & Amabile, T. M. (2015). Extrinsic and intrinsic motivation. *Wiley Encyclopedia of Management,* 1–4.

Hou, S. I. (2014). Integrating problem-based learning with community-engaged learning in teaching program development and implementation. *Universal Journal of Educational Research, 2*(1), 1–9.

Jerrett, M., Burnett, R. T., Brook, J., Kanaroglou, P., Giovis, C., Finkelstein, N., & Hutchison, B. (2004). Do socioeconomic characteristics modify the short term association between air pollution and mortality? Evidence from a zonal time series in Hamilton, Canada. *Journal of Epidemiology & Community Health, 58*(1), 31–40.

Johnston, C. M. (2015). *McMaster University, Volume 2: The Early Years in Hamilton, 1930–1957.* McGill-Queen's Press-MQUP.

Kalles, S., & Thomas, G. R. (2015). Service-learning: Promise and possibility in post-secondary education. *International Journal of Progressive Education, 11*(1), 132–48.

Kolb, D. A. (1984). *Experiential learning: Experience as the source of learning and development* (Vol. 1). Prentice-Hall.

Kolb, D. A., Boyatzis, R. E., & Mainemelis, C. (2014). Experiential learning theory: Previous research and new directions. In R. J. Sternberg, & L. Zhang (Eds.), *Perspectives on thinking, learning, and cognitive styles* (pp. 227–48). Routledge.

Latham, J., & Moffat, T. (2007). Determinants of variation in food cost and availability in two socioeconomically contrasting neighbourhoods of Hamilton, Ontario, Canada. *Health & Place, 13*(1), 273–87.

Lewis, L. H., & Williams, C. J. (1994). Experiential learning: Past and present. *New directions for adult and continuing education, 1994*(62), 5–16.

Maclachlan, J. C., & Eyles, C. H. (2011). Subglacial deforming bed conditions recorded by late quaternary sediments exposed in Vineland Quarry, Ontario, Canada. *Sedimentary Geology, 238*(3–4), 277–87.

Maclachlan, J. C., Jerrett, M., Abernathy, T., Sears, M., & Bunch, M. J. (2007). Mapping health on the Internet: A new tool for environmental justice and public health research. *Health & Place, 13*(1), 72–86.

Massey, J., Field, S. & Chan, Y. (2014). Partnering for economic development: How town-gown relations impact local economic development in small and medium cities. *Canadian Journal of Higher Education, 44*(2): 152–69.

Maurrasse, D. J. (2002). *Beyond the campus: How colleges and universities form partnerships with their communities.* Routledge.

McMaster Office of Community Engagement. (2023). *Office of Community Engagement 2023 Annual Report.* https://community.mcmaster.ca/app/uploads/2024/04/OCE-2023-Annnual-Report.pdf

Meurer, L. N., Young, S. A., Meurer, J. R., Johnson, S. L., Gilbert, I. A., & Diehr, S. (2011). The urban and community health pathway: preparing socially responsive physicians through community-engaged learning. *American journal of preventive medicine, 41*(4), S228–S236.

Mtawa, N. N., Fongwa, S. N., & Wangenge-Ouma, G. (2016). The scholarship of university-community engagement: Interrogating Boyer's model. *International Journal of Educational Development,* 49, 126–33.

O'Brien, E., Ilić, B. Ć., Veidemane, A., Dusi, D., Farnell, T., & Schmidt, N. Š. (2021). Towards a European framework for community engagement in higher education – a case study analysis of European universities. *International Journal of Sustainability in Higher Education, 23*(4), 815–30.

Parker, M., Wallerstein, N., Duran, B., Magarati, M., Burgess, E., Sanchez-Youngman, S., Boursaw, B., Heffernan, A., Garoutte, J., & Koegel, P. (2020). Engage for equity: development of community-based participatory research tools. *Health Education & Behavior, 47*(3), 359–71.

Radonic, L., Jacob, C., Kalman, R., & Lewis, E. Y. (2021). It's a sprint, not a marathon: a case for building short-term partnerships for community-based participatory research. *Qualitative Research, 23*(1), 380–98.

Rinaldi, C. (2012). The pedagogy of listening: The listening perspective from Reggio Emilia. In C. Edwards, L. Gandini & G. Forman (Eds.), *The Hundred Languages of Children: The Reggio Emilia Experience in Transformation* (3rd ed., pp. 233–46). Praeger.

Ross, L. F., Loup, A., Nelson, R. M., Botkin, J. R., Kost, R., Smith Jr, G. R., & Gehlert, S. (2010). Human subjects protections in community-engaged research: A research ethics framework. *Journal of Empirical Research on Human Research Ethics, 5*(1), 5–17.

Sandy, M., & Holland, B. A. (2006). Different worlds and common ground: Community partner perspectives on campus-community partnerships. *Michigan Journal of Community Service Learning, 13*(1), 30–43.

Serin, H. (2018). The use of extrinsic and intrinsic motivations to enhance student achievement in educational settings. *International Journal of Social Sciences & Educational Studies, 5*(1), 191–4.

Soyer, M., McCrackin, G., Ziyanak, S., Givens, J., Jump, V., & Schad, J. (2022). Leaving the lectures behind: Using community-engaged learning in research methods classes to teach about sustainability. *Teaching Sociology,* 51(3), 1–10.

Strier, R. (2011). The construction of university-community partnerships: Entangled perspectives. *Higher Education, 62*(1), 81–97.

Uprichard, E. (2008). "Children as 'being and becomings': Children, childhood and temporality." *Children & Society,* 22(4): 303–13.

Vo, H. X., & Morris, R. L. (2006). Debate as a tool in teaching economics: Rationale, technique, and some evidence. *Journal of Education for Business, 81*(6), 315–20.

Wallerstein, N., Muhammad, M., Sanchez-Youngman, S., Rodriguez Espinosa, P., Avila, M., Baker, E. A., Barnett, S., Belone, L., Golub, M., Lucero, J., Mahdi, I., Noyes, E., Nguyen, T., Roubideaux, Y., Sigo, R., & Duran, B. (2019). Power dynamics in community-based participatory research: a multiple–case study analysis of partnering contexts, histories, and practices. *Health Education & Behavior, 46*(1 Suppl), 19S–32S.

Wellman, B. (1987). *The community question re-evaluated.* Centre for Urban and Community Studies, University of Toronto.

Williams, A., Kitchen, P., DeMiglio, L., Eyles, J., Newbold, B., & Streiner, D. (2010). Sense of place in Hamilton, Ontario: Empirical results of a neighborhood-based survey. *Urban Geography, 31*(7), 905–31.

PART THREE

EL and Local Governance

9 Recasting Master's Level Geographical Education Through Experiential Learning: University-Community Connections for Social Development and Environmental Protection in the Emilia-Romagna Region of Italy

ELISA MAGNANI AND MATTEO PROTO

University of Bologna, Italy

MICHELE MANOCCHI

University of Western Ontario, Canada

Introduction

In the Italian and European contexts, experiential learning (EL) is emerging as higher education is faced with growing national and international pressures. As implemented locally, EL must negotiate local interests and connections while responding to national labour market regulations and reforms as well as European higher education harmonization. This contribution aims to discuss the role of EL in the European and Italian context by exemplifying the so-called *tirocinio formativo* implemented at the Master's Program in Geography and Territorial Processes at the University of Bologna (Italy) and its relationships with the local and regional community.

Considering that the concept of "Experiential Learning" has only recently entered the academic debate within Italian universities, the authors' main aim is to reflect on the development of this movement in the broader context of local, national, and international trends impacting higher education. The chapter begins with a discussion of existing literature and a historical overview of the role of EL in Europe and Italy through the gradual formalization of EL activities in university programs due to the European university reform process, commonly known as the Bologna Process. We then follow with an examination of EL in the specific territorial context of Bologna by presenting the case of how EL has been transposed into a set of practices within the Master's degree in Geography and Territorial Processes and the partnership with hosting community organizations. We explore the local tensions and potential for the development of EL as it confronts multi-scalar and competing pressures – international and local – in its early stages of development. This case study has been specifically identified because it offers the opportunity to observe the town-gown relation by showing off-campus interactions with the local community. Additionally, the geographical perspective is, by its very nature, strongly connected with community engagement and, as such, could offer insights into the fuller articulation of EL in other disciplines and university-community contexts. The case study also encompasses questionnaire data and semi-structured interviews with students and key community partners to collect quantitative and qualitative data to offer a comprehensive perspective.

Finally, through this chapter, the reader will be exposed to a distinctive characteristic of the Italian scenario, where the EL system is highly regulated and driven by laws and policies that standardize procedures and aim at making the system homogeneous. In other scenarios (e.g., Canada), post-secondary institutions' EL systems operate in a hybrid mode, where centralized offices (mostly focused on EL for undergraduate students) coexist with program-specific offices (mostly at the graduate and post-graduate levels). Similar to Chapters 10 and 11, then, this chapter speaks directly to the challenges and opportunities of local and associative forms of governance needed to establish and succeed with EL. The chapter concludes with discussion of the university's place in societal engagement, including relationships with partners, as well as the diversity and inclusion implications of the operation of this particular kind of EL.

Framing "Tirocinio" and Experiential Learning: The Relation Between Education and Labour Market in the European and Italian Contexts

Launched in 1998 to 1999 by the European Union through the Sorbonne and Bologna Declarations, the Bologna Process was the response of national governments to the challenges arising from the mobility of European students and graduates. It is an intergovernmental higher education reform process that includes forty-nine European countries and several European organizations with the primary purposes of: (a) bringing more coherence to higher education systems across Europe (e.g., the three-cycle degree structure – Bachelor, Master's, and Doctorate), (b) enhancing the quality and recognition of European higher education systems (e.g., the Standards and Guidelines for Quality Assurance in the European Higher Education Area), and (c) improving the conditions for exchange and collaboration within Europe and internationally (e.g., the European Credits Transfer and Accumulation System).

The Bologna process provides a forum for dialogue regarding higher education reforms and questions related to shared academic principles, such as universities' independence and students' participation in civil society activities. Among the latter, tirocinio (sometimes also referred to as "stage"; most closely aligned with unpaid internships) and co-ops have gained interest and participation from students educational institutions and employers (Reinalda & Kulesza, 2006).

Starting with an analysis of European directives regarding university-community relations and the consequent social engagement of universities, we will analyze EL opportunities provided to students from the Master's degree in Geography and Territorial Processes at the University of Bologna to trace how the process has since been implemented and formalized. It should be noted that EL, in particular, is emerging terminology that is not consistently used but gaining currently to encompass a wide variety of arrangements including those noted above. In this context, one of the instruments that can be considered as a form of EL is the so-called tirocinio, a sort of internship which cannot be straightforwardly compared to the North American experiences as it takes on several formal characteristics peculiar to the Italian case. To illustrate how the Italian scenario unfolds, we must consider the formal relationships among European, national, and local institutions and dynamics among universities, employers, and communities.

On the institutional relationships side, a significant area of investigation is the role of the European Union and its work on higher education reforms. As mentioned, through the Bologna Process and its implementation, the EU created the EHEA – European Higher Education Area. EHEA provides recommendations and indications toward more homogeneous, coherent, and comparable educational systems across countries. While the process involves working on the university's traditional missions of teaching and conducting research, for the scope of this contribution, we want to focus the attention on the notion that universities aim support the social, economic, and cultural development of local communities as well as their international reach by adapting their research interests, teaching content, and increasing knowledge/expertise mobilization (De Jong et al., 2014; Secundo et al., 2017; Agasisti et al., 2019), i.e., the so-called "Third Mission", as it is commonly referred to in the European context (Abreu et al., 2016; Urdari et al., 2017) The motivations and rationale for the third mission (TM) are many and varied, including: the rise of the knowledge economy, the impacts of globalization, financial crises, and climate change. Each in their own way began to influence the higher education sector before the Bologna Process and have since also been formalized as rationales for the development of the pan-European higher education harmonization movement (Trencher et al., 2014; El Hadidi et al., 2016; Rubens et al., 2017).

This renewed request to embrace the TM has supported and revamped the articulation of a dialogue among universities, economic actors, government institutions, and society in general (Vorley et al., 2009; Predazzi, 2012; Giuri et al., 2019) and has been recognized as increasingly important (Benneworth et al., 2015). However, its definitions and illustrations are unclear and ambiguous (Gregersen et al., 2009; Laredo, 2007; Pinheiro et al., 2015). Several concepts already adopted by the discussion on the new role of universities were present, such as the "entrepreneurial university," "technology transfer," and the "triple helix" model of partnerships (Trencher et al., 2014), making it difficult to appreciate the need for yet a further conceptualization. Furthermore, universities across Europe show a substantial level of heterogeneity persisting from pre-reform organizational arrangements, national and local laws and regulations the European level has to deal with, capabilities and resources, management styles, and community connections (among other considerations), raising concerns about the possibility of elaborating a standardized model to implement across countries (Kitagawa et al., 2016; Secundo et al., 2018). Moreover, critical analyses of how universities adopt the TM are lacking (Benneworth et al., 2016). For instance, while the use and evolution of internships have increased significantly over the past decades as a means for companies to access a talent pool and for students to gain relevant skills and experience, not all internships fulfill their purposes. According to a Eurobarometer survey, four out of ten people aged eighteen to thirty-five have had at least one internship experience, and up to 21 per cent have had four or more (European Commission, Flash Eurobarometer 378, November 2013). However, out of 4.5 million students and graduates doing an internship each year in Europe, 30 per cent have no formal learning content, 59 per cent are unpaid, less than 46 per cent of those who are paid receive financial compensation sufficient to cover basic living costs, and only 27 per cent of interns received a job offer after their internship.

The TM seems to be simultaneously a crucial turning point for higher education institutions but also an area needing innovation and organizational change (Laredo, 2007). Interestingly, on the European Higher Education Area website www.ehea.info, among the several task forces and working groups activated, none appears to focus explicitly on EL or Work-Integrated Learning (WIL). And the analysis of the implementation reports periodically published to assess the status of the process, there is no mention of EL, internship, co-op, or other such community experiences. The lack of conceptual and practical frameworks and suggestions from the EU and the absence of an articulated evaluation plan make the full adoption of this recommendation problematic and challenging at the national and local levels (Compagnucci & Spigarelli, 2020).

Despite that the Italian academic context follows these trends, where EL still lacks a shared conceptualization, there is a clear implementation of standards and regulated practices to manage the town-gown relationship, at least for curricular *tirocini* (see below). This aspect largely results from the governance characteristics and the relations among decision-making bodies in the Italian system and constitutes a distinctive feature of this system. In Italy, the university system is public (with a few private institutions operating in the sector) and primarily funded by the national government (through the *Fondo per il Finanziamento ordinario* provided by the Ministry of University and Research). Therefore, the national level is deeply involved in each local university's overall design and functioning. Specifically, the national level oversees the two pillars that guarantee degrees' and qualifications' legal value and educational quality and consistency: on the one hand, the national and public ranking of professors, which is uniform in terms of recruitment procedures and legal configurations (with some autonomy granted to universities regarding employment relationships, as per the Law 240/2010); on the other hand, the national framework of degrees' and qualifications' areas, clusters, and titles, and the didactics system. Recent examples of governmental interventions that reshaped the national system are the comprehensive reform (Law 240/2010, or "Gelmini reform") that changed universities' institutional governance and internal organization and the Ministerial decree n.270/04 (and following updates), which formalized even more the intent to focus on students' employability by tuning programs and curricula to respond to labour market needs.

Furthermore, the Italian governance system presents a regional constitutional arrangement of twenty Regions and two autonomous Provinces. Five of those Regions hold a special status (*Regioni a statuto speciale*) that grants them increased autonomy. In 2001, the constitutional reform

(Constitutional Law n. 3/2001 of October 18, 2001) provided the other fiftheen Regions with more concurrent legislative powers and the opportunity to negotiate with the central government on specific policy competencies, increasing the complexity of the decision-making processes and the heterogeneity of the general management of the educational system.

On the other side, universities are afforded significant autonomy guaranteed by the Italian Constitution (Uricchio, 2022). Article n.9 commits the Government to support the development of scientific research, and article n.33 guarantees freedom of intellectual expression and, simultaneously, universities' autonomy of research and teaching organizational and functional arrangements. This statement supports two distinct concepts: freedom of teaching regarding the methodological and content profile (the so-called "teaching autonomy") and freedom of education concerning the organizational and structural sphere, including research activities and knowledge transmission. Such a norm, linked to the tradition and history of Italian academic institutions, is peculiar to the Italian system and one of the reasons why it is challenging – let alone whether it is desirable or supported – to achieve standardization of TM relations and EL experiences. Nonetheless, as Buzzelli and Songsore (2022) highlight, capturing universities' plans is a crucial research task to inform the analysis of their commitment and direction to adapting definitions of university relevance and impact. Examining the case of the University of Bologna – one of the most advanced academic scenarios in Italy, even regarding the offer of EL – can shed some light on this topic and help identify what crucial aspects should be considered to improve while examining town-gown relations.

Within this multi-level system, the most significant form of EL is the *tirocinio formativo* (or internship). Compared to other countries and the North American experience, the tirocinio in Italy is characterized by a higher degree of formalization and standardization. As Marrone reports (2018), in Italy, most commonly, they are characterized by a top-down institutional approach. The Italian system includes two types of tirocinio: extra-curricular and curricular; the latter being our focus here. The extra-curricular tirocinio, a form of post-graduate internship, aims to create direct relations between the host company or organization and the student, aiming at enriching knowledge, acquiring professional skills and accessing the labour force. It consists of a two to six-month period of orientation and training that does not constitute a formal employment relationship (similar to an apprenticeship). For this type of internship, a cash reimbursement is established on a regional basis and the university plays the role of the promoter by encouraging companies to place graduates in the labour market, mediating between people with specific professional profiles and adequate organizations. As a form of protection from exploitation, there are some limitations by which employers and students must abide. For instance, it is prohibited for internships to involve activities that are regulated through professional boards or colleges and an organization cannot propose a tirocinio to a graduate who has worked for the host company or organization as an employee or with any other form of contract in the previous two years.

The other form of tirocinio, which is more inherent to our research, is the curricular model. This model is directly integrated into university curricula and can be recognized with degree credits. As mentioned above, this stream is based upon a high level of regulation that we consider a distinguishing characteristic of the Italian system. The reader might also appreciate the path through which the relationship between university courses and hosting organizations unfolds, with a clear leadership role played by the educational institution. Curricular practical internships are promoted following the regulations of the study course in which the student is enrolled. The study course's educational regulations define the internship schedule within the course plan, the number of credits attributed, the specific training objectives, and the assessment method. Curricular internships are promoted based on a program defining their training and organizational content and drafted in agreement between the academic tutor and the host organization's supervisor.[1] In the Italian system, it is possible to identify different types of curricular internships. The experience just illustrated is considered the typical curricular internship, where students acquire credits while receiving professional training and hands-on opportunities aligned with the educational plans of the specific study course of enrollment and characterized by the finalization of practical activities carried out in university structures (for instance, research centres) or community organizations in Italy or abroad. In addition, there are internship experiences tailored to preparing the final thesis based on a project designed with the academic tutor and the organization supervisor as well as mandatory internships in association with professions and external accreditation bodies (e.g., engineering, psychology, architecture, etc.).

Most internships are allocated to Master's students, for whom internships may be optional or mandatory due to their function as an employment opportunity. Unlike extra-curricular internships, the curricular ones are therefore characterized by their integration with training courses. Thus, the management of internships is a prerogative of educational institutions, as guaranteed by Law 92/2012. The aspect that emerges as central is the focus on internships as a tool for formalizing skills and qualifying students for the job market. Also, unlike in the US experience, where internships may continue to be activated informally (Perlin, 2011), or the Canadian scenario, in which co-ops and internships are mostly driven by employers' needs and expectations and post-secondary institutions adapt their educational offer to them, host companies or organizations in the Italian curricular tirocinio undergo a bureaucratic process involving intermediaries as prescribed by law and activated by institutions.

Another characteristic of the Italian system that must be considered because of its ability to increase complexity if not regulated is its regional fragmentation. Italian regionalism manifests here through local autonomy in regulating and promotion of internships as well as local socio-economic and labour market contexts. The different policies applied in a discretionary manner by the regions play a decisive role in characterizing the forms and number of internships, especially in the function of the substantial difference in resources invested and the different degrees of rigidity of the regulation. Companies, therefore, find themselves interacting with a non-homogeneous regulation, which encourages or discourages the opening of internships, depending on the case.

The Emilia-Romagna Region, where the University of Bologna is located, has adopted stringent regulations about internships to mitigate this complexity and discourage the abuse of this tool by implementing the formalization of the learning activities connected to *tirocini.* In this regard, a system of qualifications was standardized, i.e., a discrete division into areas of competence, which, according to the institutions, would have the role of increasing the employability of the interns and reducing the autonomy of companies in interpreting the legislation to exploit it in their favour. As a result of the reorganization of the regulations on internships carried out on a regional basis and as defined by Law 92/2012, a system of assessment of learning and skills acquired was also introduced. Once the internship has been completed, the university office meets the trainee to ascertain that the internship has been carried out according to the training plan and that these planned skills have been acquired.

In this context, the University of Bologna can be considered a large institution in a medium-small city (Lazzeroni & Piccaluga, 2015). Given the many graduates each year, the relations between educational and research structures and the community can trigger substantial development opportunities and various labour market saturation issues. The University has strongly influenced the urban conformation through its spatial organization and economic and social development. The university's presence has generated a series of relationships that have led to a dense network of relationships among community organizations, companies, and training facilities. This manifests itself in different forms. For the focus of our research, we are interested in analyzing the relationships built between the university – with educational and TM goals – and the local/regional area, being developed through the expansion of EL, as well as the consequences for both parties of such relationships.

Geographical Education and Experiential Learning: The Case of the Master's Degree in Geography and Territorial Processes

It is important to bear in mind that the University of Bologna and Emilia-Romagna experience is unique for at least three reasons: (a) for its focus on graduate level EL; (b) for the highly formalized process through which arrangements are usually made, and (c) for the involvement of stakeholders and other relevant subjects of the area/region, that offer to university students opportunities to conduct an EL activity. A mix of data and evidence offers insights into the operation of EL, again specifically curricular tirocinio, including a community partner survey undertaken by the Geography program in March and April 2021 to examine the opinions of local key actors on their experience with the trainees coming from this Master's Program. University administrative data and further in-depth interviews with survey respondents furnish additional insights.

There are various forms of EL that can be identified in this context, but as noted above the focus here is curricular tirocinio/internship. As mentioned earlier, the placement system is highly standardized. A centralized university office handles requests from students and professors while advertising opportunities arrive from community partners. In addition, each department or course of study has a list of community partners and organizations with which they have already collaborated in the past. Then, the centralized office formalizes applications and maintains relations with the host organizations.

The university program *Geografia e processi territoriali* (Geography and Territorial Processes, or simply Geography) is a two-year Master's course established in 2005 following the Italian university reform that reorganized the higher education system according to the Bologna Process and the European Higher Education Area. The curriculum provides for fifteen learning activities (eight per year) plus a final dissertation and offers two different thematic areas, the first one focusing on human geography and offering subjects such as political, economic, urban, and environmental geography; the second one aimed at developing technical expertise in the field of geomatics and specifically in GIS and remote sensing.

Since its foundation and in line with ministerial guidelines, the Master's program provides the opportunity to include an EL activity in the second year through *tirocinio curricolare* as a choice in the set of fiftheen learning activities. The tirocinio is an internship of at least 150 hours held in a public institution or a private company of the area/region (or even abroad) and is aimed at allowing students to experience some specific labour activities in a working environment, thus, enabling the exchange between the University and the territorial milieu of its area, promoting an exchange of competencies and knowledge.

The administrative records of all tirocini/internships carried out by the students since the academic year 2009/2010 that we analyzed shed light on the trends and foci of tirocinio placements. In general, the Geography program enrols about sixty to eighty students per year. Because of the structure of the curriculum, the tirocinio is an optional learning activity selected by a limited number of students per year. Since 2009/2010, a total of 137 tirocinio experiences have been carried out. Figure 9.1 overviews the distribution of these internships over the years, highlighting variable but continuous interest in this learning activity. It is also helpful to highlight the incidence of students carrying out a tirocinio as a proportion of the total amount of students per year (Figure 9.2): data on the total amount of students are available only from the academic year 2013/2014, but the trend reproduces what is shown in Figure 9.1, with a peak in 2018/2019 and a dramatic decline in 2019/2020 – due to both the effect of the COVID pandemic and a significant increase in the number of students in the Master's program (from seventy-three in 2018/2019, to ninety-five in 2019/2020, to 152 in 2020/2021, to 180 in 2020/2021).

Among the 137 tirocinio activities implemented from 2009/2010, seventy-seven concerned experiences in cartography and remote sensing and sixty encompassed experiences related to human geography. Also, eighty-three were conducted at public institutions such as municipalities, ministries, or public research institutions; nine were carried out in universities; twenty-five in NGOs, associations or foundations; and twenty at privately owned companies. Students wishing to conduct a tirocinio can choose between public institutions and private companies with an agreement with the School of Humanities. Alternatively, they can select another institution or company whose activities are congruent with the educational goals of the Master's course. In this case, a new agreement must be established between the university and the selected institution or company. In the context of ongoing research projects in collaboration

Figure 9.1. Number of Internships Carried Out by the Students of the Master's Degree in Geography and Territorial Processes Since the Academic Year 2009–10

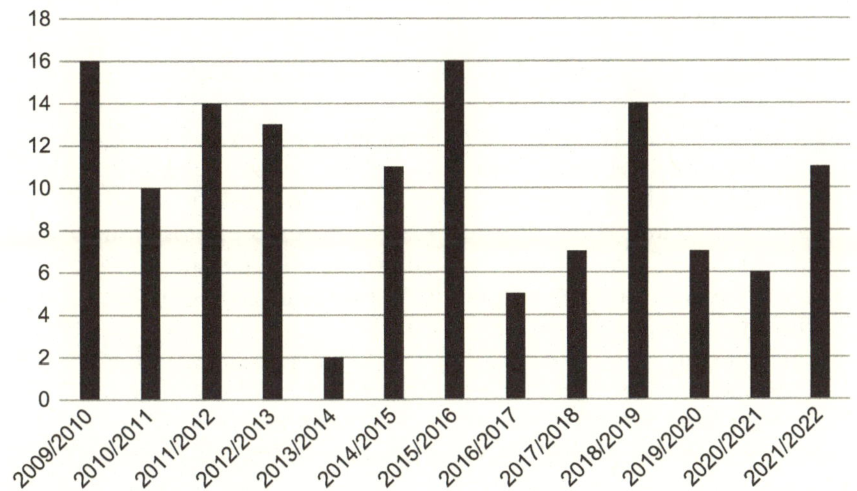

Source: Administrative data.

Figure 9.2. Incidence of the Internships Carried Out by the Students of the Master's Degree in Geography and Territorial Processes as a Proportion of Total Students of the Course per Year

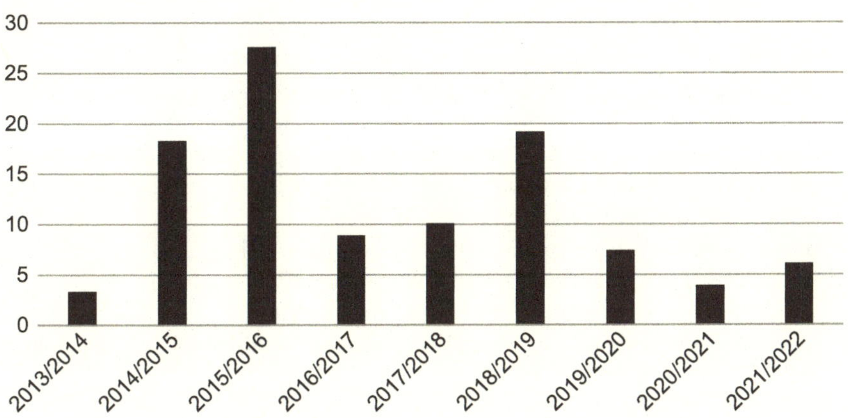

between the university and external institutions or companies, students can also apply to open calls for internships related to a specific topic.

Some examples of the EL/tirocini placements are:

- A 2017 and 2018 partnership between the Geography department and the Emilia-Romagna Regional office of the Ministry of Culture, included four internships aimed at creating a cultural heritage database to geolocate the type and location of assets of various heritage types in the region. The students' work involved GIS software and analyzing historical maps and aerial photography for implementing information on heritage sites. Three students among those involved have since signed temporary employment contracts with the same institution.[2]
- A partnership established with the *ARPAE – Agenzia Prevenzione Ambiente Energia Emilia-Romagna* (Agency for the Environmental Protection and Energy), where, since 2018, four students have conducted their internship relating to climate change impacts and power supply. In this case, technical and humanistic skills were required to develop the research projects. For instance, a study considered the impact of climate change on Protected Designation of Origin (PDO) wine production, requiring comprehensive knowledge of the economic and social geography and historical information about the production and the competence to integrate this information into a predictive model. After the tirocinio, one student received an offer for a temporary contract.
- The cartographic offices of Bologna Municipality and Emilia-Romagna Regional Government are also a consolidated place for tirocini in the field of GIS and remote sensing, with projects related to geo-referring and digitization of urban plans, urban transformation, and land planning. In this case, the required skills are related to technical competencies with reference, in particular, to the employment of GIS and remote sensing. All three students who have conducted a tirocinio at this institution were hired for temporary positions in the same office.
- Students selected to conduct their tirocinio in urban and participatory planning and physical geography and morphology studies. An example of the former is the *Fondazione per l'innovazione urbana* (Foundation for Urban Innovation). Established in Bologna in 2018, this institution originates from a collaboration between the municipality and the university and aims to develop inclusive and participatory processes in urban planning. A student who carried out a tirocinio on the topic of participatory planning was hired by

the foundation after the conclusion of his Master's course. Examples from the second field are the *INGV – Istituto Nazionale di Geofisica e Vulcanologia* (National Institute for Geophysics and Vulcanology) and the *ENEA – Agenzia Nazionale per le nuove tecnologie, l'energia e lo sviluppo economico sostenibile* (National Agency for new technologies, power supply, and sustainable economic development), where students spent their internships working on the implementation of GIS and photogrammetry projects.

- In addition, a number of tirocini experiences have been undertaken at private companies and foundations/associations. The former include technical GIS and remote sensing skills such as with E-Gea which specializes in aerial photogrammetry and remote sensing analysis in precision agriculture. For private foundations/agencies, one example is the regional network *Associazione Campi Aperti per la sovranità alimentare* (Open Field Association for Food Sovereignty), a cluster of independent farmers which produce organic food and aim at avoiding commercial supply chains, promoting local economies and sustainable food production.

In Spring of 2021, the Master's degree program undertook its first self-study of the tirocinio/internship program with a survey of partners to document and understand their views on students' education and knowledge levels. Out of sixty evaluation questionnaires sent via email, thirty-five responses were obtained. Respondents included geographical associations, public institutions, university departments or research centres, and private companies. Activities ranged from producing maps to drafting specialized texts and performing territorial and enhancement studies. A majority of the respondents were *very satisfied* with the work conducted by the trainees and, as indicated in Figure 9.3, felt their skills contributed to the organization/company. In-depth interviews were undertaken with four respondents. Insights from the interviews are limited given the small number, however, partners generally expressed that they were able to entrust the students with work and an interest in continuing to participate in the tirocinio process.

Discussion

One of the most interesting aspects of our study is related to the positive outcomes, in terms of job offers and contracts, achieved by students operating within situations of strong relationships between university courses and hosting organizations. It seems clear that spending time and resources in building a continuous and productive conversation with

Figure 9.3. Evaluation of the Pieces of Knowledge and Competencies of the Students Conducting a *Tirocinio* by the Company or Institution Hosting the Students of the Master's Degree in Geography and Territorial Processes

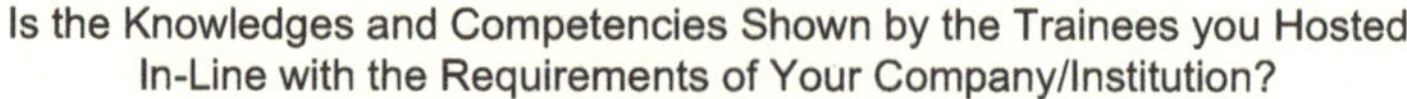

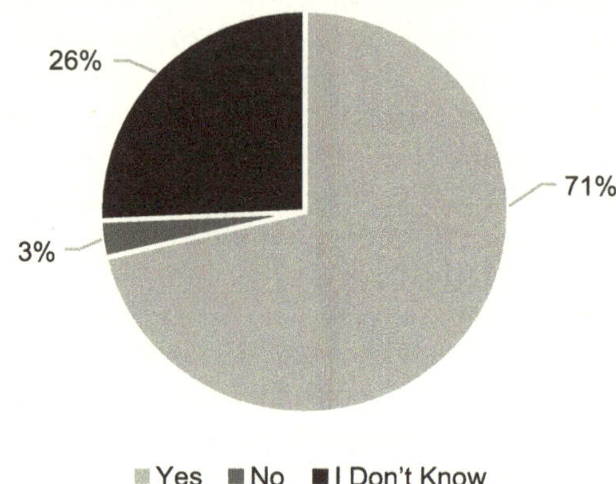

Source: Data from the survey conducted between March and April 2021.

community organizations, institutions, and businesses benefits and generates returns for all parties as students are prepared to meet hosts' needs and expectations, and organizations are ready to welcome, guide, and support students with meaningful tasks and targeted outcomes. Additionally, offering a straightforward connection between course contents and EL allows students to translate the knowledge acquired more easily into community organizations, with clear benefits for hosting organizations, communities, and the economy. Finally, strong control of processes and relationships before, during, and after the EL experience (e.g., through evaluation interviews) contributes to avoiding student exploitation, the substitution of actual workers with students, and the assignment of meaningless tasks. This benefits all the parties involved, including processes, results, behaviours, outcomes, and constant support of standardization and quality improvements. In these respects, Chapter 9 provides a first window on some of the necessary processes and resources needed for successful EL in local governance. Chapters 10 and 11 each furnish further respective windows on local and associative forms of EL stewardship.

That said, these are early moments in the development of a wider breadth of EL opportunities for Master's students at the University of Bologna. In the context of higher education reforms, the growing variety of potential partners and placement types is generating a number of challenges that must be confronted.

Multi-scalar pressures and opportunities suggest that EL will have to be understood and defined more concretely, particularly as it evolves out of the history of tirocinio as locally practiced. A particular challenge here is the pressure on the university to demonstrate its commitment to and delivery of the TM in response to European higher education reforms while also satisfying such constraints as national labour market legislation. At present, faced with the rising influence of EL as an academic movement, the Bologna case demonstrates that local history and experience will have to confront and reconcile pressures from outside the region. One question here, for example, is how student placements will evolve as universities seek to respond to EL and TM goals, particularly those concerning the institution's contribution to local economic development while avoiding undue impacts on the local labour market (Marrone, 2018).

Relatedly, a second challenge concerns the power dynamics at play among all key parties. As alluded to earlier, a large university in a relatively smaller urban region exerts influence and holds power in community relationships. The history of tirocinio bears study in its own right in this respect. Going forward, administrators and observers should be tuned to if and how power relations are reproduced or reshaped in the face of reform and regulatory pressures. Italian local and national institutions should engage in dialogues around needs and expectations but also capabilities of all the key interested actors, including students, university instructors and course developers, community organizations and local institutions, and national-level decision-makers to design policies that can support the implementation of the Bologna Process while remaining committed to local needs and priorities. If EL is the right way to support students' employability, how should university programs design it? How should community organizations and local economic networks be consulted and their needs be met? Who should initiate the process? And what should the driver be: the economic needs of companies and organizations or the learning outcomes and educational goals of the academic program? Finally, how should we reconcile universities' intellectual autonomy and long-term educational goals with partners' expectations and short-term needs? The answers to these questions not only impact the relationship between the university and various community partners but also the learner. As the Italian university system diversifies to reflect an ever-changing population, attention should be paid to the diversity and inclusiveness of these EL dynamics: for which students are selected and how they are placed with community organizations, what their self-assessment is of their experiences and what impact these opportunities have on their learning outcomes and post-graduation trajectories.

Finally, the early implementation of these wider reforms and processes suggests evaluation and course correction will play an important role beyond these initial experiences. Yet, it seems difficult to support, improve, and reproduce the EL system due, to start, to the lack of systemic evaluation plans (at the European, national, and local levels), with the consequent gap in available data. The limited data presented above may indicate the difficulty of undertaking fulsome evaluation by academic programs that are concerned primarily with the core mandate of teaching and curriculum. Self-study and evaluation are necessary for course correction. For example, as noted earlier, increasing formalization and standardization of placements have the potential to make EL placements more appealing and accessible to more students. Knowing if and how this will have transpired can only be understood through program evaluation.

NOTES

1 UniBo page: https://www.unibo.it/it/servizi-e-opportunita/tirocini/tirocini-curriculari-1.

2 In Italy, permanent jobs in public organizations can only be obtained through public selections, which involve significant resources and are relatively slow. At the same time, temporary contracts constitute a more agile tool public organizations use for specific roles or tasks (like the ones created for the hired interns).

REFERENCES

Abreu, M., Demirel, P., Grinevich, V., & Karataş-Özkan, M. (2016). Entrepreneurial practices in research-intensive and teaching-led universities. *Small Business Economy, 47*(3), 695–717.

Agasisti, T., Barra, C., & Zotti, R. (2019). Research, knowledge transfer, and innovation: the effect of Italian universities' efficiency on local economic development 2006–2012. *Journal of Regional Science, 59*(5), 819–49.

Benneworth, P., de Boer, H., & Jongbloed, B. (2015). Between good intentions and urgent stakeholder pressures: Institutionalizing the universities' third mission in the Swedish context. *European Journal of Higher Education, 5*(3), 280–96.

Benneworth, P., Pinheiro, R., & Sánchez-Barrioluengo, M. (2016). One size does not fit all! New perspectives on the university in the social knowledge economy. *Science and Public Policy, 43*(6), 731–5.

Buzzelli, M., & Songsore, E. (2022). Differentiated visions: How Ontario universities see and represent their futures. *Canadian Journal of Educational Administration and Policy*, 198, 111–23.

Compagnucci, L., & F. Spigarelli, F. (2020). The Third Mission of the university: A systematic literature review on potentials and constraints. *Technological Forecasting and Social Change*, 161, 1–30.

De Jong, S., Barker, K., Cox, D., Sveinsdottir, T., & Van Den Besselaar, P. (2014). Understanding societal impact through productive interactions: ICT research as a case. *Research Evaluation, 23*(2), 89–102.

El Hadidi, H. E., & Kirby, D. A. (2016). Universities and innovation in a factor-driven economy: The performance of universities in Egypt. *Industry & Higher Education, 30*(2), 140–8.

Giuri, P., Munari, F., Scandura, A., & Toschi, L. (2019). The strategic orientation of universities in knowledge transfer activities. *Technological Forecasting & Social Change*, 138, 261–78.

Gregersen, B., Linde, L. T., & Rasmussen, J. G. (2009). Linking between Danish universities and society. *Science and Public Policy, 36*(2), 151–6.

Kitagawa, F., Barrioluengo, M. S., & Uyarra, E. (2016). Third mission as institutional strategies: Between isomorphic forces and heterogeneous pathways. *Science and Public Policy, 43*(6), 736–50.

Laredo, P. (2007). Revisiting the Third Mission of universities: Toward a renewed categorization of university activities? *Higher Education Policy, 20*(4), 441–56.

Lazzeroni, M., & Piccaluga, A. (2015). Beyond "town and gown": The role of the university in small and medium-sized cities. *Industry and Higher Education, 29*(1), 11–23.

Marrone, M. (2018, January 25–7). *L'economia del tirocinio. Tirocinio e informalizzazione del lavoro in Emilia-Romagna* [Conference presentation]. II Convegno annuale SISEC, Milano.

Perlin, R. (2011). *Intern nation: How to earn nothing and learn little in the brave new economy.* Verso.

Pinheiro, R., Langa, P. V., & Pausits, A. (2015). One and two equals three? The third mission of higher education institutions. *European Journal of Higher Education, 5*(3), 233–49.

Predazzi, E. (2012). The third mission of the university. *Rendiconti. Lincei*, 23, 17–22.

Reinalda, B., & Kulesza, E. (2006). *The bologna process – harmonizing Europe's higher education: Including the essential original texts.* Verlag Barbara Budrich.

Rubens, A., Spigarelli, F., Cavicchi, A., & Rinaldi, C. (2017). Universities' third mission and the entrepreneurial university and the challenges they bring to higher education institutions. *Journal of Enterprising Communities*, 11, 354–72.

Secundo, G., De Beer, C., Schutte, C. S., & Passiante, G. (2017). Mobilising intellectual capital to improve European universities' competitiveness: The technology transfer offices' role. *Journal of Intellectual Capital, 18*(3), 607–24.

Secundo, G., Massaro, M., Dumay, J., & Bagnoli, C. (2018). Intellectual capital management in the fourth stage of IC research: A critical case study in university settings. *Journal of Intellectual Capital, 19*(1), 157–77.

Trencher, G., Yarime, M., McCormick, K. B., Doll, C. N., & Kraines, S. B. (2014). Beyond the third mission: exploring the emerging university function of co-creation for sustainability. *Science and Public Policy, 41*(2), 151–79.

Urdari, C., Farcas, T., & Tiron Tudor, A. (2017). Assessing the legitimacy of HEIs' contributions to society: The perspective of international rankings. *Sustainability Accounting, Management and Policy Journal, 8*(2), 191–215.

Uricchio, A. F., (2022). Autonomia universitaria e valutazione. *Osservatorio Costituzionale* 2/2022. https://www.osservatorioaic.it/images/rivista/pdf/2022_2_05_Uricchio.pdf

Vorley, T., & Nelles, J. (2009). Building entrepreneurial architectures: A conceptual interpretation of the third mission. *Policy Futures in Education, 7*(3), 284–96.

10 Experiential Learning for Sustainability: Grand Challenges and Local Communities

GUUS DIX, CORELIA BAIBARAC-DUIGNAN, AND BEN JONGBLOED

University of Twente, Netherlands

Introduction

Increasingly, universities and colleges are asked to rethink how they encourage their students to become entrepreneurial, engaged and responsible citizens who are able to tackle big societal challenges. University and college researchers, in turn, are encouraged to come up with new knowledge, technologies and tools for achieving a more inclusive and sustainable society. Surely, societal challenges constitute wicked problems (Head & Alford, 2015) around sustainable development, equity, and inclusiveness. By definition, wicked problems are complex, unpredictable, and resistant to conclusive solutions and, thus, require iterative approaches that address components of the whole problem (Head & Alford, 2015). The complexity of these problems manifests itself at many levels – from urban and regional development to national and global dimensions.

Universities have the potential – the responsibility even – to better prepare their students as future change agents with a mind and skill-set to create local solutions for such complex problems and reflect on their global consequences. To realize this potential, however, universities will need to change (some of) their education portfolio and teaching methods. Specifically, there is a need for new pedagogical content and approaches that go beyond the traditional discipline-oriented and university-internal focus. Through these new content and approaches, students can be challenged to go beyond their campus surroundings and learn outside the classroom in contexts where they can fruitfully combine practical experiences, theoretical learning outcomes, and other ways of knowing and learning.

The focus of this chapter is on current experiments with these new pedagogical approaches in teaching and learning. It asks what unites these bottom-up experiments and what *institutional transformation* on the part of the university is required to further embed and foster them? In our theory section that follows, we first discuss the call on universities to become "societally relevant" and elaborate on the idea of a "civic university" as a response to that call. Subsequently, we discuss a variety of innovative learning approaches that have been implemented in practice, such as challenge-based learning (CBL), community-engaged learning (CEL), and education for sustainable development (ESD). What all these models have in common, we argue, is the central place of experiential learning (EL): students are encouraged to address societal issues through engaging with different communities of stakeholders and to learn by critically *reflecting* on their experiences in addressing such issues.

The conceptual triad, engagement, reflection and institutional transformation, will structure our empirical sections. These sections draw on the authors' experiences with introducing pedagogical innovations at the University of Twente in the Netherlands. The common element of the three cases studied here (University of Twente, n.d.), is their emphasis on EL, which makes them different from – though not opposed to – more classical modes of teaching and learning. In each of our three cases, we focus on the objective of engagement and reflection as key elements in EL. In doing so, we particularly analyze the bottom-up motivations for such innovations as well as their institutional enablers and barriers.

In the concluding section, finally, we seek to derive general conclusions about institutional transformation from our cases that might be useful for other universities embarking on a transformative journey. We highlight some of the challenges and tensions around integrating EL into curricula: what institutional transformations are needed to further integrate and foster engaged EL approaches in universities?

A Theory of Experiential Learning

New Calls on Universities

There are increased calls made on universities and colleges to become more relevant in society – to redraw the social contract between universities and society (see Chapter 1 in this volume). In today's environment, it is not only about what a particular university is "good at" in terms of the quality of its research and teaching but also about what it is "good for" (Boulton & Lucas, 2008) in terms of its active contribution to the wider society. With roots in science policy, national and international policymakers have been pushing scientific research in the past fifteen years to contribute to the economic competitiveness of their countries and continents (Berman, 2007).

Without abandoning the strong economic focus in policymaking circles, the emphasis in the past decade has shifted towards broader societal challenges (Grau et al., 2017) and missions (Mazzucato, 2018). The societal dimension of universities is particularly relevant when universities are predominantly funded from the public purse. Funding authorities expect universities to also contribute to the public good, that is, the wider society at a regional and global level (Marginson, 2011). Bringing the university closer to society – the region, the community, external stakeholders – is manifested, for instance, in concepts such as the *civic university* (Goddard et al., 2016) and the responsible university (Biesta, 2013; Benneworth, 2019).

From Call to Action: Three Pedagogical Innovations for the Civic University

A responsible, civic university is engaged with the city, its region, and its broader communities. Such universities collaborate with public authorities and public service organizations (e.g., hospitals, social care, schools), charities and social enterprises. They integrate teaching, research and engagement with society, so that each enhances the other (Figure 10.1). Research has socio-economic impact and teaching has a strong involvement of external communities with the long-term objective of widening participation in higher education and recognizing the value of non-academic and transdisciplinary forms of knowledge produced outside the university. In this quest for university-community interaction at the civic university, several new pedagogical approaches have been developed. Below, we highlight the main characteristics of three pedagogical approaches that stand out in particular: community-engaged learning, challenge-based learning, and education for sustainable development.

As part of playing a more visible role in their local community, several universities offer their students education opportunities in the form of *community-engaged learning* (CEL) (Moore, 2010). This activity is situated in the overlapping section of the Teaching and Engagement domains in Figure 10.1. Students who choose to participate in CEL are given the opportunity to do community work, thus connecting the theories and knowledge learned in the classroom to real-world situations outside the classroom. It includes internships, cooperative education (i.e., alternating work and study), site visits, field exercises, and students' thesis work done in collaboration with external parties. These CEL activities do not necessarily have to take place in the nearby communities or town but can

Figure 10.1. The Civic University

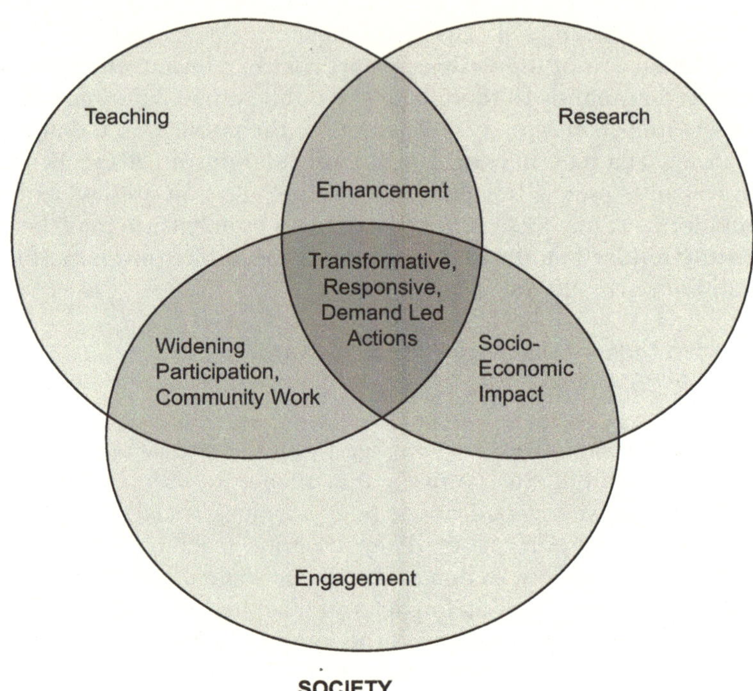

Source: Goddard, J., Hazelkorn, E., Kempton, L. and Vallance P. (2016). The Civic University: The Policy and Leadership Challenges. London: Edward Elgar. Copyright Edward Elgar Publishing. Reproduced with permission of the Licensor through PLSclear.

also happen elsewhere off-campus. Internships or student research projects carried out as part of study abroad experiences or in places beyond the immediate region are also possible.

Challenge-based learning (CBL), our second example, is a transdisciplinary approach to teaching and learning that encourages students to leverage the knowledge they gain to solve real-world wicked problems (Nichols & Cator, 2008; Gallagher & Savage, 2020). In doing so, CBL is meant to bridge the gap between science and practice, while making students aware that valuable knowledge is often produced outside the walls of the university. CBL, therefore, requires the active involvement of several external stakeholders whose perspectives and situations the students can experience. External stakeholders do not only play a role as challenge providers; they are also actively involved in the learning process, as co-creators and co-designers (of the challenge addressed) and as co-assessors (in evaluating the students' work). Moreover, the outcome is typically not centred on the solution to the challenge but rather on the mutual learning achieved through taking part in the process with the students and their co-workers/teachers.

In our third example, Education for Sustainable Development (ESD), the goal is to develop young graduates' skills in addressing sustainable development's complex challenges (Dale & Newman, 2005). The ESD approach feeds into the ever stronger demands placed on universities to address the increasingly complex societal challenges of aging, climate change, inequities, and urban regeneration. These days, these societal challenges are expressed in the language of Sustainable Development Goals (SDGs) (United Nations, 2015). ESD is not only about providing awareness and knowledge of the challenges in delivering on these SDGs but also about using that knowledge to improve local circumstances and implementing solutions in the local context (Molderez & Fonseca, 2018; Leicht et al., 2018), thus, contributing to the public good.

Conditions for Experiential Learning: Engagement, Reflection, and Institutional Transformation

What unites these three innovative pedagogical approaches is a strong experiential element in academic learning. At root, experiential learning (EL) is a process wherein students learn by engaging in hands-on practices outside of the classroom. As such, EL is meant to stimulate academic inquiry among students and promote interdisciplinarity, social engagement, cultural awareness, and leadership. Two key characteristics stand out in learning through experience: engagement and reflection. For these two characteristics to be embedded in universities, institutional transformation is a prerequisite.

Engagement

To become truly transformative in preparing students to become reflexive practitioners, the experiential element in each of the approaches (CEL, CBL, ESD) provides opportunities for students to engage with individuals and groups in a given non-academic context. CEL is a form of engaged "learning by doing". Students and teachers work together on social issues with external partners. It integrates social engagement with academic study and reflection to enrich and enhance the learning experience and contributes to community needs (Utrecht University, n.d.). Engagement is a sizeable component of CBL too. The transdisciplinary learning experience in CBL typically involves multiple stakeholders and several disciplinary perspectives. To address their challenge, students collaborate with fellow students, teachers, and external stakeholders in settings that are often outside the classroom. Education for Sustainable Development considers the gap between theory-driven and practice-based education as a key problem. ESD can take place through internships or similar placements within organizations that work to address sustainability challenges in specific ways. ESD tries to find ways to blend the theory-centred and action-centred elements of education. ESD equips learners to integrate different kinds of knowledge into actionable knowledge in order to solve place-specific local challenges – empowering and inspiring learners and community members to take action using that knowledge to improve local circumstances (Leicht et al. 2018). In other words, ESD stresses engagement.

Reflection

The second characteristic of EL in universities is that students are expected to reflect on their experience – beyond what the experience or the results means for their career development. The aim to enhance the students' ability to critically reflect on the potential implications of their actions in society stands out in all three approaches. In CEL, students are encouraged to reflect critically on their experiences and learning outcomes – at the beginning and at the completion of their EL journey. Learning objectives and competences to be acquired through EL are skills such as taking initiative, making decisions, being accountable for results, and learning from mistakes and successes. In CBL, attention is paid to teaching and practicing self-management, self-awareness, social awareness, reasoning for complexity, communication, and collaboration. These reflective skills are included in the learning goals defined for CBL programs. To acquire these skills, students and teachers take on new roles in educational settings as co-designers, and students are given more responsibility for determining their learning path (Leijon et al., 2021). In ESD, reflection feeds into the aim to create actionable knowledge and to drive change. Five key competencies are singled out to help the students reflect properly: systems thinking, futures thinking (anticipatory competencies), normative thinking, action-oriented thinking, and interpersonal (i.e., collaboration) competencies. These competencies will enable learners to participate meaningfully in local processes and to take control of their own environments (Shephard et al., 2019).

Institutional Transformation

Implementing CEL, CBL, or ESD approaches requires universities to transform their teaching and learning – their pedagogies, curriculum, and their teachers' mindsets – in order to support learners in reflecting on the knowledge acquired and communicated. This reflection can lead to changes in thinking, perceptions, beliefs, and values which can transform how the learners interpret the world around them. Introducing these new pedagogical approaches, however, requires facilitation and leadership from educational institutions – their administration and management – at different levels. The introduction of pedagogical innovations in universities often leads to challenges that can only be met at an institutional level. To address the challenges, universities will have to learn how to work in new ways, reform their teaching and learning models, and encourage their researchers to carry out multi- and transdisciplinary research. For those transformations to take place, universities need to develop new expertise and capacity among their staff. They may need to create new functions and structures, such as living labs and units for educational innovation, or introduce incentives for staff and students to support EL.

Experiential Learning in the University of Twente: Three Cases

Introduction

As discussed above, EL is an essential ingredient of community-engaged learning (CEL), challenge-based learning (CBL), and education for sustainable development (ESD). In this section, we will draw on the conceptual triad "engagement," "reflection," and "institutional transformation" to illustrate how universities are adapting their didactical model through these three pedagogical approaches. Our case is the University of Twente (UT), a mid-sized university (13,000 students) that is located in the east of the Netherlands and offers programs in engineering and social sciences. The UT takes its name from the region Twente in which it is located – a region (area: 40 square kilometers) with 620,000 inhabitants, a quarter of whom live in its largest city, Enschede. The next sections present three courses offered by the university, each of them an example of how the university has tried to incorporate elements of EL to enrich the students' learning experience – helping students become engaged and responsible graduates who are better prepared to address today's grand societal challenges. The three bachelor-level courses we focus on are:

1. *Socio-Technical Futures* – a course that is part of the Advanced Technology degree program
2. *Crossing Borders* – a minor (i.e., an elective course) accessible to all students
3. *Global Crises, Local Challenges* – a minor accessible to all students.

The three courses differ in their pedagogical approach, their partners, and their location, but all of them address the challenges around sustainable development. All three courses incorporate strong elements of engagement and reflection.

Socio-Technical Futures

Socio-Technical Futures (STF) is a course that is a part of the second year of the Advanced Technology Bachelor's program at the UT, closely aligned to a parallel course in which students work on the engineering and management of the development and commercialization of a technology (hereinafter referred to as "innovation"). Furthermore, STF is part of the university's *Reflection on Science, Technology and Society* (RESTS) education, which aims to encourage students throughout their education to reflect on, and critically think about, how science and technology is embedded in society. To support reflection, students are asked to analyze the current socio-technical context of their proposed technological innovation and develop scenarios that articulate potential futures that could unfold out of the implementation of the innovation.

Instead of following theoretical steps from textbooks, the scenario-making process is developed as a challenge-based learning (CBL) approach. Reflecting the experiential dimension of CBL, a key aspect is situating challenges within an authentic real-world context. The course places a specific focus on better defining (re-framing) the challenge for which the students seek solutions, exploring and integrating diverse stakeholder perspectives in their analysis and developing "what if" scenarios. In this approach, *reflection* and *engagement* are closely linked. To better understand the socio-technical context, dig deeper into the "problem", and formulate compelling future scenarios, students need to engage with challenge providers and other relevant stakeholders from outside the university campus. The reflection is not only aimed at students, but also at their stakeholders. To this end, students develop scenarios as tools for reflection. As such, the scenarios are not meant to be predictive but meant to expose dilemmas through plausible stories regarding who might be affected by the innovation and in what way.

Specifically, the scenarios include both narrative forms – e.g., short "what if" stories – and experiential forms – e.g., prototypes or objects from an envisaged future – that can engage a broader audience in discussions around their challenges and how to address them. Rather than having students propose solutions, the aim is to open wider debates regarding desirable courses of action. This move from a solution-oriented mindset towards an open, yet critical, mindset is one important aspect of reflection that characterizes the STF course.

Students are supported in this process through EL settings that encourage them to engage with societal stakeholders and immerse themselves in the challenges and contexts facing such challenges. Methods to be used for this engagement process are discussed and practiced during workshop-lectures. For example, citizen science (Roche et al., 2020) is explored as a way of collecting context-based data and interacting with the challenge providers to explore the different stakeholder perspectives and values. Students organize an interactive exhibition at the end of the course as a way to further engage with stakeholders and other visitors and collect their reflections.

EL feeds into the development of scenarios in three ways. First, students engage with stakeholders' experiences and perspectives, in particular their challenges. This is done in mapping sessions with challenge providers, bringing them together with students and teachers in a different setting than the usual classroom. These sessions take place at the DesignLab, a facility linked to the university that has the role of fostering connections with society and providing a platform for multidisciplinary collaboration, innovation, and creativity. Second, citizen science is used as a way for students to collect context-based data and study the challenge in its context. This activity takes place on campus in experiential sessions, but there are also student-organized site visits and ad-hoc mini-interviews that students conduct with citizens "on the street" to gauge their views on the challenges. Thirdly, in the STF course's concluding learning experiences, students are encouraged to critically think about their STF work as part of their reflection activities. This reflection takes place during the course's final exhibition event and is included in the students' final report.

Despite the fact that the CBL approach includes methods to achieve a deeper level of engagement, it tends to remain a difficult task for students. CBL requires different mindsets, learning settings and learning skills than those typically expected in mainstream text- and classroom lecture-based approaches. Developing capacities for engaging with multiple disciplinary perspectives and interacting with societal stakeholders requires a broader *institutional transformation* that gives students more opportunities for EL. Students, therefore, will directly experience the challenges facing stakeholders of different backgrounds and different roles in society. An openness for wider implementation of CBL formats at the bachelor level will then be required from the institution, including receptiveness to less traditional forms of assessment of reflection skills and group work as opposed to content-based individual assessments. Only then can CBL accomplish its transformative potential.

Crossing Borders

Crossing Borders is an elective (a *minor*) program at the University launched in 2015. Bachelor students are offered an international experience through an internship abroad, where they work with people from different cultural and disciplinary backgrounds. The program's rationale is to have students experience what it means to address an SDG-related challenge while working off-campus on a project in a private or public organization typically located in the Global South. The program's name alludes to the various kinds of borders that students must cross to successfully pass the module, including geographical and disciplinary borders, the border between technological and social innovation, and cultural borders. They will do so through team-work and multi-disciplinary project work.

While Crossing Borders builds on the idea of ESD (see above), it incorporates a broader agenda of issues, objectives and methodologies, and responds directly to the increasing interest across the university sector and among students in engaging with the SDGs. Students generally carry out an external placement (a "field study") where they individually carry out a small research project while working as a volunteer. Their host is typically a civil society organization, often a nongovernmental organization (NGO), a hospital, school, or community-based organization. Each student is allocated an academic supervisor, assisting with practical project planning and assessing two final reports. Most placements are abroad, although there is also a remote working option, with students doing a project with partners from abroad while staying in their home university.

The EL that is part of the Crossing Borders course is fostering the student's personal and professional development. The *engagement* element of the course consists of the work that students do with professionals in their host organization, where they complete a self-initiated project, collecting data and carrying out field work. They spend several hours a week volunteering in an organization, supporting it, and experiencing people and situations in environments that will differ from their own community and home university. The student's research project can be seen as a form of engaged, community-based research. Supervised by their academic supervisor and a representative of their field study organization, students cooperate with local organizations and conduct studies to meet the needs of a particular organization or community. Thus, students gain direct experience in the research process. Their projects explore how a particular SDG is being addressed in practice. Examples of tasks undertaken have included introducing interactive elements – e.g., through gamification or creative work – in a primary school's curriculum, designing facilities in an institute for disabled youth, contributing to an NGO's campaign to encourage healthy living, developing communication campaigns for a social enterprise, and participating in social credit and community investment schemes.

Key to this form of EL is a proper preparation and some type of guided *reflection*. The cultural immersion provides students with novel challenges for navigating life in a new environment and working with people from different cultural and disciplinary backgrounds. Students develop a deeper knowledge of the topics they are studying ("zooming in") and analyze, design, develop and execute the most feasible solution in order to tackle the challenge agreed upon with their host organization. As part of the program, students produce a reflection report about their learning experience. The report also provides a means for the teachers to attune their teaching approaches for subsequent cohorts and to analyze the extent to which the students have achieved the formal learning goals. During and after their project work, students are expected to then "zoom out" and reflect on what they found and experienced. Similar to the above STF course example, they are asked to assess the societal embedding of their findings, based upon their internship's experiences.

In their reflective "learning journey," students are experiencing the various ESD competencies described earlier. Students employ systems thinking to diagnose the wider causes around an SDG and to propose a potential solution. They use futures thinking when moving from a potential solution to the identification of pathways to a more just future. Normative thinking is needed for reflecting on the mechanisms that are causing societal problems around sustainability. Students use action-oriented thinking, urging themselves to align their behaviour with what they experience on the ground and propose recommendations to their host organization and its local partners on the basis of the solutions they propose. In their field work, students also demonstrate interpersonal competencies, as they must take initiative to undertake their project and collaborate with local partners in the community.

The engagement and reflection experiences during the student's EL journey imply that students in Crossing Borders integrate various ESD competencies. They are invited to reflect on their own strengths and competencies in their reflection report. The experiences allow students to better bridge between theoretical and practical learning approaches, experiencing the bridge between classroom and community. As such, Crossing Borders offers the possibility of a transformative learning experience.

Global Crises, Local Challenges

Our third case is a new elective program that was introduced in the 2023/2024 academic year: a challenge-based minor going by the name "Global Crises, Local Challenges". The program is offered to third-year bachelor's students. It is built on the conviction that the climate crisis and associated ecological crises will affect the lives of the current and future generations of students and others, particularly those living in countries and communities that have contributed least to it (Georgieva et al., 2022). As such, the program aims to provide foundational knowledge of sustainable development to students from diverse disciplines and employs CBL principles to engage students in a real-life challenge situated in a local environment.

The program design centres on providing students actionable projects that simultaneously address high-stakes issues. Students are made aware of the challenges and the nature of the crises facing our planet and get a better understanding of the deep transformation that is needed to address them. They are offered the opportunity of EL, facilitated by a pedagogical context that allows them to do so. To achieve these goals, the course includes three course components that translate the problem (global crises) to possible solutions (local challenges) while remaining open to student and stakeholder input. In a more classic "core course," students acquire the basics of systems thinking to understand how the global crises affect societies. Students get a better understanding of climate- and ecological crises and their societal consequences. They also learn about the political and economic failures of the past and the transformations needed. Alongside the core course, students learn about interdisciplinary collaboration and action research. In the "skills workshop", students learn what CBL requires in terms of *engaged* and *reflective* effort. The program stimulates students to acquire the necessary analytical skills while building competences to address societal challenges. Students are split into interdisciplinary groups, where they engage – off-campus – with external stakeholders in the local community to understand their problems and to co-develop innovative and sustainable solutions.

In the CBL component of the course, students choose one of three challenges: energy poverty, (un)sustainable food practices, or fast fashion. All three challenges lend themselves well for *engaging* with communities. In order to address the challenge, students reach out to establish working relationships with civic groups and other organizations. Surely, this is not an easy task for students, but this EL element very much makes students aware of the importance of communication and collaboration skills. For instance, when it comes to the challenge to make houses independent from natural gas for their heating, the technical solutions developed raise profound social challenges in the form of vulnerable communities being unable to afford the bill for the energy transition. Failing to include vulnerable communities in the solution could lead to decreased democratic support for a true transition. In addressing this challenge, students gain experience with the intersection of multiple issues, studying how energy poverty could be addressed in the region, which communities suffer most, and what support would be needed politically and financially to address the problem.

The course requires students to work on concrete challenges themselves but acknowledges that they cannot start from scratch in a ten-week course. To make EL successful in a limited time period, a regional network was established to help students reach local stakeholders, supporting them in gaining the intended learning experiences. Students can use a map of regional stakeholders who address and have an interest in sustainability solutions. The map includes in particular stakeholders from the Twente region who are concerned with sustainable food production, energy poverty, and fast fashion. There is an expectation that, over time and with successive cohorts of students, the ties and trust with societal partners will strengthen and students will more quickly find their way to organizations outside the university.

Given the fact that *reflective* work is an important part of the minor, the course designers encountered some institutional challenges when it came to the testing and assessment of student work. First, a balance had to be found between group assessment and assessing individual student work. Similar to the other two courses presented in this chapter, self-reflection reports by individual students are also subjected to assessment. The course designers had to respond to the university's requests for individual testing, but a fuller integration of EL requires *institutional transformation* instead of ad hoc individual adjustments. Second, the UT has been successful over the years in working with business partners and has emphasized academic and student entrepreneurship. However, a citizen- and community-oriented approach was so far not present in the university's curriculum. To overcome these limitations, a flexible ("pop-up") civic sustainability classroom was designed as a space where students and stakeholder groups can meet to address societal challenges. The pop-up classroom fosters mutual learning across and beyond academic disciplines and is integrated in the skills seminar mentioned above.

Institutional Transformation: The Challenge of Introducing Transformative Learning Models

All three programs/courses presented above constitute examples of new modes of learning, each incorporating elements of EL and requiring students to address a sustainability-related challenge provided by an external stakeholder – coming either from the university's hometown, its region, or even from abroad. The cases all require students to learn about and *engage* with organizations and societal partners located outside of the university. This implies a form of EL: student internships, students interacting with local businesses and communities, students running meetings with external stakeholders. Another common element of the three courses is their strong *reflective dimension*, which means that students have to reflect on their learning journey and place their work or project in a wider context, looking at it from different disciplinary perspectives. A lot of these elements are triggered by the experiential components in the course, when students are confronted with new practices, views, and values held by others.

The three cases and the way they try to integrate EL in CBL settings also highlighted some constraints and opportunities. These challenges, as faced by the teachers and the students involved in the courses, as well as some more broad challenges, will now be discussed. There are "internal" challenges of blending different forms of learning, as well as "external" ones around introducing a pedagogical approach that does not yet align well with the broader institutional and societal setting. Below, we address how the course designers and teachers in the programs have tried to address the challenges when (re-)developing their course.

Securing Stakeholder Engagement

Given that EL is an important component of the three courses, stakeholder engagement is a common challenge faced by the academic staff responsible for the courses. For students and lecturers, the need to identify these external partners and to establish a working relationship with them may pose some difficulties. The external partners that have a role in the three courses can be quite diverse. In the more traditional academic programs, the usual partners are often the larger nation-wide companies and, in a few cases, local public authorities. In the three cases presented here, the partners are very diverse. For the Socio-Technical Futures and Global Crises programs they range from organizations and citizen representatives located in the region, civic groups and organizations, social enterprises, to small and medium-sized enterprises. In the case of the Crossing Borders program, these are organizations such as

NGOs, schools, hospitals and charitable organizations located in the Global South. Finding the right partners and reaching out to them is quite a challenge – for students, as well as the lecturers and supervisors facilitating and assessing the students' work. However, external stakeholder presence in the programs is crucial because the stakeholders are the challenge providers who will collaborate with the students and expect to receive some benefits from the students' work. In the Crossing Borders minor, for instance, students have to take initiative, use their planning and research skills and, on top of that, have to communicate with partners from abroad who have a different cultural and professional (or disciplinary) background. While most students felt this provides an extremely useful learning experience, they do find it a very time-consuming task, and several students struggle with the demands this places on their capabilities. There always will be a role for teachers in preparing and coaching students for the task, but bachelor's students who only just started their third year in the program will find this EL experience challenging.

Language Barriers

Engaging and communicating with off-campus partners implies that some students will encounter language constraints. First, there may be a language barrier that separates students from the communities or societal partners with whom students collaborate. Clear examples can be found in the *Crossing Borders* and the *Global Crises* programs. The first may require students to travel abroad and do an internship in a country where languages spoken differ from theirs. Second, many students in the University of Twente (roughly a third) come from abroad and speak English but several local community partners (in particular the ones from vulnerable communities) in the Twente region do not master the English language well enough to communicate easily.

Expectation Management

Apart from the logistical and administrative work that comes with reaching out to external partners, other challenges arise. Relations with local stakeholders and organizations hosting students as interns must be forged early on to fit the academic calendar. Ideally, relationships should become longer term (i.e., beyond the term of one course) to ensure ownership, trust and interest from the side of the challenge providers and a better understanding of the overall goals of the students' work. The unfamiliarity of some of the external partners with the goals of the academic course and its link to a particular SDG or challenge may result in some misunderstandings and hesitancy on their side. The external challenge providers sometimes seem to expect solutions at the end of the course, and they are not immediately prepared to focus on the mutual learning process which is characteristic of CBL-type courses. In the Crossing Borders minor, for instance, the host organization has to realize that students cannot be expected to deliver a result that is ready for implementation at the end of the internship. The management of expectations on all sides is an important issue in CBL-inspired programs. In the end, CBL is a more collaborative endeavour, where students interact with communities and partners in society. Students learn by familiarizing themselves with systems thinking but also, crucially, by engaging in, and reflecting on, these real-world interactions. This requires establishing relations to non-academic communities.

Spaces for Interaction

In our first EL example, the STF course, challenge providers were brought together with students and teachers in the DesignLab, a facility that is different from an ordinary classroom but still linked to the university. However, it became clear that another physical location – a space located off-campus and "in town" – would have enabled fieldwork (say EL) better. An on-campus space limits the possibilities for the students to engage more directly with relevant external stakeholders. It appeared that relying on email or telephone contact with external stakeholders cannot replace the serendipitous encounters fostered by fieldwork. This finding led to the idea of a "pop-up civic sustainability classroom" for the Global Crises, Local Challenges program – an idea that will be linked to ChallengeLab Twente, a recent initiative by the cities in the Twente region that allows students from different education institutions to collaborate on challenges coming directly from municipalities, companies, citizens, and social organizations. Such physical interaction spaces would seem crucial for the success of CBL-type programs and can be beneficial for the students' project work and creating interaction and valuable contacts. Dedicated spaces – both physical and virtual – allow for organizing exchanges, workshops and sessions, where students experience first-hand the issues faced by the challenge providers and other stakeholders.

Institutional Transformations

The challenges above point to structural issues affecting the institutionalization of challenge-based, experiential learning in the existing organizational context of universities. As shown in our case study, there is sometimes a clash between the institutional advocacy of educational innovations and the institutional *reflexes* or *dispositions* (Bourdieu, 1996).

First, our case study university (UT) is explicitly advocating more challenge-based learning in its mission statement. However, the initial experiences with CBL and EL initiatives met with responses that show that the university is still very much adhering to the norms of more classical forms of teaching, learning, and their associated testing methods. For both minor programs discussed above, we encountered this traditional preference for testing individual students' work rather than assessing group work. The university required that at least half of a student's work be assessed individually because it maintains the idea that university diplomas are individual diplomas. Addressing challenges, however, is a collaborative and reflective endeavour and hence requires assessment of group work.

Second, the absence of institutional ties to stakeholders is an issue. With regard to citizen science and engagement, universities do not offer that much in terms of established relations. This prompted us to ask how one could responsibly reach out to communities. Given that we are often dealing with relatively short-term courses, how can one maintain a responsible and long-term relationship to communities – a relationship that communities can actually benefit from?

Finally, EL requires finding ways to institutionalize border-crossing learning communities, allowing learners to gain engagement-oriented and reflection competencies. The challenge is to facilitate learning communities where EL is integrated in ways that offer students a truly transformative learning experience. This implies that EL will need to be linked with sites of change, connecting teachers and community representatives. A stronger focus on reflection, engagement and transformative learning can only be realized when the academic institution itself transforms in ways that allow EL to be embedded more firmly in the university's organization.

Conclusions and Reflections

In this chapter, we have sought to address the research question of whether learning approaches can be constructed where learning in the university classroom is combined with practical work carried out in a local project in an EL setting. We have presented three cases drawn from our own university where practical experiences are coupled to theoretical learning outcomes. We argue that effectively delivering transformative learning experiences (through ESD, CBL, or CEL) is not a simple matter of teaching students but of confronting students with challenges found in real-life and situating students in relevant communities where they interact with practice partners or are embedded in an organization through an internship or work directly on a project. This provides for transformative learning: students undergo a learning journey where they achieve change and learn to shape that change (say innovation) in a specific local context, coupling it to wider academic and policy debates. Contextualization, critical thinking and reflection skills, and being able to zoom in and zoom out are key to addressing a problem (a "challenge") from different angles and understanding the values and norms around it.

Responding to the changing social contract for higher education (see Chapter 1) that places the SDGs more in the centre of its education and research and to help students develop future-ready skills, the University of Twente has tried to reform its educational model. It is re-thinking its role in society and tries to make its education more challenge-based. Thus, the university is trying to become more responsive to societal needs, acting as an agent of change towards solving global challenges. The three embedded case studies presented above are an illustration of this ambition.

On a speculative note, considering the changing accountability and funding environment of universities, we expect that bachelor's programs in the future will see major reforms. They will grow towards a situation where students in each bachelor's program not only experience an emphatic connection with the practice for which they are being trained but also gain the investigative and design skills that are required within that practice in order to learn to act independently, methodically and reflectively. This is important for the students' ability to acquire new knowledge in their working life as a professional and to design processes, protocols, products, and services.

We believe that the attention for challenges and EL in the university's education (and research) mission is not just a fashionable trend but a necessity. Challenges around sustainability will constitute an important driver and organizing principle for the university of the future. Our expectation is that the specific challenges of sustainable development will increasingly guide how universities organize their activities, including their curriculum and research program. This will also hold for the learning opportunities offered to students and the didactical approaches facilitating them. Universities will seek to establish new educational programs and formats with a strong emphasis on the grand societal challenges that students will encounter once they enter the labour market and, more generally, position and develop themselves as responsible citizens in society.

The education programs offered by universities, therefore, should prepare students to think systematically about the grand societal challenges using a multidisciplinary perspective. Such boundary-crossing programs will require an outward orientation and experiential elements, where students reach out to external stakeholders, companies and communities, often off-campus. It appears that this reform towards more transformative learning is not only demanded by society but also very much appreciated by students, many of them strongly motivated to take initiative in the quest for sustainable development. As shown in our case study, students are creative, energetic, idealistic individuals, concerned about the future and wishing to make global, challenging and meaningful contributions.

REFERENCES

Benneworth, P. (2019). The modernisation agenda and university irresponsibility repertoires. In M. Sørensen, L. Geschwind, J. Kekäle & R. Pinheiro (Eds.), *The responsible university* (pp. 61-86). Palgrave Macmillan. https://doi.org/10.1007/978-3-030-25646-3_3

Berman, E. P. (2007). *Creating the market university: Science, the state, and the economy, 1965–1985.* University of California Press.

Biesta, G. (2013). Responsive or responsible? Democratic education for the global networked society. *Policy Futures in Education, 11*(6), 733–44.

Boulton, G., & Lucas, C. (2008). *What are universities for?* LERU. https://www.leru.org/files/What-are-Universities-for-Full-paper.pdf

Bourdieu, P. (1996). Understanding. *Theory, Culture & Society, 13*(2), 17–37.

Dale, A., & Newman, L. (2005). Sustainable development, education and literacy. *International Journal of Sustainability in Higher Education, 6*(4), 351–62.

Gallagher, S. E., & Savage, T. (2020). Challenge-based learning in higher education: An exploratory literature review. *Teaching in Higher Education, 28*(3). https://doi.org/10.1080/13562517.2020.1863354

Georgieva, K., Gaspar, V., & Pazarbasioglu, C. (2022, March). *Poor and vulnerable countries need support to adapt to climate change.* IMF Blog. https://www.imf.org/en/Blogs/Articles/2022/03/23/blog032322-poor-and-vulnerable-countries-need-support-to-adapt-to-climate-change

Goddard, J., Hazelkorn, E., Kempton, L., & Vallance P. (2016). *The civic university: The policy and leadership challenges.* Edward Elgar.

Grau, F. X., Goddard, J., Hall, B. L., Hazelkorn, E., & Tandon, R. (2017). *Higher education in the world 6. Towards a socially responsible university.* Global University Network for Innovation.

Head, B. W., & Alford, J. (2015). Wicked problems: Implications for public policy and management. *Administration & Society, 47*(6), 711-39. https://doi.org/10.1177/0095399713481601

Leicht, A., Heiss, J., & Byun, W. J. (2018). *Issues and trends in education for sustainable development (Vol. 5).* UNESCO Publishing.

Leijon, M., Gudmundsson, P., Staaf, P., & Christersson, C. (2022). Challenge based learning in higher education – A systematic literature review. *Innovations in education and teaching international, 59*(5), 609–18.

Marginson, S. (2011). Higher education and public good. *Higher Education Quarterly, 65*(4), 411–33.

Mazzucato, M. (2018). *Mission-oriented research & innovation in the European Union: A problem-solving approach to fuel innovation-led growth.* Publications Office of the European Union.

Molderez, I., & Fonseca, E. (2018). The efficacy of real-world experiences and service learning for fostering competences for sustainable development in higher education. *Journal of Cleaner Production,* 172, 4397–410.

Moore, D. T. (2010). Forms and issues in experiential learning. In D. M. Qualters (Ed.), *New Directions for Teaching and Learning* (pp. 3–13). Wiley.

Nichols, M. H., & Cator, K. (2008). *Challenge Based Learning. White Paper.* Apple, Inc.

Roche, J., et al. (2020). Citizen science, education, and learning: challenges and opportunities. *Frontiers in Sociology,* 5. https://doi.org/10.3389/fsoc.2020.613814

Shephard, K., Rieckmann, M., & Barth, M. (2019). Seeking sustainability competence and capability in the ESD and HESD literature: An international philosophical hermeneutic analysis. *Environmental Education Research, 25*(4), 532–47.

United Nations (2015). Transforming our world: The 2030 agenda for sustainable development (A/RES/70/1). https://sustainabledevelopment.un.org/content/documents/21252030%20Agenda%20for%20Sustainable%20Development%20web.pdf

University of Twente (n.d.). *Shaping2030: technology? It's a people story.* https://www.utwente.nl/en/organisation/about/shaping2030/#strategy

Utrecht University (n.d.). *Community-Engaged Learning.* https://www.uu.nl/en/education/community-engaged-learning

11 A Dance of Dilemmas: The Local-Global Possibilities of Experiential Learning in Higher Education for Sustainable Development

PERRI TERMINE, MONI KIM, AND MARIN MACLEOD

University of Toronto, Canada

Introduction

In 2010, GlobalHigherEd (2010) featured responses to a question posed by Nigel Thrift, Vice-Chancellor of the University of Warwick: are universities optimally positioned to address fundamental global challenges and at the pace at which they deserve to be addressed? Perspectives shared by higher education (HE) leaders in response to the question varied greatly. Some reinforced "traditionalist" notes of caution against seeing universities as "agentic interventionists" outside of their general point and purpose (EDSLR, 2010). In one case, Professor Gregor McLennan of the University of Bristol defines the specific concern of universities as developing "plural communities of knowledge and understanding through discovery, controversial systematization, and rigorous reflection" (EDSLR, 2010). For him, the institution's purpose is overstepped by the notion of a collective agency. Other academics expressed support for universities as cooperators in a global web that are responsible for making commitments to sustainable development and alleviating poverty by building human and societal capacity. All contributors seemed to concur on two key points: first, the nature of universities in contemporary societies is evolving; and second, the ongoing discourse intertwining institutional mandates with the Sustainable Development Agenda inevitably carries geographical implications. From within the university learning community, there arises a curiosity regarding the tangible actions higher education institutions undertake to tackle sustainable development challenges. Additionally, there is an interest in exploring the perspectives of administrators, students, and community members, all of which contribute to the Vice-Chancellor's inquiry. The scope of this chapter serves as a starting point for this multi-faceted conversation, anchored in a global case study of experiential learning.

Universities around the world face a critical juncture in their societal engagement, sometimes referred to as a "glocal dilemma," and in improved student access to experiential and 21st-century competency-building opportunities for social and economic development. This juncture is situated within three intersecting conversations: (a) HE's contribution to the advancement of sustainable development; (b) calls to develop global competency in HE and the institution's need to keep pace with changing times and uncertainty in the 21st century; (c) the local-global implications of institutional missions and strategic plans, exemplified by Strategic Mandate Agreement sector planning in Ontario's post-secondary system in Canada. Amid simultaneously globalizing and localizing trends in student demand and research funding, we ask in this chapter, *how can universities with global reach and ambition contribute to local communities in concert through their teaching and learning mission?*

The "glocal dilemma" of HE reflects challenges and debates surrounding the balance of internationalization of public university research, enrolments and activities, and the growing socio-economic calls to leverage local community engagement for mutual university-City benefit (Knight et al., 2021; Ministry of Colleges and Universities, 2022; Buzzelli & Asafo-Adjei, 2022). Through a conceptual orientation, programmatic overview, and series of vignettes, we contribute to this dialogue by reflecting on our participation in and learning from administering the Reach Alliance – a co-curricular, multidisciplinary, experiential learning initiative that was inspired by and oriented toward advancing the Sustainable Development Agenda.

The Reach Alliance is a consortium of global universities – with partners in Ghana, South Africa, Mexico, Canada, United States, United Kingdom, Australia, and Singapore – developing the leaders we need to solve urgent local challenges of the hard to reach – those under-served for geographic, administrative, or social reasons. Working in interdisciplinary teams, the Reach Alliance's globally-minded students use rigorous research methods to identify innovative solutions to climate, public health, and economic challenges. Research is conducted in collaboration with local communities and with guidance from university faculty members, building capacity and skills among the Reach Alliance's student researchers. Resulting actionable research insights have been published in numerous journals such as Lancet and BMJ Global Health and are being used by policymakers and sector leaders, such as the Government of Canada to catalyse impact around the world.

Founded at the University of Toronto, the Reach Alliance aligns with the university's 2022–2027 International Strategic Plan. Its strategic priorities include nurturing a globally fluent university community by creating opportunities to engage globally while in Toronto, increasing the number and diversity of students participating in a broad range of learning abroad experiences, and enabling and enhancing international research collaboration to address issues of both local and global importance. Furthermore, the Reach Alliance's program tenets reflect several core principles of the strategy: "global impact and societal responsibility", "trans- and multidisciplinary collaboration," and "international fluencies ... both domestic and international" (University of Toronto, 2022). For a deeper exploration of Ontario, Canada's climate of experiential learning in higher education, see Chapter 3: When Logics Collide: Experiential Learning and Intra-Institutional dynamics. Additionally, for more on experiential learning for sustainable development, we invite you to explore Chapter 10: Experiential Learning for Sustainability: Grand Challenges and Local Communities.

Sustainable Development, Global Competencies, and Institutional Mandates

The United Nations' Sustainable Development Agenda is defined by a multi-stakeholder approach and takes a strong stance in its pledge to leave no one behind (see report of United Nations General Assembly (UNGA, 2015)). Advancing the Sustainable Development Agenda requires an integrated effort to achieve global goals, necessitating interdisciplinary and transdisciplinary research and action to engage those around the world who are seldom reached (UNGA, 2015; OECD, 2018). Within debates about the changing function and role of the university lies the argument that sustainable development cannot advance without the support of higher education and that higher education can greatly benefit from alignment with the Sustainable Development Agenda. To date, there seems to be a tentative relationship between universities and the sustainable development movement, despite the distinct role of the university as a social institution established to generate knowledge for future generations (Elkana & Klöpper, 2019; Hsueh, 2019). Many institutions, however, are implementing and engaging in relevant initiatives through research, curriculum, and international collaboration (Hsueh, 2019). Some unique initiatives at the intersection of local and global scale and scope reveal the opportunity, ambition, and potential responsibility of the university in its evolving social contract with society. These initiatives provide a compelling – and perhaps daunting – vision of what could be achieved if a post-secondary institution were to formally integrate the goals of the United Nations Sustainable Development Agenda into its strategic planning.

To foster student success in the 21st century, there has been increasing emphasis on global competency frameworks in the modern public university and their capacity to equip learners for the uncertain future of work in an interconnected world. Groups like the Organization for Economic Co-operation and Development (OECD), the European Commission, and the Partnership for 21st Century Skills (P21) have developed mutually enriching conceptualizations of global competencies or 21st-century skills. Global competencies extend beyond knowledge and skills; they encompass functional aspects, interpersonal attributes, and ethical values that address complex demands (Ontario Ministry of Education, 2016). These competencies can help learners navigate the ongoing and shifting demands of life, work, and learning. They enable individuals to actively engage with and contribute to their local and global communities, effectively utilize emerging technologies cultivate meaningful intercultural relationships, and embrace opportunities as they arise (Coyer et al., 2019; Fullan & Langworthy, 2014; OECD, 2018; Ontario Ministry of Education, 2016). Noteworthy frameworks include the OECD's Programme for International Student Assessment (PISA) global competence framework (OECD, 2018) and Dr. Michael Fullan's Six Global Competencies, or "6Cs" (formerly 4Cs), which represents a concise but powerful set of meaningful academic and personal/interpersonal qualities and capabilities: character, citizenship, collaboration, communication, creativity, and critical thinking (Fullan & Langworthy, 2014). Discussions around a 21st-century skillset are increasingly integrated into debates about the evolving nature and role of universities.

Current debates further reflect a reexamination and reimagining of higher education. This trend is exemplified by institutions in Ontario, Canada – such as the University of Toronto – operating within the context of Strategic Mandate Agreements (SMAs) to further prioritize and scale research-based, experiential, locally-engaged (while maintaining internationalized) learning. SMAs are bilateral agreements between the province's Ministry of Colleges and Universities (2022) and the forty-five publicly assisted colleges and universities, touted as a key component of the ministry's accountability framework and funding approach for the higher education system. SMAs represent a performance-based funding model that began with Phase 1 in 2014 as part of a planned three-phase process to support "differentiated improvement" among Ontario's post-secondary institutions (Buzzelli & Asafo-Adjei, 2022; Ministry of Colleges and Universities, 2022). Through SMAs, institutions are required to meet targets across ten ministry-specified metrics, which are intended to reflect their individual strengths, distinct mandates, and the role institutions play in their local communities. As such, SMAs are designed to create differentiation and specialization, encouraging competition for funding in the higher education system in Ontario and further raising questions about the role of policy and mandates in the advancement of sustainable development.

Through the lens of student experience and research excellence, we contend that international inter-university engagement can strengthen the connection between universities and their respective local contexts and communities and vice versa. This represents a departure from the traditional research paradigm and measures of excellence, which have historically prioritized scholarly contributions and citation counts in fundamental research. There is now a growing recognition of the importance of real-world impact and practical applications in research evaluation, signifying that an evolving perspective, where translational research – focused on addressing tangible, real-world challenges – is gaining prominence. Such a reconceptualization underscores the significant role of research in fostering sustainable development.

Conceptual Orientation: A "Dance of Dilemmas"

Dual themes guide our inquiry into how universities with global reach and ambition can contribute to local communities in their teaching and learning mission. We first recognize the interconnection and codependence of "local" and "global" dynamics, followed by analysis of the embeddedness and possibilities of these dynamics within the mobilization of globally-minded, locally-implemented experiential learning. Central to this discussion is the evolving model of the Reach Alliance. It represents an experiential initiative characterized by research learning in a global network of empowered local actors, particularly institutions and post-secondary students intentionally engaging in experiential curricular and co-curricular practices.

This chapter draws upon critical scholarship concerning both areas: the *local-global nexus*, sometimes referred to as "glocalism," in the role and nature of higher education for sustainable development, and *experiential learning*, namely the "disorienting dilemmas" that can drive deeper, transformative learning in experiential education that crosses geographical boundaries. The value of considering the Reach Alliance within this conversation is two-fold. First, it provides a practical means to explore the possibilities and limitations of local and global university and student engagement. Second, it incorporates transferable learning about a central notion of the public university: research excellence and student experience.

The Local-Global Nexus in Public Post-Secondary Education

Various policy- and funding-driven focus areas in universities, including the expansion of practice-based pedagogies, reveal an evolution in the core teaching and learning mission of the university. The HE sector intersects geographies and disciplines in its drive for global stature, as well as its need to mediate between foundational principles of developing an engaged citizenry and democracy and serving the learner's need to develop a livelihood for economic prosperity (Axelrod, 2002; Buzzelli & Asafo-Adjei, 2022). In the process of navigating many social, economic, political, and educative flows, post-secondary institutions find themselves attending to the local-global nexus.

In the context of sustainable development within public higher education, particularly within the framework of the Reach Alliance, understanding local-global dynamics involves consideration of spatial, temporal, and mental models and processes. Building upon the work of Houston & Lange (2018), we employ the term "local-global" to emphasize the interplay between global and local forces, which concurrently define and influence each other. Geographically, we concur that the location of learning informs the type of knowledge produced and its social impact (Knight et al., 2021). However, our use of the term "local-global" aims to transcend traditional dichotomies that often oversimplify these dynamics. Rather than portraying the local as merely regional or provincial and the global as distant and superior, we recognize the mutual constitution of these concepts. This approach avoids perpetuating notions of proximity and value that often underlie tensions between the local and global within higher education (Houston & Lange, 2018).

A local-global conceptualization gains further significance when viewed through ontological and epistemological lenses. From an ontological standpoint, encompassing political, economic, cultural, ecological, and social processes, we recognize an increasing interconnection between local and global realities. This interconnection highlights the nuanced manifestation of sustainability challenges, which are inherently global but unfold uniquely in distinct and complex local contexts (Caniglia et al., 2018). Epistemologically, the notion of local-global suggests that how we know and understand the world must connect local and global considerations, especially when addressing sustainability issues and devising solutions, such as through research-based learning programming (Caniglia et al., 2018). At the Reach Alliance, this paradigm shift resembles a transition from universal modelling to global contextualism, which suggests that interpreting knowledge is never independent of context and parts of local knowledge can be integrated into what is considered universal general knowledge (Elkana & Klöpper, 2016).

Public, research-intensive universities around the world commonly wrestle with various local-global tensions. Increased learner mobility intersects with the growing reliance of post-secondary institutions on student income due to declining public funding, resulting in a blend of domestic and international student enrolment (Knight et al., 2021). Simultaneously, market trends reflect the increasing attraction of global talent by multinational firms, whereas employers have traditionally recruited from local markets and community-engaged pedagogies are in part promoted to retain graduating students in the institution's local city or region (Knight et al., 2021). The internationalization and commercialization of research and its proposed impact are attributed to the attraction of international faculty, the reconceptualization of research excellence, and the desire to differentiate institutions in their offerings and societal engagement (Buzzelli & Asafo-Adjei, 2022, Knight et al., 2021).

In alignment with recent scholarship, we contend that HE's increasing institutional focus on local community impact does not need to forgo international reach and vice versa. Engaging with ongoing debates and critical analyses of the modern university and the neoliberal project, Knight and colleagues (2021) argue that it is the university's ability to execute local and global together that enables it to fulfil its social mission to its local communities. To pursue developmental goals, academics report working closely with the government and industry (Chankseliani et al., 2021; Buzzelli & Asafo-Adjei, 2022), and scholars further suggest that the strength and global reputation of public research universities increasingly depend on the quality of their local environment and the strength of their local partnerships (Knight et al., 2021). Similarly, how might the strength of internationalization and global partnerships influence the local reputation and opportunities of public research universities? The tensions between local and global perspectives present opportunities for innovation. The socio-economic imperatives shaping approaches to research excellence and student experience in the contemporary university, along with perceived dissonance between local and global scales, can be effectively navigated through an integrated programmatic approach wherein local and global elements are viewed as complementary rather than conflicting.

Activating Local-Global Experiential Learning and Its Benefits

To shape local-global engagement, emphasis has been placed on the suitability of experiential learning models and the readiness to offer experiential forms of education demonstrated by universities (Buzzelli &

Asafo-Adjei, 2022). From Confucius to Dewey and a whole host of current educators and scholars, there is broad agreement that participation – the heart of experiential learning (EL) – facilitates deeper learning compared to passive watching or listening. EL recognizes learning as "a process whereby concepts are derived from and continually modified by experience" (Kolb, 1984, p. 26), where "knowledge is continuously derived from and tested out in the experiences of the learner" (Kolb, 1984, p. 27). In HE, there has been a recent expansion of EL in its application and role in societal engagement, taking on many forms, such as internships, co-op placements and community engagement activities both locally and internationally (Buzzelli & Asafo-Adjei, 2022). The term is thus used broadly to include a wide range of activities and arrangements outside the classroom, including the Reach Alliance in its co-curricular, student-driven, and research-oriented nature.

The importance of global competence and the role of experiential learning as a vehicle for competency development have been highlighted by scholars in the context of the global economy and individual career success (Lee et al., 2023; Morley & Cerdin, 2010; OECD, 2018). For example, in the realm of international business, individual workers' global competence is crucial for navigating a variety of cultural and institutional complexities in business operations and determining the "effective management of business operations in global settings" (Morley & Cerdin, 2010). Furthermore, employers increasingly seek to attract adaptable learners who have engaged in deeper learning: individuals capable of applying transferable skills and knowledge to new situations and complex problems (OECD, 2018; Fullan & Langworthy, 2014). "Workforce readiness" in an increasingly digitized and interconnected world demands learners to be leaders in their own continuous learning. It requires them to develop an understanding of and critical thinking about the complex dynamics of globalization; to be open to and collaborate with people from different cultural backgrounds; to communicate respectfully; to solve problems creatively; and to actively engage in local, global, and learning communities to address issues of human and environmental sustainability (OECD, 2018; Fullan & Langworthy, 2014).

The Reach Alliance's model exemplifies a shift in teaching and mentorship toward learner-centricity, driven by a growing emphasis on "deeper learning" (Fullan & Langworthy, 2018; Ontario Ministry of Education, 2016). Deeper learning is a process that is considered increasingly relevant to the development of transferable skills and employability. It demands a shift in teaching from "focusing on covering all required content to focusing on the learning process, developing students' ability to lead their own learning and to do things with their learning. Teachers are partners with students in deep learning tasks characterized by exploration, connectedness and broader, real-world purposes" (Fullan & Langworthy, 2014, p. 7). Recent scholarship also highlights the impact of learner-centred experiences that are both on- and off-campus – a cornerstone of the Reach Alliance's student experience – in stimulating multi-layered reflections and action in the social world, with a goal of contributing to its transformation. Similar insights can be drawn from Musisi (2019), who contends that EL programs build student confidence by facilitating their ability to make connections to the larger social worlds that they inhabit in ways that go beyond what they would typically gain from traditional lecture-based pedagogy.

According to PISA, among the pedagogies for promoting global competence and deeper learning are group-based co-operative projects and organized discussions that encourage learners to analyze and reflect on the root causes of global issues (OECD, 2018; Fullan & Langworthy, 2014). The notion of Quality Education in the UN's Sustainable Development Agenda expands beyond foundational knowledge like literacy and mathematics to include an emphasis on learning to live together sustainably (OECD, 2018). PISA, considered the "global yardstick for educational success," was inspired by this lifelong, co-operative learning orientation to include global competence in its metrics for quality, equity, and effectiveness in education (OECD, 2018). To become meaningful, such a goal and its constituent pedagogies can be made visible in local implementations of global co-operative, student-driven projects, to be illustrated by the case of the Reach Alliance.

Experiential education's focus on "challenge and experience, followed by reflection, leading to learning and growth" (Association for Experiential Education, 2023) corresponds with transformative learning. The idea of transformation through adult learning involves individuals gaining an awareness of their current "habits of mind" and resulting "points of view" (Wiessner & Mezirow, 2000, p. 345), while engaging in activities that fundamentally challenge those frames of reference to adopt broader perspectives. As a result, transformative learning involves a learner's critique of their assumptions, an assessment of alternative views, and a decision to negate a previous perspective in favour of a new one or to create a synthesis of old and new (Mezirow, 1997, Gravett, 2002). The experiential component is critical, as it encourages learners to consider new and potentially uncomfortable perspectives and to consider integrating those experiences into their frames of reference (Coyer et al., 2019). Mezirow's (1997) "disorienting dilemma" element was heavily influenced by Freire's (1970) concept of conscientization: the ways in which individuals and communities recognize contradiction and "disequilibrium" and develop a critical understanding of their social reality through reflection and action, ultimately precipitating transformation. Mezirow (1978) stated that "only through reflection, active learning, and placing ourselves in an uncomfortable situation are we fully able to develop our understanding of the world and of ourselves." We observe the local-global nexus embedded in this microcosm of the student experience alongside the macro tensions and strategic activities of the university; one's local participation helps develop an understanding of oneself and the world (Knight et al., 2021).

The Reach Alliance in Practice: Implementation and Impact on a Local-Global Scale

The Reach Alliance provides local and global engagement through experiential research learning opportunities for students through participation on- and off-campus. Tensions at the local-global nexus in HE's increasing institutional focus on local community impact do not need to impede international reach. Glocality is reflected in the shaping of research excellence and student experience at the Reach Alliance, both of which are guided by experiential learning principles and an ongoing commitment to global impact. Learners and universities can engage as actors in disorienting dilemmas and learn to navigate uncertainty. This is an important element of equipping the next generation of leaders with workforce readiness. Emerging leaders will have the tools to actively participate in local, global, and learning communities to address issues of human and environmental sustainability. Student alumni of the Reach Alliance have reflected on their off-campus engagement in the program – a journey ripe with opportunities to apply knowledge and leadership skills in an experiential manner (Shafaqat et al., 2023). Alumni suggest that this approach not only challenges most study abroad or exchange programs that follow a didactic curriculum and restrict learning to a classroom but also highlights that programs of this kind are unfortunately few and far between in Canada (Shafaqat at al., 2023). Without experiential learning programs of this nature, "students are deprived of a perspective that could empower them for the rest of their careers" (Shafaqat et al., 2023).

Contextual Research Projects Focused on Impact

At the local level, each partner institution recruits students from diverse disciplines to work together in teams for nine to twelve months with the guidance of faculty mentors. These research teams investigate innovative, local solutions to pressing global challenges and translate actionable research insights through institutional partnerships. Research produced by the Reach Alliance demonstrates the interconnectedness of local and global issues, providing a deeper understanding of local realities in the context of broader global challenges. While the research centres on locally implemented innovations, it aims to generate global insights that can be applied in other relevant contexts to accelerate progress towards the Sustainable Development Goals. This local-global nexus in the research represents a shift away from universal modelling to global contextualism, demonstrating how knowledge cannot be independent of context and how parts of local knowledge can be integrated into what is considered universal general knowledge (Elkana & Klöpper, 2016).

Glocality is also reflected in the definition and shaping of research excellence by emphasizing the real-world impact and practical applications of research through active learning. Students' research about local off-campus community initiatives is disseminated in outlets with global reach through various knowledge translation activities. Students author a case study report, present at conferences, publish additional written work in leading academic journals and opinion outlets, and speak on podcasts as content experts. The application of experiential learning at the Reach Alliance demonstrates the opportunity for societal engagement and impact.

Transformation Through Reflection

Active participation and modalities to promote deeper learning – two important traits of experiential learning (Kolb, 1984) – are built into the design of the student experience at the Reach Alliance. Student researchers drive the primary research process from start to finish. They determine the scope of the research question and methodology, secure appropriate research ethics approval, conduct primary data collection, and write their findings in a case study report. The students are co-principal investigators, sharing ownership of the research process and outputs with faculty, thereby fostering deeper learning by enabling students to drive the inquiry process and make their learning visible. Developing students' ability to lead their own learning, to critically analyze and apply these learnings, and connect to broader, real-world purposes have been documented as important processes for leadership development and workforce readiness.

These concrete experiences provide opportunities for transformation through ongoing reflection. Students undergo facilitated peer feedback, team observations and reflection, and individual performance coaching by professional experts hired external to the university. Integrating intercultural research-based learning with professional and career development activities throughout the project duration encourages students to consider new and potentially uncomfortable perspectives and to consider incorporating those experiences into their frames of reference (Coyer et al., 2019). The process of undergoing this "disorienting dilemma" noted by Wiessner and Mezirow (2000) enables students to fully develop their understanding of the world and of themselves. The ability for students to understand how their local participation has global impact contributes to successful career launch for alumni from the Reach Alliance.

Faculty as Mentors Not Supervisors

The role of faculty members in student-directed experiential learning often involves the practice known as "flipping the classroom," whereby faculty members provide mentorship rather than traditional supervision (Abeysekera and Dawson, 2015; Barkley, 2009; Strayer, 2012). This approach involves faculty members from various disciplines to adopt alternative pedagogies, such as critical pedagogy, active learning, and student-centred learning, which challenge traditional hierarchies and promote student-driven learning and critical thinking. These alternative pedagogies, valued in higher education for their ability to foster student engagement and critical thinking, are particularly effective in transforming traditional learning environments at local institutions around the world. The network of faculty mentors from several global universities fosters a teaching pedagogy that operates at the local-global nexus within the international alliance.

Team-Based Skills Development

The diverse backgrounds and experiences of students and faculty participating in the Reach Alliance create a unique environment for interdisciplinary learning and inquiry, both within local teams and across the international community. This means that students with different educational and professional backgrounds, such as engineers and social scientists, approach the research questions from different perspectives and interpret data differently. Reflecting Mezirow's (1978) transformative learning orientation, students undergo transformation when they gain an awareness of their assumptions, are challenged to consider new and potentially uncomfortable perspectives, and integrate those experiences into their frames of reference. This collision and subsequent process of reorientation among Reach Alliance researchers presents a precursor to transformative learning through EL. The conditions created by this research-based EL community drives connection beyond superficial alliances and addresses deeper systemic issues and shared struggles.

Not only are students challenged by being exposed to different perspectives, they learn how to collaborate and produce research deliverables as a team. Team-based, co-operative projects are one teaching and learning method known to promote global competence and deeper understanding by encouraging learners to analyze and reflect on the root causes of global issues (OECD, 2018; Fullan & Langworthy, 2014). Research teams at the Reach Alliance work with a dedicated professional performance coach to support individual and team high performance and to build the communication, clarity, and psychological safety necessary for success. A key principle of the approach is that teamwork enhances individuals' skills, such as self-reflection, collaboration with diverse stakeholders, and the development and implementation of project management plans to produce high-quality research deliverables. This approach to leadership development necessitates that students practice the skills they are developing, such as coping with ambiguity, working across disciplines, and giving and receiving feedback. Furthermore, tending to the student researcher as a *whole person* through supports that embrace individuals professionally, personally, socio-emotionally, and within their teams, embraces a more nuanced approach to equity and inclusion in EL (Levy, 2023). By actively creating environments and facilitating learning experiences that acknowledge the nuances that shape a person's sense of self – including background, culture, values, and perspectives – EL programs like the Reach Alliance can enact this achievement (Levy, 2023). This approach fosters a deeper understanding and appreciation for the richness of human diversity, both among teams of peers and with participating stakeholders. It also aligns with the United Nations Sustainable Development Agenda's recognition that quality education goes beyond foundational subject knowledge, such as literacy and mathematics, to include an emphasis on learning to live together sustainably (OECD, 2018).

Cultivating a Global Network

Convening interdisciplinary students and faculty is important when providing experiential opportunities that contribute to cross-sector discussion focused on understanding how to reach some of the world's more remote populations. These regular in-person and online forums facilitate local and global engagement through the exchange of ideas and research insights. Ongoing professional development opportunities support translation of these actionable research insights in local and global settings. Experiential design at the Reach Alliance aspires to tangibly address the gap identified by the OECD (2018) in developing "workforce readiness" in an increasingly digitized and interconnected world. To address this gap, EL must require learners to be leaders, develop critical thinking regarding the complex dynamics of globalization, collaborate with people from different cultural backgrounds, communicate respectfully, solve problems creatively, and participate in local and global learning communities that address issues of human and environment sustainability.

Vignettes: Case Studies Illustrating Local-Global Experiential Learning

Although each partner university implements the Reach Alliance EL initiative to align with their local institutional context, the decision to conduct primary case study research locally or globally differs across universities. All partners commit to three global principles that centre on EL: (a) the research process must be student-led; (b) the research team must be interdisciplinary; and (c) the research focus must be a hard-to-reach population. Reach Alliance university partners balance their global ambitions and local community contributions through implementation of the Reach Alliance initiative.

The following vignettes vary geographically and present varying levels of program embeddedness within the university, localization, and global partnership implications (Roll et al., 2024). They further suggest that SDG-focussed initiatives benefit from both a global perspective (networked, transnational) and local perspective (context-driven, human-scale) on the SDGs, with program success ultimately tied to its overall institutional embeddedness (Roll et al., 2024). To further examine the following case studies and more, refer to the article in *Sustain Earth Reviews* titled "Learning in Action: Embedding the SDGs through the Reach Alliance." (Roll et al., 2024).

University College London (United Kingdom)

University College London conducted its first Reach Alliance case study project off-campus in the local community, the London Borough of Camden. The university recruited interdisciplinary faculty and students, including those with public policy and medical expertise, to investigate barriers faced by refugees, people seeking asylum, and undocumented migrants in accessing quality maternal healthcare in Camden. Actionable research insights from this UK-based EL research project targeted two primary local audiences. First, hospital healthcare workers were provided with insights into how hostile immigration policies may affect the access to care of pregnant refugees, asylum seekers, and undocumented migrants. Second, local government authorities were offered findings on how their work on housing and other social services impacts healthcare access for these hard-to-reach populations. Beyond the local context, lessons learned from this case study were presented to the global Reach Alliance community and are well positioned to inform healthcare practitioners and local authorities in other countries facing related healthcare challenges, such as Canada. Finally, the medical and policy students who conducted the research intend to leverage their experience and insights gained from this process as they progress in their global careers.

Tecnológico de Monterrey (Mexico)

Tecnológico de Monterrey conducted three Reach Alliance case study projects off-campus in their local community of Monterrey, recruiting interdisciplinary faculty and students from Mexico for the projects. The research topics include: the struggle and resilience of migrant Indigenous communities in irregular settlements, the appropriation of public spaces from a gender perspective, and the invisibility of children with cognitive impairment in Mexico's public education system. Actionable research insights from these Mexico-based EL research projects have been shared with key stakeholders in the country, and presented to a global audience via the Reach Alliance network. In addition to the research deliverables from this EL initiative, survey data suggests that students across the global network relish opportunities to learn from and interact with their peers at other institutions. "One of Tec's priorities has always been to have an impact on society, an impact made by both students and teachers, and also to give the students an opportunity for international exposure. This global EL network allows us to do both," reported Iza Maria Sánchez Siller, Professor, School of Government and Public Transformation, Tecnológico de Monterrey.

Lessons Learned

Ethical Partnerships

Practicing ethical partnership and co-investment is time consuming and requires addressing longstanding tensions and power dynamics between partners, especially between the so-called Global North and

Global South, within the context of colonialism, environmental racism, and other global inequities. That said, ethical partnerships are the only way for local-global initiatives to successfully operate within the higher education space. This involves asking questions before offering answers, creating time and space for co-creation, co-design, and reflection, fostering university exchanges and reciprocal visits to build understanding and trust across institutions, and demonstrating a willingness to learn from each other.

Balancing for Shared Experience

Striking a balance between standardization and customization when scaling local-global EL initiatives is difficult but critical to success. Ensuring that community members have a shared experience relative to their peers while maintaining autonomy and ownership over implementation of the initiative's components is necessary for success. Examples include student recruitment approaches, faculty mentorship practices, student engagement opportunities, and accountability mechanisms for participants. Additionally, practicing flexibility and adaptability is needed when delivering EL opportunities to students, especially those located in different geographic regions. In practice, this includes accounting for interactive hybrid collaboration opportunities and community building, facilitating virtual research practices as needed, and offering bespoke team-based support to develop key skills such as report writing.

Sustainability

Achieving sustainability for local-global experiential learning initiatives requires non-traditional advancement strategies – strategies that centre ethical partnerships, co-creation, student experience, and impact potential (i.e., knowledge translation and uptake). Time must be invested in assessing donor priorities, and universities must go beyond the "usual suspects" when it comes to making the case for limited external funding. Equally important is securing internal institutional buy-in, such as transitioning from an extra-curricular initiative to a curricular one. The option to offer course credit to participating students is particularly important for fostering equity, diversity and inclusion, as some students are unable to participate in extra-curricular initiatives due to competing academic and professional demands. In essence, EL initiatives must respond to the question: what is the value proposition for the key stakeholders involved?

Shared Priorities

Shared values among institutional partners are essential for developing and maintaining strong academic partnerships. A common understanding of what success looks like must underpin these shared values, providing a foundation for cross-institutional collaboration on EL research projects and solutions development. This in-depth collaboration allows universities to deepen their engagement with their local cities while at the same time creating meaningful impact for communities around the world through the translation of actionable research insights.

Conclusion

In recent years, commitment of higher education institutions to societal engagement and advancing the United Nations Sustainable Development Agenda has accelerated. Dialogue surrounding the imperative for post-secondary institutions to adapt to uncertain times and further conceptualize their roles in local communities and economies alongside internationalization is increasingly reflected in the evolving metrics of strategic plans. We also see that learning communities within the public university are well-positioned to contribute to the Sustainable Development Agenda as part of their teaching and learning mission and are capable of grappling with the local-global tensions underlying this mission. For a deeper exploration of sustainable development and intra-institutional transformation for experiential learning, refer to Chapter 3 (LaCroix) and Chapter 10 (Dix et al.), respectively.

The Reach Alliance is an international EL example that contributes to a key conversation in higher education teaching and learning at the local-global nexus. To shape local-global engagement, emphasis has been placed on the suitability of EL models and, furthermore, the readiness of universities to offer such opportunities (Buzzelli & Asafo, 2022). This chapter addressed the local-global nexus through the case of the Reach Alliance as a scaled EL model powered by collaboration between higher education institutions, the private, public, and civil society sectors. Four primary lessons learned through the implementation of the Reach Alliance include the following. One, there is a need to practice ethical partnership building and maintenance by co-investing time and resources to combat long-standing power dynamics between partners, especially between the Global North and Global South. Two, it is imperative to strike a balance between standardization and customization of the initiative through flexible and co-created implementation strategies in order to achieve equitable project outcomes. For more on this theme, see Chapter 8, "Experiential

Learning as Community Engagement and the Need to Attend to Equity" (Collins-Nelsen et al.). Three, beyond securing internal institutional buy-in, non-traditional advancement strategies focusing on ethical partnerships, co-creation, student experience, and impact potential are vital to sustain EL opportunities. Finally, scaling partners should be identified based on shared institutional values and aligned approaches to achieving results. Ultimately, this chapter argues that universities have a unique opportunity through policy and planning to sustain initiatives that serve both meaningful student experience and research excellence at the heart of the university mission, while advancing sustainable development at both local and global levels.

REFERENCES

Abeysekera, L., & Dawson, P. (2015). Motivation and cognitive load in the flipped classroom: Definition, rationale and a call for research. *Higher Education Research & Development, 34*(1), 1–14. https://doi.org/10.1080/07294360.2014.934336

Association for Experiential Education. (2023). *What is experiential education?* http://www.aee.org/what-is-ee

Axelrod, P. (2002). *Values in conflict: The university, the marketplace and the trials of liberal education.* McGill-Queen's University Press.

Barkley, E. F. (2009). *Student engagement techniques: A handbook for college faculty.* Jossey-Bass.

Buzzelli, M., & Asafo-Adjei, E. (2022). Experiential learning and the university's host community: Rapid growth, contested mission and policy challenge. *Higher Education,* 85: 521-38. https://doi.org/10.1007/s10734-022-00849-1

Caniglia, G., John, B., Bellina, L., Lang, D. J., Wiek, A., Cohmer, S., & Laubichler, M. D. (2018). The glocal curriculum: A model for transnational collaboration in higher education for sustainable development. *Journal of Cleaner Production,* 171, 368–76. https://doi.org/10.1016/j.jclepro.2017.09.207

Chankseliani, M., Qoraboyev, I., & Gimranova, D. (2021). Higher education contributing to local, national, and global development: New empirical and conceptual insights. *Higher Education, 81*(1), 109–27. https://doi.org/10.1007/s10734-020-00565-8

Coyer, C., Gebregiorgis, D., Patton, K., Gheleva, D., & Bikos, L. (2019). Cultivating global learning locally through community-based experiential education. *The Journal of Experiential Education, 42*(2), 155–70. https://doi.org/10.1177/1053825918824615

EDSLR. (2010, May 4). *A further response to "A question (about universities, global challenges, and an organizational-ethical dilemma)".* GlobalHigherEd. https://globalhighered.wordpress.com/2010/05/04/a-further-response/

Elkana, Y., & Klöpper, H. (2016). *The university in the twenty-first century: Teaching the New Enlightenment in the Digital Age.* Central European University Press.

Freire, P. (1970). *Pedagogy of the oppressed.* Herter and Herter.

Fullan, M., Langworthy, M., & Barber, M. (2014). *A rich seam: How new pedagogies find deep learning.* MaRS Discovery District.

GlobalHigherEd. (2010, April 8). *A question (about universities, global challenges, and an organizational-ethical dilemma).* GlobalHigherEd. https://globalhighered.wordpress.com/2010/04/08/a-question/

Gravett, S. (2002). Transformative Learning through Action Research: A Case Study from South Africa [Conference presentation abstract." Adult Education Research Conference, Raliegh, NC, United States. https://newprairiepress.org/aerc/2002/papers/22

Houston, S. D., & Lange, K. (2018). "Global/local" community engagement: advancing integrative learning and situated solidarity. *Journal of Geography in Higher Education, 42*(1), 44–60. https://doi.org/10.1080/03098265.2017.1331425

Hsueh, Chia-Ming. (2019, April 18). *Streamlining sustainability within the university.* European Association for International Education. https://www.eaie.org/blog/sustainable-development-universities.html

Knight, E., Jones, A., & Gertler, M. S. (2021). The public university and the retreat from globalisation: An economic geography perspective on managing local-global tensions in international higher education. *Environment and Planning. A, 53*(1), 210–18. https://doi.org/10.1177/0308518X20959082

Kolb, D. A. (1984). *Experiential learning: Experience as the source of learning and development.* Prentice-Hall.

Lee, J., Kobia, C., & Son, J. (2023). Improving global competence in classroom-based experiential learning activities. *Journal of Global Education and Research, 7*(2), 131–45. https://www.doi.org/10.5038/2577-509X.7.2.1116

Levy, S. (2023). *Mind the Inclusion Gap: How allies can bridge the divide between talking diversity and taking action.* Unbound Publishing.

Mezirow, J. (1978). Perspective transformation. *Adult Education Quarterly. 28(*2), 100–10.

– (1997). Transformative learning: Theory to practice. *New directions for adult and continuing education, 1997*(74), 5–12.

Ministry of Colleges and Universities. (2022). *College and university Strategic Mandate Agreements.* https://www.ontario.ca/page/all-college-and-university-strategic-mandate-agreements

Morley, M. J., & Cerdin, J. L. (2010). Intercultural competence in the international business arena. *Journal of Managerial Psychology, 25*(8), 805–9.

Musisi, N. B. (2019). The enlivened classroom: Bringing the field back to campus. In D. L. Curran, C. Owens, H. Thorson & E. Vibert (Eds.), *Out There Learning* (pp. 66–84). University of Toronto Press. https://doi.org/10.3138/9781487519469-010

OECD (2019). *Preparing our youth for an inclusive and sustainable world: The OECD PISA global competence framework.* OECD Publishing.

Ontario Ministry of Education. (2016). *21st century competencies: Foundation document for discussion. Phase 1: Towards defining 21st century competencies for Ontario.* https://theconstructionzone.wordpress.com/wp-content/uploads/2017/11/21cl_21stcenturycompetencies.pdf

Roll, K., MacLeod, M., Agbodjah, S., & Siller, I. M. S. (2024). Learning in action: Embedding the SDGs through the Reach Alliance. *Sustain Earth Reviews*, **7**, 15. https://doi.org/10.1186/s42055-024-00079-6

Shafaqat, A., Tan, D., & Zhang, P. (2023, November 6). *Canada must invest in global leadership programs within higher education institutions.* The Hill Times. https://www.hilltimes.com/story/2023/11/06/canada-must-invest-in-global-leadership-opportunities-within-higher-education-institutions/402120/

Strayer, J. F. (2012). How learning in an inverted classroom influences cooperation, innovation and task orientation. *Learning Environments Research*, 15(2), 171–93. https://doi.org/10.1007/s10984-012-9108-4

United Nations General Assembly. (2015). *Transforming our world: The 2030 agenda for sustainable development (A/RES/70/1).* https://sdgs.un.org/2030agenda

University of Toronto. (2022). *The International Strategic Plan 2022–2027.* https://global.utoronto.ca/uoft-international-strategic-plan-2022-2027/

Wiessner, C., & Mezirow, J. (2000). Theory building and the search for common ground. In J. Mezirow (Ed.), *Learning as transformation: Critical perspectives on a theory in progress* (pp. 329–58). Jossey-Bass.

12 Afterword

KRIS OLDS

University of Wisconsin-Madison, United States

Introduction

This fascinating volume has emerged at an opportune time for many universities for *their relationship to the territories they are embedded in* – be it a town, a city, a city-region, a province or state, a nation, or a supranational region – is under considerable debate and reflection. Are universities fueling the development of innovative and inclusive economies, or are they contributing to the development of processes that generate "left-behind places" and associated political cleavages? Are universities educating citizen-subjects who can contribute to the development of democratic societies, or are they becoming enclaves cut off from local communities, or, even worse, triggering processes that damage said communities?

For example, as the volume's editor and contributor Michael Buzzelli notes in Chapter 1, and as many others have too regarding their research on the impacts of the purpose-built student accommodation sector (cf. Revington and August, 2020; Revington and Wray, 2022), expanding student enrollment can concurrently displace residents as well as elevate access to housing stress. Or take the case where one scholar (Jiang, 2020; Jiang, 2021) discovered pipelines guiding southern Chinese international students into expensive securitized condominiums like "The Hub" in a large Midwestern research university which directly and indirectly reduces these students' capacity to learn about and from other students, as well as engage with their host communities. Interestingly the philanthropic arms of universities are also concerned about this type of emerging cleavage for it may reduce the emotional ties such students have to their alma mater, which could reduce their interest in donating monies in the future.

This volume has also emerged at an opportune time for universities *looking inward* via initiatives to redesign their degree requirements. In the fall term of 2024, I happened to be reading the draft text while co-chairing a 38-member task force reconsidering College of Letters & Science, University of Wisconsin-Madison, degree requirements for our tens of thousands of undergraduate students. This initiative led us to acquire data about a wide array of issues and concerns and then narrow down our priorities to ensure action could be taken. Experiential learning (EL), which we place under the umbrella term of "high impact learning experiences," came up numerous times. Our university has a long history of considering how what happens inside courses and degrees at our university impacts society and economy beyond the boundaries of the campus. The so-called "Wisconsin Idea" (a general principle that "education should influence people's lives beyond the boundaries of the classroom") (University of Wisconsin Madison, n.d.a) is fueled by the "Wisconsin Experience" vision (University of Wisconsin Madison, n.d.b):

> The Wisconsin Experience is UW-Madison's vision for the total student experience, which combines learning in and out of the classroom. Tied to the Wisconsin Idea and steeped in our long-standing institutional values – the commitment to the truth, shared participation in decision-making, and service to local and global communities – the Wisconsin Experience describes how students develop and integrate these core values across their educational experience. Through the Wisconsin Experience, our students will engage in four areas of intellectual and personal growth: empathy and humility, relentless curiosity, intellectual confidence, purposeful action.

High-impact learning experiences include:

- studying abroad, either through a UW-Madison program or a program at another university;
- living in a residential learning community;
- participating in a first-year interest group (FIG);
- enrolling in a community-based learning course;
- having an undergraduate research experience – measured by participation in organized research programs, by taking a research or thesis course or by working for pay on research activity;
- participating in an internship or other workplace-based experience for academic credit;
- working closely with a faculty member in a seminar course, honors course, or independent study;and
- completing a capstone experience within the degree-major program.

We discovered that there was a huge diversity of high impact learning experiences across schools and colleges, with the highest percentages in professional fields like Nursing, Pharmacy, Agriculture, and Life Sciences and the lowest in Business (a surprise!) and then my own college of Letters & Science. As suggested in *Experiential Learning and Community*, too, there is across the board increased interest in EL from the perspective of students (and their parents) and various stakeholders in and associated with the university.

Inspired by our discussions and debates, as well as the content of this volume, several of us pushed to consider requiring EL as part of the College's degree requirements such that 100% of our students would have to experience this type of learning to ensure graduation. However, in the end, four other degree requirements were perceived to need more immediate attention, including the ethnic studies requirement and the non-English language requirement. It is worth noting that many of our debates about EL resonated closely with the content of this volume, including about how EL ties in with our university's mission, how to institutionalize EL, how to incentivize EL, how to scale up EL, and how to resource EL. The broad tenor of the arguments that were put forward reflected a blend of academic institutional logics (see Chapter 3) and professional and community logics (see Chapter 5).

In the end, even though we are a relatively wealthy public research university, there was insufficient support for mandating EL as a new degree requirement for all students until *adequate resources* could be dedicated to such practices and *equitable* student access to them could be ensured. Equity is a particular concern within our university and college, and the institutionalization process is not typically triggered and resourced unless equity concerns are adequately managed. Our deliberations resonated with the content in multiple chapters and helped me better understand just why we have been achieving successes on some levels (much high impact learning is indeed underway) but also not on other levels (especially institutionalizing in non-professional fields that do not require EL for accreditation purposes). This is the mark of an effective and timely publication.

UW-Madison is, of course, not the only university wrestling with EL right now. Given this, let's consider some of the main contributions and key ideas associated with this book.

Main Contributions, Key Ideas

The substantive chapters of this twelve-chapter volume focus on, as the title and subtitle make clear, how EL reflects universities' teaching and learning missions and how these forge relationships in and with their local communities.

Logics and Governance

Taken as a whole, it is clear that over the past two to three decades, universities have been faced with major structural and strategic challenges. These have resulted in significant transformations in the scope of their mission, governance, knowledge production and circulation, and relations with wider national, regional and global economies, and societies. These transformations are part of a wider "paradigmatic transition" facing all societies and universities, around the world.

What needs to be asked is *why*: why are universities advocating for the creation and/or enhancement of EL in the ways they are? A focus on logics is critically important to understand these "why" questions.

Chapter 3, for example, helped shed light on the presence, within universities, of multiple logics associated with EL. These include:

- the Managerial Institutional Logic, which places universities in competition with each other; and
- the Academic Institutional Logic, which values universities and associated programs as reflective of the university as an institution that values autonomy, the production of knowledge, and the production of knowledgeable citizen-subjects.

Chapter 4 connects with Chapter 3, though unpacks five logics, rooted in sources of legitimacy and authority, as well as bases of norms, attention, and strategy for establishing and maintaining EL:

- State Logics
- Market Logics
- Corporate Logics
- Professional Logics
- Community Logics

Suffice it to say each differs significantly and also that most EL offerings reflect a combination of some or all of these logics and these evolve over time. Each of these logics also shapes if and how EL is institutionalized within universities. As Emerson LaCroix notes (Chapter 3), institutionalization is:

> essentially an organizational process whereby a practical idea or practice becomes sedimented within an organization to the point that it becomes taken for granted (Tolbert and Zucker, 1996). From an organizational perspective, institutionalization of experiential learning would allow

universities to demonstrate that there has been actual effort to foster and develop the pedagogy, as opposed to responding more ceremonially to external funding pressures (e.g., rebranding existing initiatives instead of developing new ones).

State logics, for example, once legitimized the exploitation of what are now deemed the First Nations (see the history of the "Land Grab University" in Lee & Atone, 2020), yet now in most jurisdictions, in combination with Professional and/or Community logics, state logics drive or at least enable EL to contribute to the dismantling of decolonization (as clearly scoped out in Chapter 7) or at least attend to reconciliation in a variety of ways. Or take the case where State logics and Corporate logics align to support both innovation systems and city-region development with respect to advanced industrial production but also 'workplace ready' competencies for students.

Experiential Learning and Community also does a wonderful job of shedding light on the logic-mission relationship (see Chapters 4, 9, and 10) at the broader university level. EL emerges in a conducive context in which the logic and mission both work together to support particular forms of EL, thereby providing both legitimacy and resources (broadly defined) for this agenda. EL is not necessarily, therefore, focused on one outcome over another; it depends on how logic and mission align.

Mechanisms and Sites of EL

But what is EL, and how does it operate? *Experiential Learning and Community* sheds light on the amazing diversity of approaches to EL, including both paid and unpaid:

- clinical placements
- co-operative education
- community engaged placements
- field placements
- internships
- practice-based learning
- practicums
- service learning
- workplace learning/work-integrated learning

As Buzzelli acknowledges in the Introduction, the inclusion of chapters that focus on all of these, and more, forms of EL, reflects an "inclusive definition" that is necessary due to the current flux in EL across university campuses in most countries but also that EL takes part, for the most part, off campus and instead in the community and in a structured way. The focus on "structured ways" brings discussions about these mechanisms into a related discussion about curricular matters. EL takes place in the terrain of curricular decisions about degree, majors and minors, certificates, and so on, which in turn are brought to life via credit-granting courses. This said, there are also numerous non-course-based opportunities to provide EL for students in a manner that benefits both students and the communities the student is engaged with. I am dating myself here, though I clearly recall the absence of EL opportunities in the social sciences when I was an undergraduate at the University of British Columbia (UBC) in the early 1980s. Given this, I simply managed myself and volunteered for the Downtown East Side Residents Association (DERA), as well as for Carnegie Centre (a community centre) in Vancouver in what was Canada's poorest census district (Hassan & Ley, 1994). These were life transforming experiences, but they were not acknowledged nor even registered by my department (Geography), nor UBC.

Experiential Learning and Community also helps shed light on the nature of the debate about the *where* of EL. At first glance, EL seems like it is surely, and perhaps solely, an off-campus form of learning that is facilitated by the formation of relationships between universities and off campus organizations, firms, and the like. The University of Waterloo's world famous cooperative education program, for example, is structured such that undergraduate students spend "four and six work terms (four months in length) throughout the duration" (University of Waterloo, n.d.; see also Chapters 1, 3, 5 and 10 in this volume) of their co-op degree and involves a progressive scaffolding of experiences that ramp up over time, testing the skills and expertise of students while concurrently (and ideally) forming trusting relationships that could end up in permanent employment upon graduation.

Off campus sites of EL include offices, labs, incubators, research centres, social innovation hubs, and so on. These sites and their relationship to EL logics, curriculum, and pedagogic practices are discussed throughout the book (see Chapter 2 in particular).

A complementary and much needed discussion also flags the ways in which EL can take place on campuses too. Chapter 7, for example, focuses on the role of critical pedagogy and indigenous communities that bring together on-campus and field work experiences, while Chapter 11 engages with the role of global consortia of universities that bring together faculty, students, staff, and multi-sited communities. These discussions reminded me of another initiative I was involved with regarding the development of a memorandum of understanding that would enable

UW-Madison's University Research Park (URP) to have the authority to become active in leveraging their skills and expertise and applying them to transforming our main campus (University of Wisconsin Madison. 2021). For example, university research parks are often quite sterile, hard to reach (for students who depend upon public transport), and are lacking in the vibrancy of a bustling main campus. In the brainstorming phase, research-active chemists suggested that the URP should work with the campus planning authorities to enable the creation of industry labs on campus and ideally in or adjacent to the Department of Chemistry, the School of Pharmacy, and the Department of Chemical Engineering. The vision included student lab placements within on-campus industry labs, and was partially inspired by the strong relationship between GE Healthcare and our School of Medicine and Public Health that has students working with GE Healthcare on our campus to support and learn from "developments in magnetic resonance (MR), computed tomography (CT), ultrasound, interventional radiology (IR), theranostics and molecular imaging (MI) modalities. as well as patient care solutions" (University of Wisconsin Madison, 2023).

Interestingly, these conversations fed into the development of a new West Campus District Plan that is currently being implemented on our campus. The design principles include (University of Wisconsin Madison, n.d.c):

- spark discovery (by enhancing critical mass of research and innovation in close proximity to one another);
- create a sense of place (providing a mix of uses to foster connection and a welcoming campus environment);
- transportation and mobility (essential elements to developing a modern and accessible district);
- enhance the natural landscape (creating open spaces and connections to Lake Mendota);
- embrace cultural and historical significance (invest in our area's rich and complex history, acknowledging the ties to the original Native Nations land, Teejop); and
- prioritize walkability (strengthen the pedestrian network and create a network of close destinations).

These design principles for the new West Campus District Plan support and legitimize the progressive blending and blurring of "town and gown," including via enhanced opportunities for EL *on* campus in mixed use areas that are planned to be livelier at all times of the day and week.

Such on-campus partnerships to support EL need not only be associated with STEM fields, as was clear, again, in Chapters 7, 9, and 11. Or take the case of Cardiff University in Wales that has created a Social Science Research Park (SPARK). Cardiff University's approach involved "adapting and evolving the traditional science park model" and in so doing it "creates new infrastructure for combining our social science know-how with those of our partners" (Price & Delbridge, 2015).

Of course, all books include silences and absences regarding select relevant topics. Given the debates we engaged with, as noted above, in our recent degree requirements initiative, it was interesting to see that most authors in *Experiential Learning and Community* focused on traditional versus non-traditional students. EL, like study abroad, at least in its current form, grew in importance in the era of massification in Western countries and was, therefore, configured on assumptions about age (young), familial status (single), and capacity to be mobile. Discussions about the "non-traditional" tend to be focused on expanding the breadth and depth of community partnerships versus the student (see Chapters 5 and 11). More on this issue below.

Overall, then, *Experiential Learning and Community* has generated considerable insights for those engaged with debates and programming regarding not just EL but also the future of the university itself, as well as the "town-gown" relationship. The contributions are pitched at a number of key levels (from the conceptual to the empirical) and deal with a wide variety of geographies. And it is a timely volume, indeed.

The Future of the University vis-à-vis Experiential Learning

The future of the university vis-à-vis EL will obviously be shaped by the structural forces shaping the higher education sector in general and then associated dynamics regarding mission, governance, strategy, and practices.

Clearly, emerging patterns regarding the economic health of universities will shape their capacity to develop, support, and/or indeed abandon EL programming. Over the last decade, we have seen broad patterns reflecting disinvestment by the state, increased dependence upon revenue via international students (especially in Canada), and emerging cleavages associated with high demand (from students) and resource rich (via tuition revenue and endowment income) universities versus declining demand (from students) and resource poor universities. The fiscal constraints associated with these changes, including the spread of Activity-Based Budgeting (ABB) as well as Responsibility Center Management (RCM) budgeting (Hanover Research, 2023), cannot help but reduce the appetite for supporting high impact learning, including via EL. As is evident in *Experiential Learning and Community*, EL requires support beyond a synchronization with institutional mission; it needs to be institutionalized, supported by student and community/employer-facing academic staff, and by faculty members who have the capacity to prioritize EL as part of their teaching portfolio. (While they differ regarding where ultimate authority rests, Activity-Based Budgeting (ABB) as well as Responsibility Center Management (RCM) budgeting both tend to incentivize units – schools, college and departments – to seek higher levels of revenue generating-activity, which often includes scaling up numbers [of majors and/or course credits taught]. One can argue that high impact modes of teaching and learning like EL will help boost major numbers, but scaling up via expanded student numbers per course is much easier to facilitate and has a more direct impact on improving budget positioning. One simple budget models primer is available at Hanover Research, 2023.

The future of the university vis-à -vis EL will also be impacted by public perceptions regarding the value of a university degree, including whether universities are producing "work-ready" graduates, as well as "work changing" graduates. As noted by Ville Björck in Chapter 2, the latter term means "graduates who are critical and creative enough to challenge and change established work practices and work trends in a profession or in working life in general." EL arguably is a major contributor to producing both types of graduates, and EL opportunities are often viewed positively by both parents and students during the educational process. However, public perception regarding the value of a university degree is an increasingly politicized phenomenon, especially in the United States where evolving culture wars and ideological battles reverberate through the public sphere and into budgetary negotiations with state legislatures, for example. While conditions are clearly more polarized in the United States compared to most Western countries, the assumed relationship between high quality and high impact teaching and learning practices and enhanced support for higher education is not a guaranteed one. Over the last decade, I've spoken with dozens of university leaders and leaders of associations of universities in numerous countries, and they are frequently concerned regarding the capacity of politicians to demonstrate genuine malice when negotiating about governance issues, while also rarely speaking publicly about the value and impact of universities upon society and economy. And at the most extreme level, the presence and impact of tech billionaires like Peter Thiel is forming a cancerous relationship between some powerful figures and the formal higher education sector. In a forthcoming co-authored chapter, one of my colleagues, Christopher Muellerleile, delves into the highly antagonistic approach Thiel and others are pursuing vis-à-vis higher education (Robertson et al. in press). Muellerleile notes:

> It does not take long after diving into the texts written by Thiel and similar thinkers of his ilk to see how central the Western university is to their diagnosis of the ills of Western society. Thiel and others, like Curtis Yarvin, Nick Land, and Petrie Friedman (Milton Friedman's grandson), all argue that universities in the West are institutions of the left-wing elite, a ruling class obsessed with diversity that has corrupted science and slowed technological development (Smith and Burrows 2021). Along with the administrative or "deep" state, they argue that elite universities have captured the levers of American state power. One solution for Thiel is complete secession or libertarian "exit" from the nation-state to either cyberspace, outer space, or into the ocean (Craib 2022, 181-208). Thiel has, for instance, generously funded the Seasteading Institute, chaired by Friedman, whose projects include building independent pods on the ocean beyond the reach of the state and its territorial waters. Thiel's message is always the same. Universities: stifle innovation because they are overly bureaucratic and risk-averse; discourage radical innovation; and are out of touch with the real-world challenges faced by entrepreneurs and innovators. But most importantly, Thiel has also accused universities of indoctrinating students with politically correct and left-leaning ideologies, hampering their critical thinking.

To what degree does EL matter to highly influential antagonists like Thiel, Elon Musk, and others? It does not, or I should say it does but only as a target. And it is too easy for advocates of EL and higher education more generally outside of the United States to assume they are not interested in what is going on in other Western countries. This should be a concerning question to consider, and believers of the intrinsic value of EL would be wise to keep it in mind that ideologically driven malice is a current and present danger around the world.

Dangers aside, EL is here to stay. As noted above, we see EL being incorporated into more and more plans to develop "innovation districts" on and off campuses, as well as in campus adjacent zones (see, for, example, Baldwin, 2021). We see EL being used to legitimize evolving university missions in increasingly resource constrained contexts. And we see EL increasingly tied into one of the key growth segments within universities – student services, including career services. And as I noted above, EL is being bundled into a wider range of "high impact" learning programming, experiences and practices. But this begs the question: as EL is increasingly valued, institutionalized, profiled, umbrellaed, and present both on campuses, off campuses, and in campus adjacent zones, will the number of EL-related issues to grapple with expand exponentially?

For example, are EL learning outcomes being assessed, and, if so, in the most effective ways? How is EL contributing, if at all, to city-region innovation processes? And how are those responsible for managing, coordinating, and teaching in EL spaces being supported, assessed, and vetted, especially given the large percentage of contingent (temporary) faculty who are working under relatively precarious conditions? Higher education institutions, especially in Western counties, flag and praise shared governance systems and procedures: this is largely, I would argue, positive. But the challenges associated with shared governance include ensuring that widely distributed EL is effectively supported, managed, resourced, and effectively governed. The successful spread and deepening of EL on and off our campuses are a double edged sword; we see it present on a myriad of levels and forms and in a myriad of geographies, but does distributed responsibility for EL enhance its resilience or leave it open to risks during an increasingly risky era? Or perhaps both! These are but just a few questions worth grappling with regarding the nature of EL in universities as well as "with" the local community. This volume provides those interested in EL and higher education more generally with a strong levelling up base upon which to consider these questions, issues, concerns, and future trajectories.

REFERENCES

Baldwin, D. (2021). *In the Shadow of the Ivory Tower: How universities are plundering our cities.* Bold Type Books.

Cardiff University. (n.d.). *Social Science Research Park (SPARK).* https://www.cardiff.ac.uk/social-science-research-park/about-us

Hanover Research, (2023, October 23). *6 alternative budget models for colleges and universities,* https://www.hanoverresearch.com/insights-blog/higher-education/6-alternative-budget-models-for-colleges-and-universities/

Hasson, S. & Ley, D. (1994) *Neighbourhood Organizations and the Welfare State* (pp. 172–204). University of Toronto Press.

Lee, R., & Ahtone, T. (2020, March 30). *Land-grab universities.* High Country News. https://www.hcn.org/issues/52-4/indigenous-affairs-education-land-grab-universities/

Jiang, S. (2020). Diversity without integration? Racialization and spaces of exclusion in international higher education. *British Journal of Sociology of Education, 42*(1), 32–47.

– (2021). The Call of the Homeland: Transnational Education and the Rising Nationalism among Chinese Overseas Students. *Comparative Education Review, 65*(1), 34–55.

Price, A., & Delbridge R. (2015). *Social science parks: Society's new super-labs.* Nesta. https://media.nesta.org.uk/documents/social_science_parks_paper.pdf

Revington, N. & August, M. (2020). Making a market for itself: The emergent financialization of student housing in Canada. *Environment and Planning A: Economy and Space, 52*(5), 856–77.

Revington, N., & Wray, A. J. D. (2022). Land-Use Planning Approaches to Near-Campus Neighborhoods and Student Housing Development Patterns in Ontario, Canada. *Housing Policy Debate, 34*(5), 668–94.

Robertson, S., Muellerleile, C., Wu, J. & Olds, K. (in press). Perforated nations, universities, and the zonal politics of knowledge production. In K. Brogger, H. Moscovitz, S.L. Robertson & J. Lee (Eds.), *Geo-Politics of Higher Education, World Yearbook 2025.* Routledge.

University of Waterloo. (n.d.). *About co-op.* https://uwaterloo.ca/co-operative-education/about-co-op

University of Wisconsin Madison. (n.d.a). *Wisconsin idea.* https://www.wisc.edu/wisconsin-idea/

– (n.d.b). *Wisconsin experience.* https://wisconsinexperience.wisc.edu/

– (n.d.c) *Finance and Administration.* https://finadmin.wisc.edu/westcampus/concept/

– (2021, October 8). *Regents approve university research park agreement.*

– (2023, November 17). *UW–Madison and GE HealthCare broaden shared commitment to health care innovation.* https://news.wisc.edu/uw-madison-and-ge-healthcare-broaden-shared-commitment-to-health-care-innovation/

List of Contributors

Corelia Baibarac-Duignan, PhD, is an Assistant Professor at the University of Twente, Netherlands, in the Knowledge, Transformation and Society (KiTeS) section. She is co-founder of the university's RUrban Futures Collective, a platform dedicated to studying the role of science and technology in rural-urban interactions. Originally trained as an architect, Corelia is a transdisciplinary researcher and educator working at the intersection between sustainability, commons, and creative approaches to civic engagement in inclusive transformations towards sustainable futures.

Roy Bear Chief, LLD, BSW, MSW, is the Espoom Taah or Helper for the Department of Health, Community and Education at Mount Royal University. He has been involved in Decolonization and Indigenization at Mount Royal by sharing his Blackfoot language and culture with students and faculty to create understanding as well as raising awareness and consciousness. He also goes into classes upon request to share his knowledge of the residential schools, child welfare, child studies regarding family and kinship, and uses creation stories to integrate knowledge around Blackfoot culture.

Carolyn Bjartveit, BSc, MEd, PhD, is an Associate Professor and coordinates the Bachelor of Child Studies/Early Learning and Child Care program at Mount Royal University. She has experience teaching pre-K to post-secondary graduate levels in early childhood education. Her research areas include curriculum studies, cultural studies, history and philosophy of early childhood education, and teacher education. Her current research focuses on social justice, human rights, and how immigrant and international students' cultural identities intersect with the curriculum in Canadian post-secondary education settings.

Ville Björck, PhD, is a Senior Lecturer in Education at University West in Trollhättan, Sweden. He serves as the acting editor of University West's research blog, WILReflections, which focuses on Work-integrated Learning (WIL). Ville's research critically examines how popular terms such as Work-integrated Learning, Experiential Learning and Graduate Employability are understood and conceptualized in both research and the marketing discourse of higher education institutions.

Michael Buzzelli, BA (Hons), MA, MEd., PhD, is Director of the Centre for Urban Policy and Local Governance at the University of Western Ontario. After completing graduate work at McMaster University, Michael held academic appointments at the University of British Columbia, Vancouver, and Queen's University, Kingston, and has been a visiting scholar at the Universities of Melbourne and Glasgow as well as the Alma Mater Studiorum – Universita di Bologna. He has led several national and international research projects as well as applied graduate policy training and consulting work. His current SSHRC-funded research focuses on higher education system policy and planning, research on teaching and learning, and knowledge mobilization in the sector.

Rebecca Collins-Nelsen, BA(Hons), MA, PhD, is a teaching and research lead at McMaster Children and Youth University (MCYU) housed in the Department of Pediatrics at McMaster University. Rebecca has solidified a pedagogical philosophy that foregrounds student engagement and critical thinking, throughout her teaching at various post-secondary institutions around Ontario. Much of her current teaching centres on Community Engagement. As such, she is actively involved in building and nurturing community partnerships throughout the city of Hamilton. As a scholar, she is committed to research that identifies and eradicates various forms of inequality using a critical intersectional lens. Her research has been supported by multiple grants and it currently focused on social inequality, teaching and learning, and children's rights.

Guus Dix, PhD, is an Assistant Professor of sociology of science and technology at the University of Twente, the Netherlands, in the Knowledge, Transformation and Society (KiTeS) section. As a researcher and teacher, he is concerned with the climate and ecological crisis as a social, political, and economic problem. As a climate activist with Extinction Rebellion and Scientist Rebellion, he is committed to a better future in which we no longer drill for new fossil resources, in which universities only work with partners who are also serious about the transition, and in which solidarity with people who are struggling here is on a par with people's right to a just and habitable planet elsewhere.

Kaylee Eady, PhD, is an Assistant Professor in Health Professions Education at the University of Ottawa. Kaylee's research aims to improve the teaching and learning of health professionals and, with this, the care provided to and the health of our communities. Specifically, her research focuses on advancing and enhancing theory and practice, assessment strategies, teaching strategies, program evaluation, and methods in Health Professions Education.

Hannah Egert, BA (Hons), MA, is the Performance Analyst in the Housing & Conference Services Department at McMaster University. Her work bridges practical analysis and assessment to enhance both student experience and departmental performance. She holds a Bachelor's degree in Geography & Environmental Studies and a Master's in Geography, both from McMaster University. Hannah is also a Sessional Instructor at McMaster, and worked in the field of water-quality education after her Master's degree. With a passion for teaching pedagogy, she focuses on creating accessible and engaging courses for the evolving landscape of higher education.

Catherine M. Giroux, PhD, is a Postdoctoral Fellow at McGill University's Faculty of Medicine and a Part-time Professor in the Faculty of Education at the University of Ottawa. Catherine previously completed a SSHRC-funded Postdoctoral Fellowship at the Institute of Health Sciences Education at McGill University. Her program of research explores whether and how health professionals use social media as a mechanism of knowledge mobilization. She has expertise in qualitative, digital, and ethnographic research methods and scoping review methods.

Hannele Gordon, BSocSc, BEd., has held various roles in primary and early childhood education, teaching children on reserves in Ontario and in public preschools in Alberta. While working as an educator and cultural diversity coordinator in a community organization in Calgary, there were opportunities for Hannele to mentor and work with postsecondary undergraduate students on community-based projects. Her current role involves supporting licensed child care centres in Alberta. Hannele's academic studies and professional experience in sociology and education have fostered an interest in how culture, intersectional identities, and policy inform educators' pedagogical practice in the classroom.

Ben Jongbloed, PhD, is an Associate Professor at the University of Twente in the Netherlands. From 1992, he has been working at the university's Center for Higher Education Policy Studies (CHEPS) – now part of the KiTeS (Knowledge, Transformation and Society) section. He teaches *Crossing Borders*, an elective course on international internships tied to the Sustainable Development Goals. His research, often for clients like the European Commission and national Education ministries, focuses on performance-based funding and integrating entrepreneurship and sustainability into higher education.

Moni Kim, BASc (Hons), MPH, is the Senior Research Program and Engagement Officer at The Reach Alliance, University of Toronto. She leads the research and leadership development initiative, equipping emerging global leaders with the skills to drive impact across Reach's global partner institutions. With extensive experience in international development and global health, Moni has worked across sectors – including civil society, academia, government, and the private sector – to mobilize strategic partnerships and advance equity-focused initiatives. Her work has contributed to high-impact projects, with a focus on public health, human rights, and community-centred practice.

Emerson LaCroix, BA (Hons), MA, PhD, is the Senior Researcher at the Ontario Council on Articulation and Transfer. Emerson completed his graduate studies at the University of Waterloo, focusing on the intersection of experiential education and organizational theory. Emerson's research has been supported by both SSHRC and Ontario Graduate Scholarships and has been published in key journals such as *Higher Education*, the *Canadian Journal of Higher Education*, and the *Journal of Experiential Education*. His current research examines the various facets of student mobility in Ontario higher education and provides key insights to sectoral stakeholders.

John Maclachlan, BSc (Hons), MA, PhD, serves as the Manager of Educational Initiatives and Assessment for McMaster University Housing and Conference Services and holds an appointment as an Adjunct Assistant Professor in the School of Earth, Environment, and Society at McMaster University. With extensive experience in higher education, John has developed and instructed courses at several Ontario universities, including McMaster University, Wilfrid Laurier University, and the University of Guelph, focusing primarily on climate change and community engagement. His research has been supported by multiple grants, with his current work examining the impacts of climate change on communities in

Peru and investigating the relationship between students' sense of belonging and their academic success in higher education.

Marin MacLeod, BA (Hons), MPH, is a relationship builder across academic, government, private, and community organizations. She leads the Reach Alliance, a consortium of global universities developing the leaders we need to solve urgent local challenges of the hard to reach. Prior to joining the Reach Alliance, Marin led Grand Challenges Canada's approach to impact measurement across their maternal, newborn, and child health innovation portfolio. Her focus was on the systems and processes used to capture results and to share knowledge generated by grantees through the organization's unique innovation platform. Marin's experience in partnership development, leadership growth, and community engagement, has contributed to many successful interdisciplinary projects around the world.

Elisa Magnani, PhD, is Professor of Human Geography at the Department of History and Cultures of the University of Bologna. She coordinated the master's degree in Geography and territorial processes of the University of Bologna from 2018 and 2024 and has been supervising internship experiences for the students of the master's for several years. Her research interests deal with two main topics: on one side, cultural and critical heritage tourism, with a focus on the places connected to the slave trade in Africa; on the other side, the nexus between climate change and mobility, both tourism and migration.

Michele Manocchi, PhD, is an Adjunct Professor in the Department of Psychology at Western University (London, ON), co-founder of the Project Global Impact Initiative (USA) to Accelerate a Healthier World and an Inner Development Goals co-creator within the UN Sustainable Development Goals framework. After earning his PhD in Comparative Social Research (University of Turin, Italy) and publishing his book on the experiences of asylum seekers and the Italian and European refugee systems, Michele arrived in Canada in 2013 to collaborate on several research projects: promoting and protecting migrant women's rights in Mexico, Moldova and the Philippines (International Migration Research Centre, Wilfrid Laurier University); undocumented migrants and sanctuary cities (Department of Criminology, Toronto Metropolitan University); higher education, microcredentials, and international students' paths; up-skilling and re-skilling strategies for newcomers and domestic workers; and experiential learning models within town-gown relations (Western University).

Peter Milley, PhD, is a Professor in the Faculty of Education and Director of the Centre for Research on Educational and Community Services (CRECS) at the University of Ottawa. His teaching and research focus on educational administration, policy, and evaluation. His recent Social Sciences and Humanities Research Council-funded work explores social innovation leadership in Canadian universities. Before academia, Peter was a Senior Advisor in the Canadian federal public service on executive leadership development programs domestically and internationally. He also served as Director of Research in an international network of public senior officials, academics, and experts aimed at shaping future directions in public administration and policy.

Katherine A. Moreau, PhD, is a Full Professor in Health Professions Education. Katherine's research focuses on (1) patient and family engagement in the teaching and assessment of medical students and residents, (2) patient, family, and community involvement in program evaluation and research, and (3) experiential learning across all levels of education.

Kris Olds, PhD, an economic and urban geographer, as well as urban planner, is the Vilas Distinguished Achievement Professor in the Department of Geography, University of Wisconsin-Madison. He has been at the University of Wisconsin-Madison since 2001. He is a "first generation" university attendee and graduate. He has worked as an academic in England, Canada, Singapore (1997–2001), and the United States (2001 to present). He was also based at Sciences Po in Paris from 2007–8, and also taught at Schwarzman College at Tsinghua University in 2018. His current research focuses on the transformation of higher education and research vis-à-vis city-region and supranational development processes and politics. He also serves as board member on the UniverCity Alliance at UW-Madison, as well as Board Chair of Educational Credential Evaluators, Inc. (a public service nonprofit organization).

Matteo Proto, PhD, is an Associate Professor of Geography at the University of Bologna. His research contributes to historical geography and cartography, political geography, and socio-spatial transformations in contemporary cities. He focuses on geographical theories related to the processes of bordering and nation-building. Other research topics include water studies, specifically the historical transformations of Northern Italy's waterscapes and a critical analysis of urban regeneration. He has served as the Principal Investigator for the SIR research project River Frames. Matteo received his PhD in the History of Europe in 2009 from the University of Bologna. He has held positions as a Research Fellow at the University of Bologna, the Leibniz Institut für Länderkunde in Leipzig (Germany), and the University of Trento. Additionally, he has collaborated on research projects or spent time as a visiting researcher at the University of Verona, Innsbruck (Austria), Budapest (Hungary), Edinburgh (UK), and Erfurt (Germany).

Sandeep Raha, BSc, (Hon), MSc, PhD, is an Associate Professor in the Department of Pediatrics at McMaster University. He is also the co-founder and current Director of McMaster Children and Youth University. Through this program, Sandeep and his team have developed curricular content to engage undergraduate and graduate students in the pedagogy of collaborative learning with young people. These courses uniquely engage young people as well teachers and families in interdisciplinary interactive learning opportunities. This work has earned him the President's Award in Teaching and Learning, McMaster University highest teaching award, as well as the King Charles Coronation Medal, for service to community and Canada. His current research focuses on evaluating and supporting openness to learning and critical thinking in young people through interdisciplinary experiential learning.

Perri Termine, BA (Hons), MEd., is a community development and organizational learning practitioner committed to lifelong learning, social care, and transformative research. Her focus is on translating and mobilizing knowledge to promote positive impact and inclusion. Perri earned a Master of Education in Adult Education and Community Development from University of Toronto and a Bachelor of Arts in Global Studies from Wilfrid Laurier University. From 2020–2, Perri was a Researcher at the Reach Alliance, where she collaborated with a multidisciplinary team at the University of Toronto to explore effective cross-sector partnership practices in global health interventions, particularly in Mozambique. Perri's background in education, community engagement, and global development has facilitated successful program development and delivery, as well as research collaborations, across multiple sectors and countries.

Index